Business Dynamics Models

Advances in Design and Control

SIAM's Advances in Design and Control series consists of texts and monographs dealing with all areas of design and control and their applications. Topics of interest include shape optimization, multidisciplinary design, trajectory optimization, feedback, and optimal control. The series focuses on the mathematical and computational aspects of engineering design and control that are usable in a wide variety of scientific and engineering disciplines.

Series Volumes

Kaszkurewicz, Eugenius and Bhaya, Amit, *Business Dynamics Models: Optimization-Based One Step Ahead Optimal Control*
Pedregal, Pablo, *A Variational Approach to Optimal Control of ODEs*
Garon, André and Delfour, Michel C., *Transfinite Interpolations and Eulerian/Lagrangian Dynamics*
Martinelli, Agostino, *Observability: A New Theory Based on the Group of Invariance*
Betts, John T., *Practical Methods for Optimal Control Using Nonlinear Programming, Third Edition*
Rodrigues, Luis, Samadi, Behzad, and Moarref, Miad, *Piecewise Affine Control: Continuous-Time, Sampled-Data, and Networked Systems*
Ferrara, A., Incremona, G. P., and Cucuzzella, C., *Advanced and Optimization Based Sliding Mode Control: Theory and Applications*
Morelli, A. and Smith, M., *Passive Network Synthesis: An Approach to Classification*
Özbay, Hitay, Gümüşsoy, Suat, Kashima, Kenji, and Yamamoto, Yutaka, *Frequency Domain Techniques for* $\mathcal{H}_\infty$ *Control of Distributed Parameter Systems*
Khalil, Hassan K., *High-Gain Observers in Nonlinear Feedback Control*
Bauso, Dario, *Game Theory with Engineering Applications*
Corless, M., King, C., Shorten, R., and Wirth, F., *AIMD Dynamics and Distributed Resource Allocation*
Walker, Shawn W., *The Shapes of Things: A Practical Guide to Differential Geometry and the Shape Derivative*
Michiels, Wim and Niculescu, Silviu-Iulian, *Stability, Control, and Computation for Time-Delay Systems: An Eigenvalue-Based Approach, Second Edition*
Narang-Siddarth, Anshu and Valasek, John, *Nonlinear Time Scale Systems in Standard and Nonstandard Forms: Analysis and Control*
Bekiaris-Liberis, Nikolaos and Krstic, Miroslav, *Nonlinear Control under Nonconstant Delays*
Osmolovskii, Nikolai P. and Maurer, Helmut, *Applications to Regular and Bang-Bang Control: Second-Order Necessary and Sufficient Optimality Conditions in Calculus of Variations and Optimal Control*
Biegler, Lorenz T., Campbell, Stephen L., and Mehrmann, Volker, eds., *Control and Optimization with Differential-Algebraic Constraints*
Delfour, M. C. and Zolésio, J.-P., *Shapes and Geometries: Metrics, Analysis, Differential Calculus, and Optimization, Second Edition*
Hovakimyan, Naira and Cao, Chengyu, $\mathcal{L}_1$ *Adaptive Control Theory: Guaranteed Robustness with Fast Adaptation*
Speyer, Jason L. and Jacobson, David H., *Primer on Optimal Control Theory*
Betts, John T., *Practical Methods for Optimal Control and Estimation Using Nonlinear Programming, Second Edition*
Shima, Tal and Rasmussen, Steven, eds., *UAV Cooperative Decision and Control: Challenges and Practical Approaches*
Speyer, Jason L. and Chung, Walter H., *Stochastic Processes, Estimation, and Control*
Krstic, Miroslav and Smyshlyaev, Andrey, *Boundary Control of PDEs: A Course on Backstepping Designs*
Ito, Kazufumi and Kunisch, Karl, *Lagrange Multiplier Approach to Variational Problems and Applications*
Xue, Dingyü, Chen, YangQuan, and Atherton, Derek P., *Linear Feedback Control: Analysis and Design with MATLAB*
Hanson, Floyd B., *Applied Stochastic Processes and Control for Jump-Diffusions: Modeling, Analysis, and Computation*
Michiels, Wim and Niculescu, Silviu-Iulian, *Stability and Stabilization of Time-Delay Systems: An Eigenvalue-Based Approach*
Ioannou, Petros and Fidan, Barış, *Adaptive Control Tutorial*
Bhaya, Amit and Kaszkurewicz, Eugenius, *Control Perspectives on Numerical Algorithms and Matrix Problems*
Robinett III, Rush D., Wilson, David G., Eisler, G. Richard, and Hurtado, John E., *Applied Dynamic Programming for Optimization of Dynamical Systems*
Huang, J., *Nonlinear Output Regulation: Theory and Applications*
Haslinger, J. and Mäkinen, R. A. E., *Introduction to Shape Optimization: Theory, Approximation, and Computation*
Antoulas, Athanasios C., *Approximation of Large-Scale Dynamical Systems*
Gunzburger, Max D., *Perspectives in Flow Control and Optimization*
Delfour, M. C. and Zolésio, J.-P., *Shapes and Geometries: Analysis, Differential Calculus, and Optimization*
Betts, John T., *Practical Methods for Optimal Control Using Nonlinear Programming*
El Ghaoui, Laurent and Niculescu, Silviu-Iulian, eds., *Advances in Linear Matrix Inequality Methods in Control*
Helton, J. William and James, Matthew R., *Extending* $\mathcal{H}^\infty$ *Control to Nonlinear Systems: Control of Nonlinear Systems to Achieve Performance Objectives*

Business Dynamics Models
Optimization-Based One Step Ahead Optimal Control

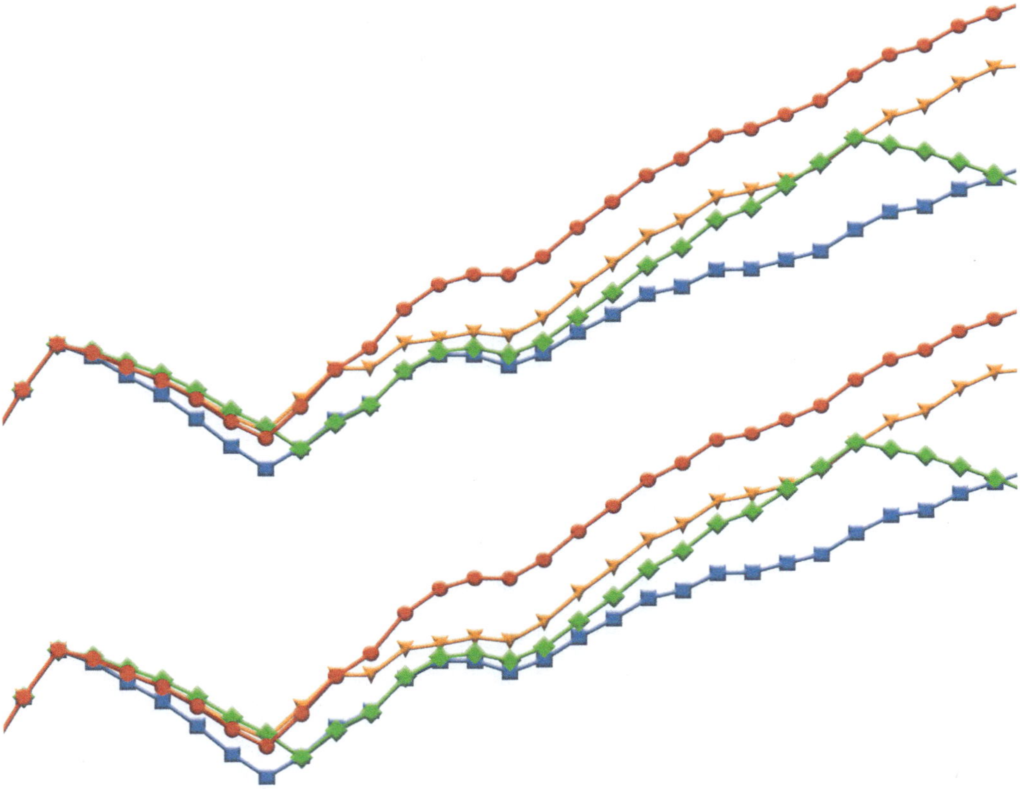

Eugenius Kaszkurewicz
Federal University of Rio de Janeiro
Rio de Janeiro, Brazil

Amit Bhaya
Federal University of Rio de Janeiro
Rio de Janeiro, Brazil

siam.

Society for Industrial and Applied Mathematics
Philadelphia

10 9 8 7 6 5 4 3 2 1

Publications Director	Kivmars H. Bowling
Executive Editor	Elizabeth Greenspan
Managing Editor	Kelly Thomas
Production Editor	Lisa Briggeman
Copy Editor	Gary Davidoff
Production Manager	Donna Witzleben
Production Coordinator	Cally A. Shrader
Compositor	Cheryl Hufnagle
Graphic Designer	Doug Smock

Library of Congress Cataloging-in-Publication Data

Names: Kaszkurewicz, Eugenius, author. | Bhaya, Amit, author.
Title: Business dynamics models : optimization-based one step ahead optimal control / Eugenius Kaszkurewicz and Amit Bhaya.
Description: [Philadelphia] : [Society for Industrial and Applied Mathematics], 2022. | Includes bibliographical references and index. | Summary: "In this book business dynamics refers to a combination of business management and financial objectives embedded in a dynamical system model. The model is subject to a control that optimizes a performance index that takes both management and finance into account. The central idea in this book is the concept of one step ahead optimal control and its global version, which is referred to as omniscient control and serves as a theoretical benchmark. The solutions presented in this book are intended to provide a rationale for the use of optimal control and to provide guidelines for further investigation into more complex models . It is also possible to use the formulations presented in a so-called "flight simulator mode" to investigate different complex scenarios"-- Provided by publisher.
Identifiers: LCCN 2022029235 (print) | LCCN 2022029236 (ebook) | ISBN 9781611977301 (paperback) | ISBN 9781611977318 (ebook)
Subjects: LCSH: Business--Mathematical models. | Industrial management--Econometric models. | AMS: Systems theory; control -- Instructional exposition (textbooks, tutorial papers, etc.). | Systems theory; control -- Research exposition (monographs, survey articles). | Game theory, economics, social and behavioral sciences -- Instructional exposition (textbooks, tutorial papers, etc.). | Game theory, economics, social and behavioral sciences -- Research exposition (monographs, survey articles). | Game theory, economics, social and behavioral sciences -- Computational methods. | Operations research, mathematical programming -- Mathematical programming -- Linear programming. | Game theory, economics, social and behavioral sciences -- Game theory -- Dynamic games. | Operations research, mathematical programming -- Instructional exposition (textbooks, tutorial papers, etc.). | Operations research, mathematical programming -- Research exposition (monographs, survey articles).
Classification: LCC HD30.25 .K37 2022 (print) | LCC HD30.25 (ebook) | DDC 658.001/51--dc23/eng/20220712
LC record available at *https://lccn.loc.gov/2022029235*
LC ebook record available at *https://lccn.loc.gov/2022029236*

This book is dedicated to

all our great teachers,

our parents being the first ones

Contents

List of Figures

List of Tables

List of Algorithms

Preface

In this book, business dynamics refers to a combination of business management and financial objectives embedded in a dynamical system model subject to a control that optimizes an index that takes both management and financial aspects into account. For example, a supply chain model can be viewed from the point of view of inventory level control, avoiding stock-outs, etc. (management problems) or from a purely financial viewpoint (optimizing economic value added). We seek to combine both aspects by proposing an index (to be optimized in the short term [one step ahead]) which combines both management and financial concerns and, at the same time, is computationally tractable. Financial objectives usually involve wealth maximization, possibly constrained by risk aversion.

This book was born out of two courses offered to advanced undergraduates. While preparing the first, entitled Business Dynamics and Control, the authors realized that the standard texts on business dynamics emphasized modeling aspects but did not really develop systematic approaches based on the well-developed theory of optimal control. The second course, an introduction to optimization for senior undergraduates, was presented from the perspective of modeling and emphasizing the formulation of problems in a format permitting solution by standard mathematical programming software. This led the authors to formulate many of the problems presented in the first course in an optimal control/optimization setting. This book makes an attempt to weave these two strands of control and optimization into a systematic approach. Our hope is that it can be used in a capstone course, either for business or control majors, who have had some exposure to optimization and some basic ideas of control and dynamical systems.

The book is written around a collection of examples that are illustrative and characteristic of the area of business dynamics, in which the control action and its effects are emphasized, particularly in regard to its role in achieving optimality of an appropriate performance index.

In fact, the formulation of this class of problems usually involves an optimal control problem, although not necessarily one that admits a closed form or analytical solution. A control perspective on economics or business dynamics is not new; in fact, the choice of topics in this book has been influenced by the books of McGarvey and Hannon [MH04], Sterman [Ste00], and Sethi and Thompson[ST00]. Bertsimas, O'Hair, and Pulleyblank [BOP16] use linear optimization on resource allocation and revenue management problems (portfolio construction, allocation policies, and online advertising), but the models in [BOP16] are static, as opposed to the dynamic models considered in this book. Furthermore, problems and data are the main focus of [BOP16], while models and methods play a supporting role, for students "with no assumed background knowledge." Duggan [Dug16] focuses exclusively on modeling and statistical model validation when real data are available, using the language R, but there is no discussion of control of the dynamical models considered.

In contrast, this book makes more extensive use of optimization and control tools, presenting one unifying idea or method, namely, one step ahead optimal control. This method is shown to be applicable to a broad class of dynamic business models and results in tractable real time control policies. The level of the book is appropriate for senior undergraduate and first-year graduate students and features examples in MATLAB and Julia (used, for example, in quantitative economics [PSS22]).

We make no claim that the chosen problems are real-life ones, although the problem formulations and solution techniques presented in this book are certainly conducive to scalability, in terms of size as well as complexity.

The optimal solutions presented in the book are obtained through the use of numerical methods for optimal control problems, with special emphasis placed on the formulation of optimal control problems as standard mathematical programming problems, as proposed by Canon, Cullum, and Polak in their pioneering book [CCP70].

More specifically, the central idea in this book is the concept of one step ahead optimal control and its global version, which is referred to as omniscient control. These concepts can be explained as follows. Given a performance criterion, myopic or greedy decisions are those taken on a short horizon, using the current value of the state and exogenous inputs to compute the best or optimal control with respect to the given performance criterion. The shortest horizon, in discrete time, is exactly one step ahead of current time and is the one used in this book. The computed control, which maximizes the objective function one step ahead, is then plugged into the dynamics to determine the next state. In the next step, the updated state and the new exogenous input, which has just become available, are used to determine the new optimal control. This continues, step by step, until the final time is reached. One advantage of this repeated online optimization is its use of feedback, unlike conventional optimal control over a given horizon, which is typically open loop. Dynamic programming based solutions of optimal control problems can be put into feedback form in some cases but otherwise suffer from the curse of dimensionality. Hence another significant advantage of the proposed one step ahead optimal approach is that it always has low computational complexity.

The solutions presented in this book are intended to provide a rationale for the use of optimal control and also to provide guidelines for further investigation into models which are more complex, have more parameters, and include more constraints. In this context, it is also possible to use the formulations presented in a so-called "flight simulator mode" to investigate different complex scenarios.

In published papers, it is often the case that after a specific modeling approach and solution technique are chosen, the model is simplified or modified in such a way that application of the chosen technique yields analytical results. For example, in the literature on supply chains using control techniques, considerable emphasis is placed on the use of a particular control structure (proportional-integral-derivative) and on control objectives (such as regulation to specified stock levels), so that existing techniques from feedback control can be applied. Another example comes from the literature on market share dynamics under advertising expenditure, in which much effort has been spent on the application of optimal control tools (e.g., the maximum principle) to obtain analytical results, often tweaking the dynamics to make this possible.

In contrast, the examples chosen in this book favor models that contain some realistic features, even if they are not conducive to the application of theoretical tools in order to establish analytical results. Thus the examples rely on an appropriate problem formulation and efficient modern optimization software to obtain numerical solutions, rather than analytical ones. Of course, this also implies that effort is needed to interpret numerical results in more general terms, extracting a suitable control or management philosophy from them, and this is done wherever possible. A further aid to the reader's comprehension and interpretability of the different dynamics and strategies studied in the book is a profusion of graphs accompanying the numerical examples. Code for all the examples in the book is posted at bookstore.siam.org/dc40/bonus. The codes should be regarded as illustrative rather than definitive, since they come with no guarantees.

For several of the dynamical models considered in the book, numerical examples show that the one step ahead optimal solution is identical to the omniscient optimal one. This suggests deeper investigation, leading to theoretical results. The authors made the decision, in the interest of a broader audience, to avoid the classical definition-theorem-proof format, adopting instead a formulation-algorithm-example approach in this book, leaving the former to future technical publications, or even a future edition. Thus, this book does not give comprehensive theoretical treatments of the problems studied in each chapter. On the contrary, there is a narrow focus on showing the simplicity and wide applicability of the one step ahead optimal control approach. The Notes and References sections at the end of each chapter attempt to paint a somewhat broader picture of the related approaches to the problem, citing references that develop methods similar in spirit to the ones in the book. Once again, there is no claim to completeness, and the authors apologize in advance for omissions, which should be understood to have occurred merely as a result of lack of awareness.

Acknowledgments

We would like to acknowledge the help of our former student Leonardo Valente Ferreira for overall computational support and coding and running numerical examples in MATLAB in Chapter 5, as well as the assistance of our current student Luiz Carlos de Barros Roth for coding and running numerical examples in Julia in Chapter 6. We thank Ana Claudia Ribeiro of E-papers Serviços Editoriais Ltda. for help with the index and the cover art. It is a distinct pleasure to acknowledge, for the second time around, the ever-accommodating Elizabeth Greenspan, Executive Editor at SIAM, who handled our book with her customary good cheer and efficiency, as well as SIAM's excellent copy-editing staff. We also thank two anonymous reviewers for constructive comments on the draft of this book.

We acknowledge and thank Benito van der Zander, Jan Sundermeyer, Daniel Braun, and Tim Hoffmann for their excellent LaTeX editor TeXstudio; The Inkscape Project; Ottfried Cheong for the Ipe extensible drawing editor; Alan Edelman, Viral Shah, and the Julia team for making Julia available; and Iain Dunning, Joey Huchette, and Miles Lubin for the algebraic modeling language JuMP (written in Julia), which is the computational workhorse used throughout the book. We are immensely grateful to Portal Periódicos and Alexandra Elbakyan.

As always, special thanks are due to Chean (EK) and Lucia (AB), who tolerated our absences, both physical and mental, with great patience and energy, all the way from the conception of the book, through the difficult times of the pandemic, to its completion.

The research leading to this book was financed in part by the Coordenação de Aperfeiçoamento de Pessoal de Nível Superior - Brasil (CAPES) Finance Code 001. AB's research was partially supported by the research grants BPP/PQ 310646/2016-2 and Universal 406106/2016-9 from the Brazilian National Council for Scientific and Technological Development (CNPq). EK's research was supported by a grant from Foundation Carlos Chagas Filho Research Support of the State of Rio de Janeiro (FAPERJ) Bolsa PVE E-26/201.972/2016. The authors would like to acknowledge and thank all these funding agencies, as well as their home institution, the Federal University of Rio de Janeiro (UFRJ), where all the work described in this book was carried out, in the Center for High Performance Computing (NACAD) and the Department of Electrical Engineering (PEE), at the Graduate School of Engineering (COPPE).

Rio de Janeiro, September 21, 2022

Chapter 1

An overview of some models in business dynamics

This chapter gives brief verbal descriptions of the business dynamics models that will be studied in the subsequent chapters, where they will be represented by discrete-time dynamical systems, which are also referred to as ordinary difference equations or recurrences. The models studied in this book are not intended to be fully realistic. However, all contain enough elements of the corresponding real-world problems so as to capture the essential dynamics, and hence the important behavioral features, of the former.

1.1 ▪ Debt amortization problem

The simplest version of the debt amortization problem is nicknamed the credit card problem and described as follows. An individual wishes to use monthly income to pay off (amortize) a fixed credit card debt over a given period of time, without compromising whole income (i.e., limiting the amount of monthly amortization payment), and wishes to find the best schedule of payments to achieve this goal. In Chapter 3, this simple model is generalized to the debt amortization problem for a firm, for debts that may not be fixed, through payments from different investment accounts, subject to corresponding transaction costs. Some debts may be allowed to grow in certain periods, provided that the overall assets of the firm are maximized over a given planning horizon. The decision maker must determine the monthly amortization payment schedule (i.e., how much, and from which investment accounts), in order to achieve the objective of zeroing the debt over a given period of time. The amortization payment schedule is interpreted as the control sequence, found using the one step ahead optimal control as well as the omniscient optimal control formulations, in order to permit comparison of performances. The mathematical formulations are followed by numerical examples.

1.2 ▪ Cash balance problem

The simplest cash balance problem is one in which an individual has a current account which receives incoming flows of bills to pay and of deposits (sales and other dividends), as well as an investment account, from which withdrawals may be made in order to avoid an overdraft on the current account, and into which excess cash from the current account may be deposited, to earn interest for the individual. The individual's objective is to maximize wealth, while avoiding overdraft in the current account and shorting in the investment account. In this problem, the cash transfers, which incur transaction costs, are the control inputs, to be determined using the one step ahead optimal control. The omniscient optimal control formulations are also studied, for comparison. In Chapter 4, this is generalized to a cash management problem for a firm, with more than one investment account, transaction costs for cash transfers, and risk minimization all taken into account. Numerical examples follow the mathematical formulations of the cash balance problems considered.

1.3 ▪ Dynamic trading

Suppose that, at time k, an investor holds a certain amount of assets and a certain quantity of cash. Each asset has a price at time k and can be sold and converted into cash at this price. In the reverse direction, the investor can buy assets with cash, at their current prices, converting cash into assets. Cash is held in an account that accumulates interest at a given rate. Withdrawals from this account to buy assets are subject to a transaction cost that is proportional to the amount withdrawn. Given asset price series which vary with time according to the market, the simplest version of the dynamic trading problem, over a specified horizon, is that of determining the sequence of asset and cash holdings, at each instant in this horizon, that will lead to the maximization of the total wealth (cash plus cash value of assets held at the end of the trading horizon). Needless to say, the investor or trader is only aware of the past price and the current price at the time they have to make each decision over the trading horizon. Chapter 5 shows how to apply the one step ahead optimal control approach to this problem, under this realistic information constraint. Comparison is made, as usual, of the one step ahead with the omniscient approach, where the latter assumes that the asset prices are known *a priori* over the entire planning horizon. In addition, the chapter also proposes a simple approach to include risk reduction in the one step ahead optimization problems. As usual, numerical examples illustrate the proposed solution methods.

1.4 ▪ Inventory control and management

McGarvey and Hannon [MH04] describe a simple supply chain problem in the following terms:

> One of our most difficult issues involves understanding the complex way in which the world of the customer connects with the world of retail business. The vagaries of pleasing customers on the one hand while dealing with suppliers on the other can sometimes seem overwhelming. Charge too much or not have the article in stock, and you may never see the customer again. Order too much or too often, and you may run up the inventory cost, causing profits to vanish. This is a balancing act if ever there was one. How can you walk that tightrope and survive? Reliance on mental models of a process fraught with randomness, feedbacks, and delays makes the most astute of mental management models unreliable.

We take a retail store as the simplest example of a supply chain. The store manager's objective is to choose an ordering sequence, in response to the demand, that maximizes cumulative profit over a given time horizon, assuming that there are costs associated with handling, shipping, storage, and shortage (being out of stock affects sales negatively, since customers are turned away). Finally, profits (= sales revenues minus costs) are discounted using a fixed interest rate and then added over the given horizon to obtain the cumulative profit.

More specifically, given a known fixed delivery delay in receiving goods to restock inventory, the inventory control problem can be formulated as that of maximizing the overall profit, which is the difference between the sales revenue and the sum of shipping, inventory, and lost sales costs, given an uncertain demand. In Chapter 6, the one step ahead optimal control approach will be applied to a suitably formulated cost function, and numerical examples are given to show that it performs reasonably well with respect to the omniscient optimal control approach.

1.5 ▪ Market share dynamics under advertising

The classical Vidale–Wolfe continuous-time dynamical system models the evolution of market share, of a single firm (monopoly), under advertising. This model has been much studied from the perspective of optimal control over a fixed horizon to solve the problem of finding optimal advertising expenditure over the entire horizon, for example (see [ST00]), in order to maximize an objective function consisting of the market share combined with a negatively weighted advertising expenditure rate, and a terminal constraint on the market share, while satisfying an interval constraint on the advertising expenditure rate. In Chapter 7, the Vidale–Wolfe model and a recent generalization are discretized and subjected to one step ahead optimal control as well as omniscient optimal control advertising policies, for comparison. This is an example of the application of the one step ahead optimal control approach to a dynamical system model which is nonlinear, and more will be said about this in Chapter 7.

Deal [Dea79] generalized the Vidale–Wolfe model to duopolies, and other generalizations have been proposed. Chapter 8 examines discrete-time versions of these duopoly market share models, under one step ahead optimal control advertising policies, in the context of competitive dynamic games. Several numerical examples illustrate the problems discussed in Chapters 7 and 8.

Notes and references

Optimal control has long been applied to problems in business, finance, economics, and management science, an early survey being [Tra68], while book length treatments of the theory have been given in [KS91; Set19; ST00]. The books [MH04; Mor07; RH12; Ste00] focus on modeling issues in business dynamics, with little or no attention given to actual design of controls.

The debt amortization problem is inspired by a similar problem called the credit card problem in [CŻ13], which is solved using an omniscient control based approach. The cash balance problem has a long history: the model used in this book is based on the one presented in [ST00], although the treatment and solution method proposed in this book are quite different. The dynamic trading problem has been treated extensively in the literature, using a wide variety of techniques: the simplified version treated in this book is inspired by a similar, but more complex (and realistic) treatment in [Boy+17], and also by the simple moving average methods, variants of which are widely used in the literature [Cha13]. The supply chain model treated in this book is based on [MH04], in which a proportional, integral, and derivative-type control is used. Finally the models of market share under advertising are based on those presented in [ST00] and variations, such as those in [ABK20].

Chapter 2

Omniscient and one step ahead optimal control

This chapter gives a formal description of the central idea in this book, explaining the concept of one step ahead optimal control and its global version, which is referred to as omniscient control.

2.1 ▪ Omniscient optimal control problems

A discrete-time dynamical system describes the evolution of a state vector $\mathbf{x}$ in $\mathbb{R}^n$, and is usually specified as a discrete-time recurrence or difference equation, with a given initial condition for its state vector. For all cases of interest in this book, the right-hand side of the difference equation, in addition to depending on the state vector $\mathbf{x}$, also depends on a vector $\mathbf{u} \in \mathbb{R}^m$, referred to as the control, and possibly an exogenous input vector $\mathbf{e} \in \mathbb{R}^\ell$.

Consider the following **discrete-time dynamical system**:

$$\mathbf{x}(k+1) = \mathbf{F}(\mathbf{x}(k), \mathbf{u}(k), \mathbf{e}(k), k), \quad k = 1, \ldots, K_f, \tag{2.1}$$

where $\mathbf{x}(k)$ is the state variable, $\mathbf{u}(k)$ is the control input that can be chosen by the decision maker, usually subject to some constraints, and $\mathbf{e}(k)$ is an exogenous input, which is known at time k, but is not known for future times, and is not under the control of the decision maker.

Suppose that the decision maker has to determine control inputs $u(k)$ over a given planning horizon, say $k \in [1, K_f]$. In order to do this, the decision maker defines a certain objective function J that they wish to optimize over the planning horizon. This function J depends on the control $\mathbf{u}(k)$, the exogenous input $\mathbf{e}(k)$, and the state $\mathbf{x}(k)$: specific examples of different choices of J will be given later. In classical control theory, the optimal control problem is that of optimizing the performance index J over some given interval of time, subject to the dynamics (2.1) and possibly some additional constraints on the state and input vectors. The solution to this problem, assuming of course that one exists, determines the optimal control sequence over the entire planning horizon and, in this sense, can be thought of as a global solution.

Thus, the omniscient optimal control problem is defined as the standard optimal control problem of optimizing the objective function J_{om} over the whole planning horizon, by choice of the control sequence $\{\mathbf{u}(k)\}_{k=1}^{K_f}$. Clearly, in order to be able to do this, the entire sequence of exogenous inputs $\{\mathbf{e}(k)\}_{k=1}^{K_f}$ must be known *a priori*, and this is the reason for the adjective "omniscient." To fix ideas, suppose that the optimal control problem is of the Mayer type

[CCP70], [ST00, Chaps. 2, 8], namely, the terminal value of the objective function is to be maximized.

The **omniscient optimal control problem** can then be written as follows:
Given the exogenous input sequence$\{\mathbf{e}(k)\}_{k=1}^{K_f}$,

$$\begin{aligned} &\text{maximize } J_{om}(K_f+1) \\ &\text{subject to the dynamics (2.1) for } k=1,\dots,K_f \\ &\text{by choice of } \mathbf{u}(\mathbf{k}), k=1,\dots,K_f. \end{aligned} \tag{2.2}$$

An important observation, formalized and studied in [CCP70], is that the dynamics in (2.2) can be regarded as K_f equality constraints, turning the optimal control problem into a mathematical programming problem, provided that all the states $\mathbf{x}(k)$ and all the controls $\mathbf{u}(k)$ over the entire horizon, $k = 1,\dots,K_f$, are regarded as decision variables, making up a total of $mK_f + n(K_f + 1)$ decision variables. This means that the entire arsenal of mathematical programming methods can be used to solve optimal control problems; indeed, this will be the main approach taken in this book. The structure of the dynamical system and the objective function will determine the tractability of the mathematical programming problem that results from an optimal control problem. For instance, if the objective function is linear and the dynamical system is linear (i.e., in state and control), then the resulting problem is just a linear programming problem. In more general settings, it will also usually be the case that additional constraints need to be imposed on the state variables $\mathbf{x}(k)$ and the control variables $\mathbf{u}(k)$ and, in these cases, the nature of these constraints will also influence the computational tractability of the mathematical programming problem (2.2).

The adjective omniscient reveals the practical limitation of attempting to use the approach just outlined to compute the optimal control sequence, since a real-world decision maker is not omniscient and will not have the sequence of future exogenous inputs at their disposal. More specifically, they can record past values of the exogenous input, and the current or present value becomes known at the instant of choosing the current control input, but the decision maker never has access to future values of the exogenous input. The next section deals with this practical constraint on the availability of information.

2.2 ▪ The one step ahead optimal control problem

One possible approach to optimal control under the causal information constraint (of not knowing future inputs) is to use **one step ahead optimal control** (OSAOC), in the terminology of this book. Note that, given the exogenous input $\mathbf{e}(k)$ and the state $\mathbf{x}(k)$ at time k, from the dynamics (2.1), the control $\mathbf{u}(k)$ at instant k determines the value of the state at the next time instant, $\mathbf{x}(k+1)$.

First, we define the one step ahead optimal approach in words. Given a performance criterion, myopic or greedy decisions are taken on a short horizon, in the limit, just one step ahead, using the current value of the state and exogenous inputs to compute the best or one step ahead optimal control with respect to the given performance criterion. This computed control is then plugged into the dynamics to determine the next state. In the next step, the updated state and the new exogenous input, which has just become available, is used to determine the new optimal control. This continues, step by step, until the final time or end of the horizon is reached. One advantage of this repeated online optimization is that it incorporates state feedback, unlike conventional (i.e., omniscient) optimal control over a given horizon, which is typically an open-loop control (i.e., does a computation of the control sequence over the entire horizon and does not use feedback).

Let the one step ahead performance index be denoted $J_{os}(\mathbf{x}, \mathbf{u}, \mathbf{e})$.

The **one step ahead optimal control problem** at time k is then defined as follows:
Given the exogenous input $\mathbf{e}(k)$ and the current state $\mathbf{x}(k)$,

$$\begin{aligned}&\text{maximize } J_{os}(\mathbf{x}(k+1), \mathbf{u}, \mathbf{e}(k))\\&\text{subject to the dynamics } \mathbf{x}(k+1) = F(\mathbf{x}(k), \mathbf{u}, \mathbf{e}(k))\\&\text{by choice of } \mathbf{u}.\end{aligned} \tag{2.3}$$

Substituting for $\mathbf{x}(k+1)$ by $F(\mathbf{x}(k), \mathbf{u}, \mathbf{e}(k))$ in the performance index J_{os},

the **one step ahead optimal control at instant** k, denoted $\mathbf{u}_{os}(k)$, can be defined compactly as follows:

$$\mathbf{u}_{os}(k) := \text{argmax}_{\mathbf{u}} J_{os}(F(\mathbf{x}(k), \mathbf{u}, \mathbf{e}(k)), \mathbf{u}, \mathbf{e}(k)). \tag{2.4}$$

The **model dynamics under one step ahead optimal control** can then be written as

$$\mathbf{x}(k+1) = F(\mathbf{x}(k), \mathbf{u}_{os}(k), \mathbf{e}(k)). \tag{2.5}$$

Formulation (2.3) is clearly usable to compute an optimal sequence of controls in real time, using only the current value of the exogenous input $\mathbf{e}(k)$ and the current state $\mathbf{x}(k)$. At each instant k, after computing the optimal control, denoted $\mathbf{u}_{os}(k)$, the next state can be found from (2.1), and, as soon as the next exogenous input becomes known, (2.4), with k replaced by $k+1$, solved again, to compute the optimal control $\mathbf{u}_{os}(k+1)$. The process is repeated as long as desired, for example, until the end of the planning horizon. Note that this makes it clear that the dynamics (2.5) represents the dynamics (2.1) under a type of feedback control that is computed from (2.4). It should also be noted that the one step ahead optimal control problem is computationally much simpler to solve than the omniscient optimal control problem, since it has only m decision variables, compared with $mK_f + n(K_f + 1)$ for the omniscient optimal control problem. Of course, the one step ahead optimal control problem has to be solved K_f times in order to compute the control sequence over the entire horizon. However, as K_f (horizon) and n (dimension of the state vector) both increase, the number of decision variables in the omniscient optimal control problem increases like the product nK_f, while the one step ahead optimal control problem has the same number m of decision variables at each step. This confers a significant computational advantage on one step ahead optimal control, making it very suitable for real time control.

If the objective functions J_{om} and J_{os} coincide, for example, in the case when J_{om} is the value of some function of the state variables at the end of a simulation horizon, and the one step J_{os} is the same function, over a single time unit, then it is clear that the one step ahead optimal control problem is a suboptimal version of the omniscient optimal control problem and, moreover, that the optimal value of J_{om} is the largest value attainable by J_{os} at the end of a planning horizon. Finally, as with the omniscient optimal control problem, any constraints that need to be imposed on state and control variables can also be included in the one step ahead optimal control formulation. Once again, there are fewer constraints for the one step ahead optimal control problem than for the omniscient optimal control problem; for instance, if there are p constraints for the one step ahead optimal control problem at each time instant k, then there will be pK_f constraints for the omniscient optimal control problem.

Figure 2.1 presents the one step ahead optimal control scheme in a pictorial format.

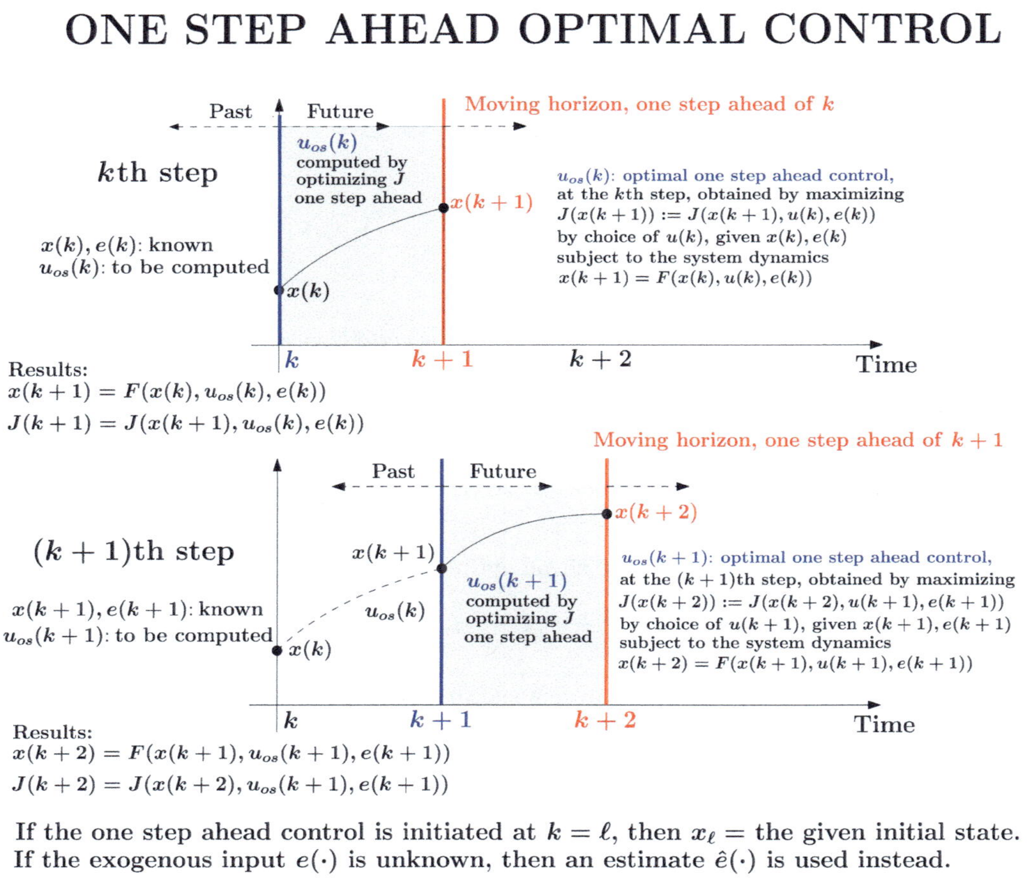

Figure 2.1. *Pictorial description of the one step ahead optimal control approach.*

2.2.1 ▪ Connection between one step ahead optimal control and predictive control

This section points out the connection between one step ahead optimal control and predictive control.

Consider the **time-invariant version of the discrete dynamical system** (2.1)

$$\mathbf{x}(k+1) = \mathbf{F}(\mathbf{x}(k), \mathbf{u}(k), \mathbf{e}(k)), k = 1, 2, \ldots, K_f. \tag{2.6}$$

Assume that, at each step (also referred to as a stage), the index to be maximized is denoted $J_{os}(\mathbf{x}(k), \mathbf{u}(k), \mathbf{e}(k))$. *One step ahead optimization*, called *one step ahead lookahead* in [Ber05, sect. 5], refers to the maximization of J_{os}, by choice of $\mathbf{u}(k) \in \mathcal{U}$, at each step k, subject to the dynamics (2.6) and the state constraints $\mathbf{x} \in \mathcal{X}$. The sets $\mathcal{U}, \mathcal{X}, \mathcal{E}$ are, respectively, the input, state, and exogenous input constraint sets. Note that, in this one step ahead problem, it is assumed that the exogenous input $\mathbf{e}(k)$ is known and, furthermore, belongs to some set $\mathcal{E}$. This aspect of the problem will be discussed further below.

This procedure can be generalized to **an m-step ahead scheme**, in which **the performance index J_{ms} to be maximized**, at step k, is given by

$$J_{ms}(\mathbf{x}(k), \mathbf{u}(k), \mathbf{e}(k)) := \sum_{i=k}^{k+m+1} J_{os}(\mathbf{x}(i), \mathbf{u}(i), \mathbf{e}(i)), \tag{2.7}$$

also subject to the dynamics (2.6) and the constraints $\mathbf{x}(i) \in \mathcal{X}$, $\mathbf{u}(i) \in \mathcal{U}$, $\mathbf{e}(i) \in \mathcal{E}$, for $i = k, k+1, \ldots, k+m-1$.

In other words, at step (or stage) k, given the current state $\mathbf{x}(i)$ and current exogenous input $\mathbf{e}(i)$, a control sequence, denoted $\{\mathbf{u}_{ms}(i)\}_{i=k}^{k+m-1}$, is found by solving the following **m-step ahead deterministic optimal control problem, denoted $P_m(k)$**:

$$\begin{array}{l} \text{maximize } J_{ms} \\ \text{subject to the dynamic constraints } \mathbf{x}(i+1) = \mathbf{F}(\mathbf{x}(i), \mathbf{u}(i), \mathbf{e}(i)), \\ \text{as well as the constraints } \mathbf{x}(i) \in \mathcal{X}, \mathbf{u}(i) \in \mathcal{U}, \mathbf{e}(i) \in \mathcal{E}, \\ \text{for } i = k, k+1, \ldots, k+m-1. \end{array} \tag{2.8}$$

The **m-step ahead predictive control scheme** can now be formulated concisely as follows:

$$\begin{array}{l} \text{Step 1: } k = 1. \\ \text{Step 2: Solve problem } P_m(k) \text{ to obtain } \{\mathbf{u}_{ms}(i)\}_{i=k}^{k+m-1}. \\ \text{Step 3: Apply control } \mathbf{u}_{ms}(k) \text{ to the dynamics (2.6) and update the state.} \\ \text{Step 4: } k \leftarrow k+1 \text{ and return to Step 2, until } k = K_f. \end{array} \tag{2.9}$$

The following observations are important:

- For $m = 1$, the index J_{ms} reduces to J_{os} and the problem $P_1(k)$ is the one step ahead optimization problem.

- In order to be able to solve problem $P_m(k)$, the exogenous inputs $\mathbf{e}(i)$ need to be known for $i = k, k+1, \ldots, k+m-1$. If they are not, they need to be predicted, and this is one reason for the name predictive control.

- Step 3 of (2.9) makes it clear that m-step ahead predictive control is a feedback control scheme. Also note that the computed controls $\mathbf{u}_{ms}(i), i = k+1, \ldots, k+m-1$, are discarded, and only the computed control $\mathbf{u}_{ms}(k)$ is actually used at step k. This also makes it clear that the one step ahead control scheme (i.e., $m = 1$) is the least expensive (and least wasteful) from a computational viewpoint.

- The classical optimal control computed in one shot over the entire horizon is referred to in this book as omniscient optimal control, because it requires knowledge of the entire exogenous control sequence $\mathbf{e}(i)$, $i = 1, \ldots, K_f$, at the outset of the computation. In contrast, the m-step ahead optimal control scheme (2.9) only requires knowledge of the exogenous inputs over a limited horizon: from $i = k$ up to $i = k+m-1$. It is thus clear that m-step ahead optimal control is suboptimal with respect to omniscient optimal control and, furthermore, that the latter serves as a benchmark for the former, in the sense that it represents the best possible performance achievable assuming perfect knowledge of the exogenous inputs.

In practical applications of m-step ahead optimal control, three basic questions arise and serve to highlight the distinction between its use in control problems [Ber05; CA07], as opposed to its use in the business dynamics problems treated in this book.

The first question is with respect to uncertainty in the dynamics of the system under study. In control theory, it is always assumed that the plant (physical object to be controlled) is represented by a mathematical model which, invariably, simplifies the real-world dynamics and thus introduces uncertainty, also called unmodeled dynamics. The m-step ahead optimal control is, of course, computed using the mathematical model and then applied to the plant. This leads to the name model predictive control to emphasize this situation and alert the user to the fact that, once the computed control is applied to the real plant, both modeling uncertainties and disturbances determine the actual next state of the plant, which is measured and fed back to the next step of optimal control computation. Caution and common sense, in the face of uncertainties, dictate that only one step (or, at best a few steps) of the computed optimal control sequence is (are) actually applied to the plant. In contrast, the "plant" in most of the business dynamics models treated in this book represents a kind of bookkeeping (e.g., cash balance, accumulation of credit or wealth, subject to interest) and there is no modeling uncertainty, in this respect.

The second question has to do with prediction of the exogenous inputs when they are unknown. At step k, these exogenous inputs, in control applications, are treated as unknown disturbances, to be rejected, meaning that they should not affect the overall objective of control, which is usually the stabilization of system states in the neighborhood of specified reference values. In the business dynamics models in this book, the exogenous inputs have different characteristics. For instance, they could be cash deposits or withdrawals, sales demands, etc., and are to be accommodated, rather than rejected, while maximizing some performance index. Furthermore, depending on when the control action at step k is taken, it might be reasonable to assume that the exogenous demand is known. As an example, if the control is an ordering decision in a store supply chain and is taken after the close of business for the day (i.e., closing the store), then it is legitimate to assume that the day's demand (total number of sales) is known, and no prediction is needed to calculate the one step ahead optimal control.

The third question involves stability of the state variables. In control applications, given the fact that physical variables are required to remain bounded or tend asymptotically to zero, as well as the presence of model uncertainty and disturbances, there is a strong emphasis on proving some relevant stability result for the system under the feedback (closed-loop) m-step ahead control scheme, often over an infinite horizon. In most of the business dynamics applications in this book, the problems treated are finite horizon problems, and, in addition, it is desirable that some state variables grow exponentially. For example, in problems involving management of debt and investments, ideally the debts should decay to zero over the horizon, while the investment account balances should increase exponentially rather than remaining within some lower and upper bounds.

In some problems, it may be convenient to use a certain objective function, denoted J in the omniscient optimal control problem and one step ahead optimal control problem, and a different function, denoted W, to evaluate performance of a given control sequence. In this case too, supposing that $U_{\mathrm{om}}, U_{\mathrm{os}}$ denote the optimal omniscient and one step ahead sequences, comparison will be made between $W(U_{\mathrm{om}})$ and $W(U_{\mathrm{os}})$ in order to determine the level of suboptimality of the one step ahead optimal control. In words, the omniscient solution is used as a reference to evaluate the degree of suboptimality of the one step ahead optimal control. In some of the business models studied in this book, it will be found that one step ahead optimal controls are, in fact, optimal. In other cases, even though one step ahead optimal control is suboptimal, the level of suboptimality turns out to be acceptable, in view of its tractability and computational simplicity. This, together with the flexibility of the one step ahead optimal control method that permits its application in a wide variety of problems, is one of the main messages of this book.

The concept of one step ahead optimal control is also utilized in numerical algorithms; for example, in the search for an optimal step size for the "next" step (i.e., one step ahead) to be taken by an algorithm. An important constraint, for numerical algorithms, is that of convergence, which can be expressed as a nonpositivity constraint on the decrement of a suitably defined function, called a Liapunov function. For more on this subject, which also served as one of the inspirations for the approach adopted in this book, the reader is referred to [BK06, Chapter 3].

2.3 ▪ Simple numerical example of one step ahead and omniscient optimal control

This section illustrates the transcription of an optimal control problem of a discrete dynamical system into a mathematical programming problem. The first example, inspired by [CCP70, Chap. 4, Ex. 37, p. 81], is deliberately chosen to be as simple as possible, with the performance index and the dynamical system both being linear.

The **dynamical system is an integrator or accumulator of the input** $u(k)$ and written as follows:

$$x(k+1) = x(k) + u(k), \quad k = 1, 2, \ldots. \tag{2.10}$$

The **omniscient optimal control problem** is to maximize the final state, given a horizon $K_f = 4$. Formally, **the performance index** associated with this problem is thus written as

$$J_{om}(x, u) = x(K_f). \tag{2.11}$$

In addition, the controls are subject to the constraint $|u(k)| \leq u_{max} = 1$, and the states are constrained to be nonnegative $x(k) > 0$ with the initial state $x(1) = x_{init} = 1$. Framed in this manner, it is clear that this problem is an instance of a finite horizon optimal control problem.

Thus, the mathematical formulation of the **omniscient optimal control problem** is as follows:

$$\begin{aligned} &\text{maximize } J_{om}(x, u) \\ &\text{subject to the dynamics (2.10)} \\ &\text{with } x(k) \geq 0, \\ &\qquad x(1) = x_{init}, \\ &\text{by choice of } |u(k)| \leq 1, k = 1, 2, \ldots, K_f. \end{aligned} \tag{2.12}$$

This example is simple enough to find the **omniscient optimal control**, denoted $u_{om}(\cdot)$, by inspection:

$$u_{om}(1) = u_{om}(2) = u_{om}(3) = u_{max} = 1. \tag{2.13}$$

In other words, the performance index is maximized by using the maximum allowable value of the control at each step. Once the optimal controls are obtained, the omniscient optimal states are also easily computed from the dynamics (2.10).

Following [CCP70], this optimal control problem can clearly be interpreted as a (static) problem of mathematical optimization, which is actually a linear programming problem. The key to this interpretation is to realize that, if all the state variables, $x(i), i = 1, 2, 3, 4$, as well as the controls $u(i), i = 1, 2, 3$, are treated as decision variables, then the dynamics are just linear equality constraints involving these variables, in addition to the nonnegativity constraints on the states and the box constraints on the controls, which are linear inequality constraints. More formally, the vector of decision variables is defined as

$$\mathbf{z} = (x(1), x(2), x(3), x(4), u(1), u(2), u(3))^{\mathsf{T}}. \tag{2.14}$$

The following additional notation is needed:

$$\begin{aligned} \mathbf{w} &= (0, 0, 0, 1, 0, 0, 0), \\ \boldsymbol{\beta} &= (0, 0, 0, 0, -u_{max}, -u_{max}, -u_{max})^{\mathsf{T}}, \\ \boldsymbol{\gamma} &= (0, 0, 0, 0, u_{max}, u_{max}, u_{max})^{\mathsf{T}}, \end{aligned} \tag{2.15}$$

$$\mathbf{R} = \begin{bmatrix} 1 & 0 & 0 & 0 & 0 & 0 & 0 \\ -1 & 1 & 0 & 0 & -1 & 0 & 0 \\ 0 & -1 & 1 & 0 & 0 & -1 & 0 \\ 0 & 0 & -1 & 1 & 0 & 0 & -1 \end{bmatrix}, \quad \mathbf{c} = (x_{init}, 0, 0, 0)^{\mathsf{T}}, \tag{2.16}$$

$$\mathbf{M}_1 = \begin{bmatrix} \mathbf{I}_4 & \mathbf{0}_{4\times 3} \\ \mathbf{0}_{3\times 4} & \mathbf{0}_3 \end{bmatrix}, \quad \mathbf{M}_2 = \begin{bmatrix} \mathbf{0}_4 & \mathbf{0}_{4\times 3} \\ \mathbf{0}_{3\times 4} & \mathbf{I}_3 \end{bmatrix}, \tag{2.17}$$

where $\mathbf{I}_k$ denotes the $k \times k$ identity matrix, $\mathbf{0}_k$ a $k \times k$ matrix of zeros, and $\mathbf{0}_{m\times n}$ an $m \times n$ matrix of zeros.

In this notation, the objective function, $J_{om} = \mathbf{w}^{\mathsf{T}}\mathbf{z}$, and the **omniscient optimal control problem** (2.12) can be written **as the following linear program**:

$$\begin{aligned} &\text{maximize } \mathbf{w}^{\mathsf{T}}\mathbf{z} \\ &\text{subject to } \mathbf{Rz} = \mathbf{c}, \\ &\qquad \mathbf{M}_1\mathbf{z} \geq \mathbf{0}_7, \\ &\qquad \boldsymbol{\beta} \leq \mathbf{M}_2\mathbf{z} \leq \boldsymbol{\gamma}. \end{aligned} \tag{2.18}$$

The one step ahead version of the omniscient problem is defined by choosing the one step ahead analogue of the omniscient performance index J_{om}, namely, maximizing, at each instant k, the state at the next instant $x(k+1)$.

The **one step ahead performance index**, at instant k, is denoted $J_{os}(x(k), u(k))$ and defined as follows:

$$J_{os}(x(k), u(k)) := x(k+1). \tag{2.19}$$

The mathematical formulation of the **one step ahead optimal control problem** for (2.10), at instant k, can now be written as

$$\begin{aligned} &\text{maximize } J_{os}(x(k), u(k)) \\ &\text{subject to the dynamics } x(k+1) = x(k) + u(k) \\ &\text{with } x(k) = \text{known current value} \\ &\text{and } |u(k)| \leq 1, \end{aligned} \tag{2.20}$$

which, by (2.19) and (2.10), is the same as

$$\begin{aligned} &\text{maximize } x(k) + u(k) \\ &\text{with } x(k) = \text{known current value} \\ &\text{and } |u(k)| \leq 1, \end{aligned} \tag{2.21}$$

making it clear that, for each k, the one step ahead optimal control, denoted $u_{os}(k)$, is equal to 1. Thus the one step ahead optimization problem leads to the same result as omniscient optimization, namely, that the one step ahead optimal controls $u_{os}(k) = 1, k = 1, 2, 3$, result in the maximization of the final state $x(4)$. Note that $J_{os}(x(4), u(4)) = J_{om}(x(4), u(4)) = 4$.

In many problems, a natural choice of performance index $J_{om}(x, u)$ involves both the final state and the controls, i.e., the class of Bolza problems [Set19]. For instance, a common choice would be to maximize the terminal state, while using as little control effort as possible, which is encapsulated by the following performance index:

$$J^1_{om}(x, u) = x(K_f) - \alpha \sum_{i=1}^{K_f-1} u(i). \tag{2.22}$$

In this case, if $J^1_{os}(x(k), u(k))$ were chosen to be equal to $x(k) - \alpha u(k)$ for $\alpha > 0$, which is the one step ahead version of the omniscient performance index $J^1_{om}(x, u)$, then the result would evidently be $u^1_{os}(k) = 0, k = 1, 2, 3$, with final state $x(4)$ equal to the initial state $x(1) = 1$. The situation with the omniscient optimal control with performance index $J^1_{om}(x, u)$, however, is the same as before (with index $J_{om}(x, u)$), for $\alpha \in [0, 1)$, with omniscient optimal controls all equal to one and optimal final state $x(4) = 4$. This can be verified by observing that, over the entire horizon, the dynamics (2.10) can be written out in full as follows:

$$\begin{aligned} x(2) &= x(1) + u(1), \\ x(3) &= x(2) + u(2), \\ x(4) &= x(3) + u(3), \end{aligned} \tag{2.23}$$

which implies that

$$x(4) = x(1) + \sum_{i=1}^{3} u(i). \tag{2.24}$$

This, in turn, implies that the performance index can be written solely in terms of the controls $u(\cdot)$ and the initial condition $x(1)$ as

$$J^1_{om}(x, u) = x(1) + (1 - \alpha) \sum_{i=1}^{3} u(i), \tag{2.25}$$

showing clearly that the omniscient optimal control is still $u^1_{om}(k) = 1, k = 1, 2, 3$, as long as $\alpha \in [0, 1)$. However, if $J^1_{os}(x(k), u(k))$ is chosen as before, i.e., equal to $J_{os}(x(k), u(k)) = x(k+1)$, then it is easy to see that the one step ahead optimal control $u^1_{os}(k) = 1, k = 1, 2, 3$, is the same as the omniscient optimal control $u^1_{om}(k) = u_{om}(k), k = 1, 2, 3$.

This discussion brings up an essential point that will reappear in subsequent chapters, namely, that it is necessary to choose the one step ahead optimal index carefully, so that one step ahead optimal control, although suboptimal, achieves results that are reasonably close to those obtained using omniscient optimal control.

2.3.1 ▪ Computational implementation of the simple example

This section shows how the omniscient and one step ahead optimal control problems, formulated as linear programming problems, can be implemented in the algebraic modeling language JuMP (**Ju**lia **M**athematical **P**rogramming) [DHL17], created for use in conjunction with Julia, a relatively new language for scientific computation [Bez+17]. The interesting feature of JuMP is that it permits the user to write code that is very close to the natural mathematical formulation of the problem, without the need to rewrite it in some standard form. In the simple problem (2.10), (2.11), this means that the natural optimal control formulation (2.12) can be coded in JuMP directly, as shown below, without the need for the reformulation (2.18) as a standard linear program.

```
# Omniscient optimal control computation of (2.12)
# Invoking the Algebraic Modeling Language (AML) JuMP
# and the COIN-OR LP solver Clp
using JuMP, Clp

# Naming the model and specifying the solver
m = Model(Clp.Optimizer)

# Parameters
Kf = 4        # Horizon
x_init = 1    # Initial state

# Defining the decision variables for omniscient optimization
@variable(m, x[1:Kf] >= 0 )    # nonnegative decision variables (states)
@variable(m, u[1:Kf-1] )       # decision variables (controls)

# Box constraints on controls
for i in 1:Kf-1
  @constraint(m, u[i] <= 1 )
  @constraint(m, u[i] >= -1 )
end

# Dynamics written as linear constraints
# on the decision variables x[.],u[.]
for i in 1:Kf-1
  @constraint(m, x[i+1] == x[i] + u[i] )
end

# Initial condition imposed as constraint
@constraint(m, x[1] == x_init )

# Objective function
J = x[Kf]
@objective(m, Max, J )

# Carrying out the omniscient optimization
optimize!(m)

#Retrieving and printing the results
println("Omniscient optimal controls, u = ", JuMP.value.(u) )
println("Omniscient optimal states, x = ", JuMP.value.(x) )
println("Omnisc. optimal perf. index, Jom = ", JuMP.objective_value(m) )
```

The output from this code is as follows:

```
Omniscient optimal controls, u = [1.0, 1.0, 1.0].
Omniscient optimal states, x = [1.0, 2.0, 3.0, 4.0].
Omnisc. optimal perf. index, Jom = 4.0.
```

For comparison, the code for one step ahead optimization is shown below.

```
# One step ahead optimal control computation of (2.20)
# Invoking the Algebraic Modeling Language (AML) JuMP
# and the COIN-OR LP solver Clp
using JuMP, Clp
```

```

# Parameters
Kf = 4                # Horizon
x_init = 1            # Initial state
x = zeros(Kf)         # allocating memory for states
uOS = zeros(Kf-1)     # allocating memory for controls
Jos = zeros(Kf)

# Initial condition
x[1] = x_init

# Main one step ahead (OSA) optimization loop
for t in 2:Kf
  #Naming the model and specifying the solver
  mOS = Model(Clp.Optimizer)

  # Decision variables for OSA optimization
  @variable(mOS, xL[1:2])   #state (in OSA loop)
  @variable(mOS, uL)        #control (in OSA loop)

  # Nonnegativity constraint on states
  for k in 1:2
     @constraint(mOS, xL[k]>= 0)
  end

  # Current state imposed as initial condition for OSA optimization
  @constraint(mOS, xL[1] == x[t-1])

  # One step ahead dynamics
  @constraint(mOS, xL[2]== xL[1] + uL )
  # Box constraints on OSA control
  @constraint(mOS, uL <= 1 )
  @constraint(mOS, uL >= -1 )

  # One step ahead objective function, JL
  JL = xL[2]
  @objective(mOS, Max, JL )

  # Carrying out the one step ahead optimization
  optimize!(mOS)

  #Retrieve optimal control and state in OSA loop
  xL_opt = JuMP.value.(xL)
  u_opt = JuMP.value.(uL)

  # Update state and control with OSA optimal values
  x[t] = xL_opt[2]
  uOS[t-1] = u_opt
  Jos[t] = x[t]
end

# Printing out the results
println("One step ahead optimal controls, u = ", uOS )
println("One step ahead optimal states, x = ", x )
println("One step ahead optimal performance index Jos[Kf] = ", Jos[Kf] )
```

The output from this code is as follows:

```
One step ahead optimal controls, u = [1.0, 1.0, 1.0].
One step ahead optimal states, x = [1.0, 2.0, 3.0, 4.0].
One step ahead optimal performance index at Kf, Jos[Kf] = 4.0.
```

Thus, for this simple example, by appropriate choice of the one step ahead performance index J_{os}, it is possible to achieve the same trajectory as that of the omniscient optimal control obtained by using the performance index J (2.11). Similar cases will be seen in subsequent developments in this book.

2.4 ▪ One step ahead optimization with a nonlinear cost function

The second example revisits a classical one from [CCP70, Chap. 4, Ex. 37, p. 81], where it was considered only in the omniscient context. The problem is reproduced here for the reader's convenience:

$$\begin{array}{l} \min \ \sum_{i=1}^{2} \left(x(i)^2 - \frac{1}{2}(-2)^{i-1}\left[(u(i)+2)^2 - 1\right]\right) \\ \text{such that } x(i+1) = x(i) + u(i), \quad i = 1,2, \\ x(1) = 1, \\ -3 \leq u(i) \leq 1, \quad i = 1,2. \end{array} \tag{2.26}$$

Following [CCP70], this simple omniscient optimal control problem can be solved explicitly. Since $x(1) = 1$, from the dynamics, $x(2) = x(1) + u(1) = 1 + u(1)$. Denoting the objective function to be minimized as J_{om}, and substituting for $x(1)$ by 1 and $x(2)$ by $1 + u(1)$, yields, after simplification,

$$J_{om} = \frac{1}{2}u(1)^2 + (u(2)+2)^2 - \frac{1}{2}, \tag{2.27}$$

whence it is clear that $u_{om}(1) = 0$, $u_{om}(2) = -2$, $x_{om}(1) = 1$, $x_{om}(2) = 1$, which give $J_{om} = -\frac{1}{2}$.

First approach to OSA optimization

The omniscient cost function J_{om} is written, in the most straightforward manner, as the sum of two (OSA) functions, denoted $J_{os}(1)$, $J_{os}(2)$, i.e.,

$$J_{os}(i) = x(i)^2 - \frac{1}{2}(-2)^{i-1}\left[(u(i)+2)^2 - 1\right], \quad i = 1,2,$$

so that, clearly,

$$J_{om} = J_{os}(1) + J_{os}(2).$$

Writing out these expressions in full,

$$J_{os}(1) = x(1)^2 - \frac{1}{2}\left[(u(1)+2)^2 - 1\right] = 1 - \frac{1}{2}\left[(u(1)+2)^2 - 1\right],$$

$$J_{os}(2) = x(2)^2 + \left[(u(2)+2)^2 - 1\right],$$

so that the problems of minimizing $J_{os}(1)$ (resp., $J_{os}(2)$) by choice of $u(1)$ (resp., $u(2)$) are decoupled from each other. By inspection, it is clear that the minimizing values, denoted $u_{os}(1)$ (resp., $u_{os}(2)$), are $u_{os}(1) = 1$, $u_{os}(2) = -2$, yielding $x_{os}(1) = 1$, $x_{os}(2) = 2$, and $J_{om}(2) = 0$.

Second approach to OSA optimization

Once again, the idea is to write the omniscient cost function as the sum of two (OSA) functions, denoted $J_{os}(1)$, $J_{os}(2)$, but with a different arrangement of the terms, i.e.,

$$J_{os}(1) = x(2)^2 + x(1)^2 - \frac{1}{2}(-2)^{i-1}\left[(u(1)+2)^2 - 1\right]$$

and

$$J_{os}(2) = -\frac{1}{2}(-2)^{2-1}\left[(u(2)+2)^2 - 1\right] = \left[(u(2)+2)^2 - 1\right]$$

so that, again

$$J_{om} = J_{os}(1) + J_{os}(2).$$

Substituting for $x(1)$ by 1 and $x(2)$ by $1 + u(1)$ in the expression for $J_{os}(1)$ yields, after simplification,

$$J_{os}(1) = \frac{1}{2}u(1)^2 - \frac{3}{2},$$

which implies $u_{os}(1) = 0$. From the expression for $J_{os}(2)$, it is obvious that $u_{os}(2) = -2$, from which it follows that, with this choice of the stage cost functions $J_{os}(i), i = 1, 2$, the one step ahead optimal control is the same as the omniscient optimal control, namely, $u_{os}(1) = 0$, $u_{os}(2) = -2$, $x_{os}(1) = 1$, $x_{os}(2) = 1$, which give $J_{om} = -\frac{1}{2}$.

The values of the cost function J obtained at the end of the horizon ($K_f = 2$) by the different techniques are given in Table 2.1 for easy comparison.

Table 2.1. *Values of the cost function at the end of the optimization horizon, using omniscient optimization, as well as two versions of one step ahead optimization.*

	Omniscient	OSA Approach 1	OSA Approach 2
J	$-\frac{1}{2}$	0	$-\frac{1}{2}$

The Julia code for the second approach to one step ahead optimization is given below.

```
#Define the stage cost function
function ccp70_ex4_37(x,u,i)
  return x^2 -0.5*(-2)^(i-1)*((u+2)^2 -1 )
end
#Define parameters
# Parameters
Kf = 1 #11, for second part of the example    # Horizon
x_init = 1;  # Initial state
#One step ahead optimal control
# Invoking JuMP and the COIN-OR LP solver Ipopt
using JuMP, Ipopt
x = zeros(Kf)
x[1] = x_init
u = zeros(Kf-1)
for i in 1:Kf-1
  # Naming the model and specifying the solver
  m = Model(Ipopt.Optimizer)
  set_optimizer_attributes(m, "print_level" => 0 )
  # Defining the decision variable for OSA optimization
  @variable(m, uOS )          # decision variable (control)
  # Box constraints on controls
  @constraint(m, uOS <= 1 )
  @constraint(m, uOS >= -3 )
  if i != Kf
    J = (x[i] + uOS)^2 + ccp70_ex4_37(x[i], uOS , i)
  else
    J = (uOS + 2)^2 - 1
  end
  @objective(m, Min, J)
  # Carrying out the OSA optimization
  optimize!(m)
  u[i] = JuMP.value.(uOS)
```

```
  x[i+1] = x[i]^2 + u[i]
end

#Retrieving and printing the results
println("One step ahead optimal control, u = ", u )
println("One step ahead optimal states, x = ", x )

J_calc = 0
for i in 1: Kf-1
  J_calc = J_calc + ccp70_ex4_37(x[i],u[i],i)
end
println("One step ahead optimal performance index, J = ", J_calc )
```

The output from this code is

```
One step ahead optimal control, u = [-1.6731827041533548e-9],
One step ahead optimal states, x = [1.0, 0.9999999983268173],
One step ahead optimal performance index, J = -0.4999999966536346,
```

confirming the results obtained analytically.

Finally, the difference between the one step ahead optimal control and the omniscient control becomes more evident over a larger horizon. Figure 2.2 below shows the controls and state trajectories for the omniscient and one step ahead optimal approaches for a horizon of 10 steps. After the initial steps, the omniscient and one step ahead controls become essentially identical. The corresponding states, though they track each other, are not identical.

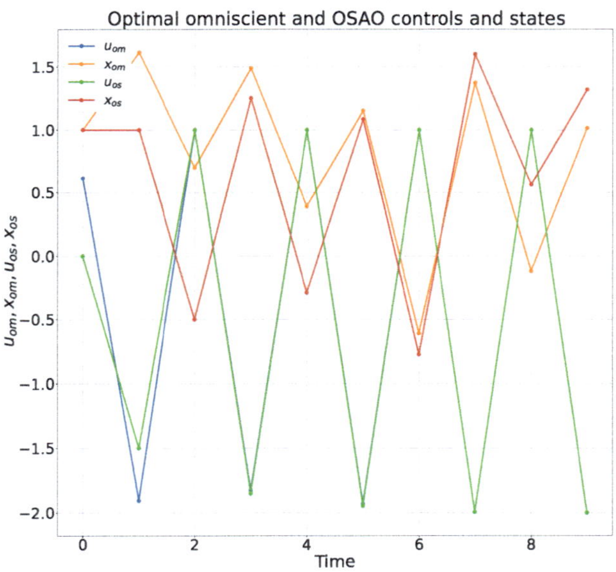

Figure 2.2. *Comparison of one step ahead optimal control and states with omniscient control and states. After the initial steps, the omniscient and one step ahead controls become essentially identical. The corresponding states, though they track each other, are not identical.*

The overall conclusion is that, although one step ahead optimization is suboptimal, there could exist choices of the stage cost functions that result in one step ahead optimization achieving results quite close to the omniscient optimal trajectory. In fact, in most of the applications that arise in this book, the objective function for the one step ahead optimal control problem is expressed as $J_{os}(x(k+1), u(k))$ and thus similar to the second approach described in the above example.

Notes and references

As far as the authors could determine, in a business/finance context, the first mention of what is referred to in this book as one step ahead optimal and omniscient optimal control occurs in the literature on portfolio optimization. Mossin [Mos68] refers to one step ahead optimization as one period optimization and to omniscient optimization as multiperiod optimization. Mossin notes that, in the context of multiperiod optimization, it is generally nonoptimal to make decisions for one period at a time without looking ahead, and he refers to one-period-at-a-time decision making as *myopic*. However, he also shows that, for a class of utility functions (linear, logarithmic, exponential, and power [which includes quadratic]), myopia is optimal. In a recent paper, Dokuchaev [Dok07] confirms Mossin's results in a stochastic setting.

Lavretsky [Lav00], in the context of discrete-time control-affine systems, used the term *greedy control* to denote minimization of the instantaneous quadratic cost function, rather than the cumulative one used in conventional optimal control. He also established a relation between greedy and conventional optimal control, for a class of linear discrete-time systems.

The contributions of Mossin and Lavretsky are the precursors, in the finance and control literature, of the concepts of one step ahead and omniscient optimal control, although neither author exploits these concepts in the manner proposed in this book.

Other, more recent contributions are [WH18] in the context of duopolies with eWOM (electronic Word-of-Mouth) advertising, [Qin+16] who propose the online modified greedy (OMG) algorithm for storage control, [ZC17] in supply chain planning, and [LSZ16] in supply chains with revenue sharing. In the last cited reference, the terminology for one step ahead (resp., omniscient) is myopic (resp., farsighted). A general discussion of myopic methods in management can be found in [Miz10]. The paper [Wan+19] compares farsighted and myopic strategies in a continuous-time manufacturer-retailer supply chain model. The farsighted strategies or controls are calculated by using the Hamilton–Jacobi–Bellman equations for equilibrium solutions of a Stackelberg differential game model. In this book, the authors prefer to use the term *omniscient* instead of *farsighted*, since the latter term may lead to the misleading impression that a farsighted strategy is actually implementable, when in fact it is not, since, at any given instant, the values of all variables (such as demands, costs, and prices) need to be known at all future instants. There have also been other comparisons of myopic versus farsighted behavior in several different contexts [LSZ16; SM06; WH18; ZC17; ZC21], and all these papers use the term farsighted instead of, as in this book, omniscient.

The theoretical underpinnings of limited lookahead policies, which are m-step ahead generalizations of one step ahead optimal control, are discussed in great depth in the classic text [Ber17].

In some dynamical systems, state vectors may be accessible only with bounded delays, and in such systems, it may still be possible to use the one step ahead approach, using the latest available data. An example of this type occurs in the one step ahead approach to the inventory control problem in Chapter 6. A general model of a discrete-time dynamical system with bounded delays in the states is discussed in [KB00], in the context of partially asynchronous (= bounded delays) computation.

For readers who are new to the programming language Julia [Bez+17], in addition to the wealth of material available at https://discourse.julialang.org/, an excellent introduction, in a context similar to the one in this book, can be found in [PSS22]. Similarly, for JuMP [DHL17], which is a domain-specific modeling language for mathematical optimization embedded in Julia, in addition to the official website https://jump.dev/JuMP.jl/stable/, we also recommend [KW19], with optimization codes written in Julia, and [Kwo21], which contains an introduction to JuMP. Both books [KW19] and [Kwo21], as well as the accompanying codes and notebooks, are available online.

For a recent study comparing algebraic modeling languages, such as GAMS, AMPL, JuMP, etc., see [JOP21]. These authors conclude that "in the context of the reviewed algebraic modelling languages, JuMP allows formulating an optimization problem most concisely."

Chapter 3

The debt amortization problem with wealth maximization

This chapter discusses the application of the one step ahead optimal control approach to various models of the debt amortization problem. This is the problem of amortizing given initial debts, in a scenario where there are limits on the amortization payments made from one or more investment accounts, a target date by which the debts should be paid off, as well as the possibilities of incurring additional debts and receiving deposits and dividends in the investment accounts during the planning horizon. It is often the case that the decision maker desires to drive a given debt to zero over a specified horizon and simultaneously has the objective of maximizing wealth (total investment accounts balance less debts) over the same horizon: this is referred to as the debt amortization problem with wealth maximization.

3.1 ▪ Description of the debt amortization problem

To fix ideas, the single debt, single investment account version of the general debt amortization problem is considered first. In this problem, it is assumed that a debt $\{x(k)\} \geq 0$, subject to interest rate α, is increased by a sequence of expenditures $\{c(k)\} \geq 0$ made by its holder (referred to alternatively as the debt manager), who also operates an investment account with balance $\{y(k)\} \geq 0$, which has an associated interest rate of β, and from which transfers are made to amortize the debt. Each transfer $u(k) \geq 0$ out of the investment account is subject to a transaction cost, proportional to the amount being transferred (i.e., $\gamma u(k)$), and there is a cash flow (of deposits $\{d(k)\} \geq 0$) into the investment account. In order to set this problem up as one of optimal control, it is necessary to specify three things: the dynamics, i.e., describe exactly how the amortization payments affect the evolution of the debt and the investment account balance; the control, which, in this case, is clearly the amortization payment sequence; and finally, the performance index that encapsulates the objectives of the debt manager. Some possibilities in regard to the computation of the evolution of the debt and the investment and appropriate performance indices are detailed next. A particular choice of dynamics and performance index leads to a specific optimal control problem.

The omniscient and one step ahead control problems discussed in general terms in Chapter 2 are made more precise in the context of debt amortization as follows. For any one step ahead index, knowledge of the current debt $x(k)$, the current investment account balance $y(k)$, the current expenditure $c(k)$, and the current deposit $d(k)$ is all that is required in order to compute the current one step ahead optimal debt amortization payment $u(k)$. This means that one step ahead schemes can be used in real time or online mode, by which it is meant that the optimal decision depends only on available information (current and past). The optimization of omniscient indices, on the other hand, requires knowledge of the expenditure and deposit sequences over the entire interval, referred to as the planning horizon. This implies that the resulting omniscient control sequences cannot be used for real time debt amortization but only in situations in which there is complete knowledge of future expenditures and deposits, without any uncertainty. In control terminology, one step ahead strategies lead to feedback control, whereas optimal omniscient strategies produce open-loop control. As is well known, feedback controls are equipped to deal with uncertainty (in this case, about the future), since they incorporate the effect of uncertainties, as they occur, into the control decisions. Optimal omniscient controls, in contrast, use exact knowledge of future data in order to find the control at the current time. This presumes that future data are not subject to any uncertainty and, furthermore, implies that optimal omniscient control is noncausal and thus not implementable in any practical situation in which perfect knowledge of the future is unavailable. Nevertheless, it is a useful abstraction permitting the calculation of a hypothetical globally optimum solution against which implementable (suboptimal) solutions can be measured.

3.1.1 ▪ Dynamical models of the debt amortization process

Two models of the debt amortization process are considered, differing only in the order in which the payment is discounted and the interest calculated.

First calculate interest, then discount payment model

In this model the interest α on the current debt $x(k)$ is calculated before the amortization payment $u(k)$ is deducted from the amount owed. Spending $c(k)$, which adds to the overall debt, is also assumed to occur after the interest calculation. The amortization payment $u(k)$ is made by transferring from an investment account, which has current balance $y(k)$ and interest rate β. The transfer is subject to a transaction cost proportional to its amount, with proportionality constant $\gamma > 0$.

The resulting **calculate interest then discount payment (CIDP) dynamical system model** is as follows:

$$x(k+1) = (1+\alpha)x(k) - u(k) + c(k), \tag{3.1}$$
$$y(k+1) = (1+\beta)y(k) - (1+\gamma)u(k) + d(k). \tag{3.2}$$

First discount payment, then calculate interest model

This section considers a debt amortization model, which is similar in all details to the CIDP model, except that the interest α on the current debt $x(k)$ is calculated after the amortization payment $u(k)$ is deducted from the amount owed.

The dynamics of this **discount payment, then calculate interest (DPCI) model**, is as follows:

$$x(k+1) = (1+\alpha)(x(k) - u(k)) + c(k), \tag{3.3}$$
$$y(k+1) = (1+\beta)(y(k) - u(k)) - \gamma u(k) + d(k). \tag{3.4}$$

In both models, the **wealth** $w(k)$ **at instant** k is defined as the investment account balance less the debt:

$$w(k) = y(k) - x(k). \tag{3.5}$$

Remark. The models (3.1), (3.2) and (3.3), (3.4) are simple, and several variants are possible in which, for example, the computation of the investment account balance is made after transfers and transaction costs are deducted and before the deposit has occurred. The one step ahead optimal control approach can be applied to all these variants.

3.1.2 ▪ Performance indices for debt amortization problem with wealth maximization

We first describe possible strategies for debt amortization with wealth maximization in words, and then give the formal mathematical performance indices that are conducive to such strategies.

A straightforward strategy is to choose amortization payments, respecting an upper bound, in such a way that the debt is reduced to zero as fast as possible. On the other hand, if the final wealth $w(K_f)$ is to be maximized, then the interest rate of the investment account may determine that it is not optimal to reduce the debt to zero as fast as possible. This discussion makes it clear that the debt amortization problem can be treated as a multiobjective optimization problem, if the debt $x(k)$ and the investment account balance $y(k)$ are regarded as two performance indices, where the first is minimized and the second is maximized. We use the conventional notation J for performance indices and consider the one step ahead optimization framework,

$$J_1(k+1) := -x(k+1), \tag{3.6}$$

$$J_2(k+1) := y(k+1), \tag{3.7}$$

where J_1 has been defined as the negative of the current debt, in order to consider the case in which both indices are to be maximized. Substituting the right-hand sides of (3.6) and (3.7) by the respective right-hand sides of (3.1), (3.2), in the one step ahead optimization context, it is clear that both J_1, J_2 are functions of the single decision variable $u(k)$, since $x(k), y(k), c(k), d(k)$ are all known at time instant k. Thus the trade-off curve or Pareto frontier in the J_1-J_2 coordinate plane can be found by optimizing a weighted sum of J_1 and J_2, for different choices of weights, with respect to u, and plotting the optimal values of J_1, J_2. The total wealth can be written as the sum $(J_1 + J_2)$; thus maximizing this sum corresponds to maximizing wealth.

In order to investigate the trade-off between indices J_1 and J_2, weighted performance indices are now defined. It should also be noted that the use of weighted performance indices allows the debt amortization with wealth maximization problem to be approached in the one step ahead and omniscient optimal frameworks, which are defined in terms of a single objective function.

Two **weighted debt amortization performance indices**, to be **maximized**, are defined:

$$J_{os}^{sd,\omega}(k+1) := \kappa y(k+1) - \mu x(k+1) = \kappa J_2 + \mu J_1, \tag{3.8}$$

$$J_{om,f}^{sd,\omega} := \kappa y(K_f+1) - \mu x(K_f+1). \tag{3.9}$$

The superscript sd indicates that a single debt is being considered, while superscript ω indicates that the index is weighted, the weights being κ and μ, i.e., $\omega = (\kappa, \mu)$. The subscript os

pertains to the one step ahead case, om to the omniscient case, and, for the omniscient case, the subscript f indicates the fact that only the final values of x and y, i.e., those at the end of the planning horizon, are taken into account. It should also be noted that, for the index $J_{os}^{sd,\omega}$, the choice of weights $\kappa = 0, \mu = 1$ corresponds to what might be referred to as strict debt amortization, namely, the problem of driving the debt to a minimum value, ideally zero, without any concern for the final wealth achieved. The choice $\kappa = 1, \mu = 1$ corresponds to the maximization of total wealth. Any other choice of nonnegative weights implies that neither debt minimization nor wealth maximization will necessarily occur when the index is maximized. However, if κ is chosen larger than μ, then the tendency of the optimal control will be to maximize wealth. Conversely, with μ much larger than κ, the optimal control will tend to drive the debt to zero. In these cases, when the weights (κ, μ) are equal to neither $(0, 1)$ nor $(1, 1)$, since the value of the optimal performance index is not directly interpretable, it is reasonable to use the final wealth as well as the final debt achieved by the optimal control as measures of its success.

For future reference, when the weights are chosen as $\kappa = 0, \mu = 1$ (resp., $\kappa = 1, \mu = 1$) the index and related optimal control problem will be qualified with the adjectives *debt amortization* (resp., *wealth maximization*). All other choices of nonnegative weights correspond to problems of *debt amortization with wealth maximization*; for example, the choice $\kappa = 1$, $\mu = 5$ corresponds to the objective of maximizing the investment account balance, while simultaneously driving the debt to zero.

There are important differences between the one step ahead and omniscient performance indices. The first is that the one step ahead index only requires knowledge of the current debt $x(k)$, the current investment account balance $y(k)$, the current expenditure $c(k)$, and the current deposit $d(k)$ in order to compute the current debt amortization payment $u(k)$. Thus, it is possible to use the one step ahead scheme of minimizing $J_{os}^{sd,\omega}(k)$ at each k in a real time debt management scheme. Using the omniscient index $J_{om,f}^{sd,\omega}$ to compute the sequence of debt amortization payments, on the other hand, requires knowledge of the initial debt, the initial investment account balance, and the expenditure and deposit sequences over the *entire* planning horizon $[1, K_f]$. This index can only be used in situations in which there are no unforeseen expenditures or deposits in the whole planning period. In this chapter, as in the rest of the book, even though omniscient knowledge is almost never available in most real situations, the omniscient scenario is used as an ideal case or benchmark against which performance of the one step ahead schemes is evaluated.

The indices (3.8) and (3.9) are linear. It can be shown that quadratic indices lead to the same optimal amortization payments, but of course they involve the use of solvers for quadratic problems, whereas the indices (3.8), (3.9) require only the use of linear programming solvers, which are more scalable.

Note also that the omniscient index (3.9) could allow the debt to grow during the interval $[1, K_f]$, as long as the (weighted) final wealth is maximized. A large intermediate growth of debt would alarm most debt managers, even though the amortization policy is known to be long-term optimal. In other words, the choice of the weights κ and μ allows a debt manager to trade off the speed of debt amortization for the growth of investment account balance. Numerical examples, as well as the determination of the Pareto frontier, will clarify this further.

3.2 ▪ Omniscient optimal control formulation of debt amortization and wealth maximization

The omniscient optimal control problem is formulated as the maximization of the performance index $J_{om,f}^{sd,\omega}$ over a given planning horizon $[1, K_f]$, subject to the debt amortization dynamics D, where D = CIDP (equations (3.1) and (3.2)) or DPCI (equations (3.3) and (3.4)).

Thus the **omniscient optimal control debt amortization problem** is

$$\begin{aligned} &\text{maximize } J^{sd,\omega}_{om,f} \\ &\text{subject to debt amortization dynamics } D, k = 1, \ldots, K_f, \\ &0 \leq u(k) \leq u_{\max}, k = 1, \ldots, K_f, \\ &x(k) \geq 0, k = 1, \ldots, K_f + 1, \\ &0 \leq y_{\min} \leq y(k), k = 1, \ldots, K_f + 1. \end{aligned} \tag{3.10}$$

The upper bound $u_{\max}$ is imposed because in most practical cases the initial debt is large enough to make it difficult to be paid off in one installment right after it is contracted. Also such a strategy would leave the debtor with very little liquidity for expenditures other than debt servicing. On the other hand, the minimum investment account balance $y_{\min}$ is usually stipulated by the financial institution handling the investment.

3.3 ▪ One step ahead optimal control formulation of debt amortization with wealth maximization

In this section too, the notation D is used for debt amortization dynamics D, where $D =$ CIDP (equations (3.1) and (3.2)) or DPCI (equations (3.3) and (3.4)).

The **one step ahead optimal control debt amortization problem** is formulated as follows:

$$\begin{aligned} &\text{maximize } J^{sd,\omega}_{os}(k+1) \\ &\text{subject to debt amortization dynamics } D \text{ at instant } k, \\ &0 \leq u(k) \leq u_{\max}, \\ &x(k) \geq 0, \\ &0 \leq y_{\min} \leq y(k). \end{aligned} \tag{3.11}$$

3.3.1 ▪ Analytical determination of one step ahead optimal control for the CIDP and DPCI models

The single debt models CIDP and DPCI are simple enough to permit analytic calculation of one step ahead optimal control. This section shows the calculation for the CIDP model, since it allows the determination of the entire Pareto frontier, as the weights κ and μ in the performance index $J^{sd,w}_{os}$ are varied.

The following temporary notation will be used: variables at instant $k+1$ will be indicated with a superscript $+$, and variables at instant k will be written without the (k); thus $x(k+1)$ will be denoted x^+ and $x(k)$ written simply as x. In this notation, $J^{sd,\omega}_{os} = \kappa y^+ - \mu x^+$ and substituting for x^+, y^+ by the right-hand sides of (3.1), (3.2) yields

$$J^{sd,\omega}_{os} = \underbrace{(\kappa(1+\beta)y - \mu(1+\alpha)x + \kappa d - \mu c)}_{A} + \underbrace{(\mu - \kappa(1+\gamma))}_{B}\, u, \tag{3.12}$$

which is the equation of a straight line with intercept A and slope B, so that the one step ahead optimal control, denoted as u^*_{CIDP}, depends only on the slope B and can be written as

$$u^*_{CIDP} = \begin{cases} u_{\max} & \text{if } B > 0, \\ 0 & \text{if } B < 0. \end{cases}$$

Finally, if $B = 0$ (i.e., $\mu = \kappa(1+\gamma)$), then (3.12) shows that the control u has no effect on the index, which can be interpreted to mean that all values of $u \in (0, u_{\max})$ are optimal for this particular choice of weights.

Thus, the complete expression for the one step ahead optimal control u^*_{CIDP} can be written as

$$u^*_{CIDP} = \begin{cases} u_{\max} & \text{if } \mu > \kappa(1+\gamma), \\ 0 & \text{if } \mu < \kappa(1+\gamma), \\ \in (0, u_{\max}) & \text{if } \mu = \kappa(1+\gamma). \end{cases} \tag{3.13}$$

Some important observations about the optimal control u^*_{CIDP} in (3.13) are as follows:

- It is independent of the interest rates α and β.
- Although it superficially resembles an all or nothing bang-bang type control, the transition between 0 and $u_{\max}$ is predicated on the relation among the parameters μ, κ, γ and not on values of the state variables $x(k)$, $y(k)$, which is the usual case with bang-bang control.
- From (3.13), in the **special case** $\kappa = \mu = 1, \gamma > 0$, the **one step ahead optimal control** u^*_{CIDP} **is identically zero**, which indicates that the choice of equal weights is not a good one in this case. In the numerical examples in the following section, this particular choice of weights will be used only to calculate the omniscient solution, and the associated value of final wealth attained by it, since this represents a global optimum for final wealth, to be used for comparative purposes.

The values of J_1, J_2 for the two possible optimal values of u from (3.13) are

$$J_1 = \begin{cases} J_1^{\bar{u}} := -[(1+\alpha)x(k) - u_{\max} + c(k)] & \text{for } (\mu > \kappa(1+\gamma)), \\ J_1^0 := -[(1+\alpha)x(k) + c(k)] & \text{for } (\mu < \kappa(1+\gamma)), \end{cases} \tag{3.14}$$

$$J_2 = \begin{cases} J_2^{\bar{u}} := (1+\beta)y(k) - (1+\gamma)u_{\max} + d(k) & \text{for } (\mu > \kappa(1+\gamma)), \\ J_2^0 := (1+\beta)y(k) + d(k) & \text{for } (\mu < \kappa(1+\gamma)). \end{cases} \tag{3.15}$$

The Pareto frontier can now be drawn and is shown in Fig. 3.1. Let P denote the point $(-J_1^{\bar{u}}, J_2^{\bar{u}})$, and Q the point $(-J_1^0, J_2^0)$. Then the slope of the line PQ can be calculated from (3.14), (3.15) to be $(1+\gamma)$. The frontier is as depicted in Fig. 3.1(A), if

$$(1+\beta)y(k) - (1+\gamma)u_{\max} + d(k) < (1+\alpha)x(k) - u_{\max} + c(k)$$

and, otherwise, as in Fig. 3.1(B), if

$$(1+\beta)y(k) - (1+\gamma)u_{\max} + d(k) > (1+\alpha)x(k) - u_{\max} + c(k).$$

In Fig. 3.1, the trade-off can be seen by observing that point P, which corresponds to $u = u_{max}$, represents the best value for index J_1 and the worst for index J_2, while point Q, corresponding to $u = 0$, represents the exact opposite. Points between P and Q represent intermediate values of u in the interval $(0, u_{\max})$, which are optimal when $\mu = \kappa(1+\gamma)$, as explained above. This means that the feasible points and the Pareto points coincide in this case. Point P is optimal for the choice $(\kappa, \mu) = (0, 1)$, while point Q is optimal for $(\kappa, \mu) = (1, 1)$.

Similar calculations for the DPCI case yield

$$u^*_{DPCI} = \begin{cases} u_{\max} & \text{if } \mu(1+\alpha) > \kappa(1+\beta+\gamma), \\ 0 & \text{if } \mu(1+\alpha) < \kappa(1+\beta+\gamma). \end{cases} \tag{3.16}$$

Note that u^*_{DPCI} does depend on the parameters α, β, γ and that, for $\kappa = \mu = 1$, $u^*_{DPCI} \equiv 0$ only if $\alpha < \beta + \gamma$. A final observation is that in more complex models, such as those involving multiple debts and investment accounts, it becomes difficult to find the OSA optimal control

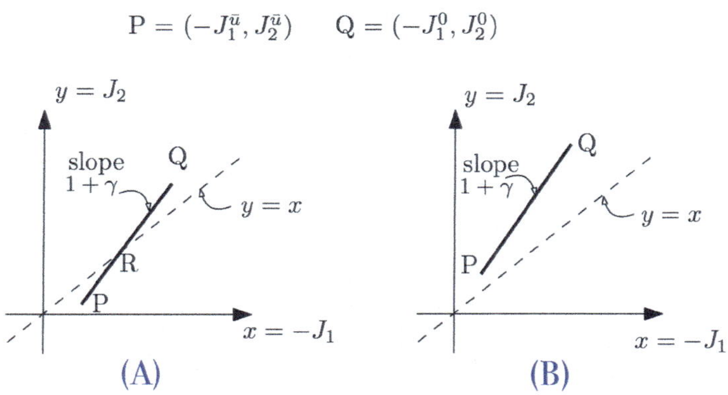

Figure 3.1. *The Pareto frontier for the indices J_1, J_2 in the one step ahead optimal formulation is the straight line joining points P and Q, with slope $(1+\gamma)$. (A) Wealth is positive for the segment QR, which lies above the zero wealth line $y = x$. (B) Wealth is positive for the whole Pareto frontier PQ.*

analytically, and it is necessary to resort to numerical solutions, obtained by the use of optimization software.

3.4 ▪ Numerical examples of debt amortization with wealth maximization

This section presents some numerical examples of OSAOC applied to the CIDP and DPCI models of the debt amortization problem, compared with the omniscient solutions. The expenditure and deposit sequences are given below, with their statistics and properties listed in Table 3.1. For all the numerical examples, the initial debt x is 10,000 and the initial investment account balance y is 15,000. Note that the initial conditions (debt and balance) are crucial in determining if the debt amortization problem possesses a viable solution. For example, assuming zero deposits and expenditures, if the initial debt is considerably larger than the initial investment account balance, then the debt amortization problem may not have a feasible solution, maintaining the investment account balance as nonnegative. Parameters for the numerical examples are in Table 3.2.

Table 3.1. *30-day expenditure and deposit sequences: statistics and properties.*

	Mean	Standard deviation	Property
Expenditures c	1135.3	707.1	Random
Deposits d_1	1500	3411.4	Periodic, period 7
Deposits d_2	1200	3111.7	Periodic, period 10
Deposits d_3	1179.1	757.8	Random

Results of numerical experiments corresponding to the parameter values in rows 1, 3, 6, 9, and 10 of Table 3.2 are shown graphically in Figs. 3.2 through 3.6.

Example 1: Debt amortization, period 7 deposit sequence d_1

In Example 1, shown in Fig. 3.2, the investment account receives the deposit sequence, d_1, and the expenditure sequence, $\{c(k)\}$, described in section 3.4 and Table 3.1, with parameter values given in row 1 of Table 3.2.

Table 3.2. *Parameter values for the numerical examples in section* 3.4.

Example	α	β	γ	κ	μ	$u_{\max}$	$y_{\min}$	Expenditure	Deposit	Model
1	0.07	0.03	0.01	0	1	3000	0	d_1	c	CIDP
2	0.07	0.03	0.01	1	1	3000	0	d_1	c	CIDP
3	0.07	0.03	0.01	1	5	3000	0	d_1	c	CIDP
4	0.07	0.03	0.01	0	1	3000	0	d_2	c	CIDP
5	0.07	0.03	0.01	1	1	3000	0	d_2	c	CIDP
6	0.07	0.03	0.01	1	5	3000	0	d_2	c	CIDP
7	0.07	0.03	0.01	0	1	3000	0	d_3	c	CIDP
8	0.07	0.03	0.01	1	1	3000	0	d_3	c	CIDP
9	0.07	0.03	0.01	1	5	3000	0	d_3	c	CIDP
10	0.07	0.03	0.01	0	1	3000	0	d_1	c	DPCI
11	0.07	0.03	0.01	1	1	3000	0	d_1	c	DPCI
12	0.07	0.03	0.01	1	5	3000	0	d_1	c	DPCI

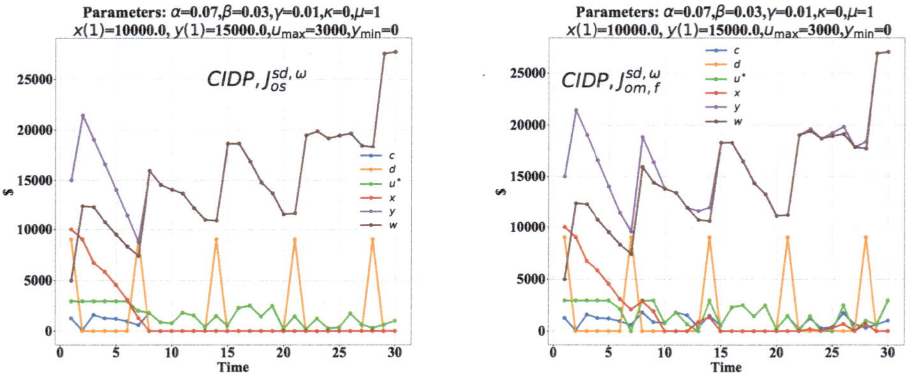

(a) One step ahead amortization payments

(b) Omniscient amortization payments

Figure 3.2. *Amortization payments for Example* 1, *with parameters as in row* 1 *of Table* 3.2, *maximizing the indices* (a) $J_{os}^{sd,\omega}$ *and* (b) $J_{om,f}^{sd,\omega}$, *respectively. The one step ahead and omniscient strategies are almost identical, except for the turnpike effect in the latter, with the initial transient lasting to instant* $k = 15$, *and the final transient occurring from* $k = 25$ *to* $k = 30$. *Payments* u *(green line) track the expenditure* c *(blue line) exactly after an initial transient in the one step ahead case.*

Example 3: Debt amortization and wealth maximization, period 7 deposit sequence d_1

In Example 3, shown in Fig. 3.3, the investment account receives the deposit sequence, d_1, and the expenditure sequence, $\{c(k)\}$, described in section 3.4 and Table 3.1, with parameter values given in row 3 of Table 3.2.

Example 6: Debt amortization and wealth maximization, period 10 deposit sequence d_2

In Example 6, shown in Fig. 3.4, the investment account receives the periodic deposit sequence, d_2, and the expenditure sequence, $\{c(k)\}$, described in section 3.4 and Table 3.1, with parameter values given in row 6 of Table 3.1.

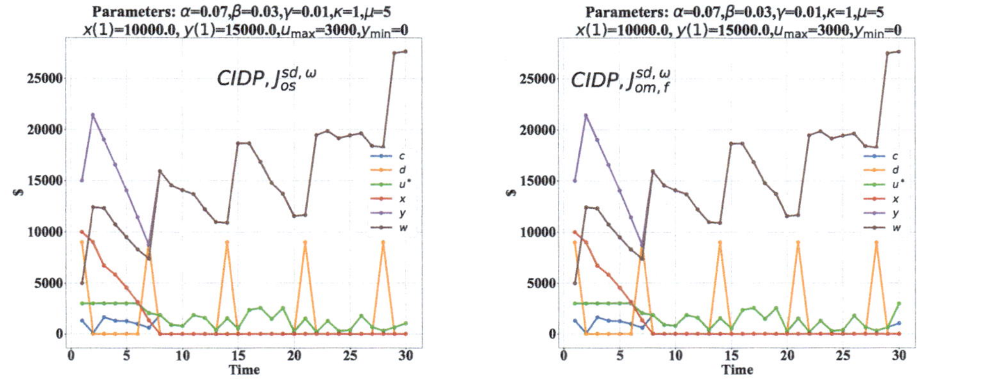

(a) One step ahead amortization payments (b) Omniscient amortization payments

Figure 3.3. *Amortization payments for Example* 3*, with parameters as in row* 3 *of Table* 3.2*, maximizing the indices* (a) $J_{os}^{sd,\omega}$ *and* (b) $J_{om,f}^{sd,\omega}$*, respectively. The investment account receives a periodic (weekly) deposit sequence* $\{d(k)\}$ *of* 9000 *units. The one step ahead and omniscient strategies are identical (except for the turnpike effect), with payments* u *(green line) tracking the expenditure* c *(blue line) exactly after an initial transient.*

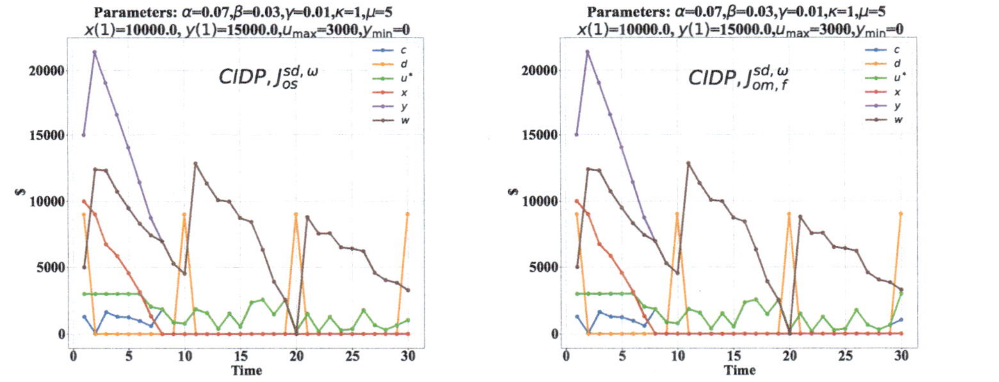

(a) One step ahead amortization payments (b) Omniscient amortization payments

Figure 3.4. *Amortization payments for Example* 6*, with parameters as in row* 6 *of Table* 3.2*, maximizing the indices* (a) $J_{os}^{sd,\omega}$ *and* (b) $J_{om,f}^{sd,\omega}$*, respectively. The investment account receives a periodic deposit sequence* $\{d(k)\}$ *of* 9000 *units every* 10 *days. The one step ahead and omniscient strategies are identical (except for the turnpike effect), with payments* u *(green line) tracking the expenditure* c *(blue line) exactly after an initial transient. Both strategies thus attain the same final wealth value, at* $k = 30$*, of* 3268 *units, which is much lower than the corresponding value in Fig.* 3.3*; this is to be expected, since the period of the deposits has been increased from* 7 *to* 10*.*

Example 9: Debt amortization and wealth maximization, random deposit sequence d_3

In Example 9, shown in Fig. 3.5, the investment accounts for both the deposit sequence $\{d(k)\}$ and the expenditure sequence $\{c(k)\}$ are randomly generated, with their respective mean values as in Table 3.1.

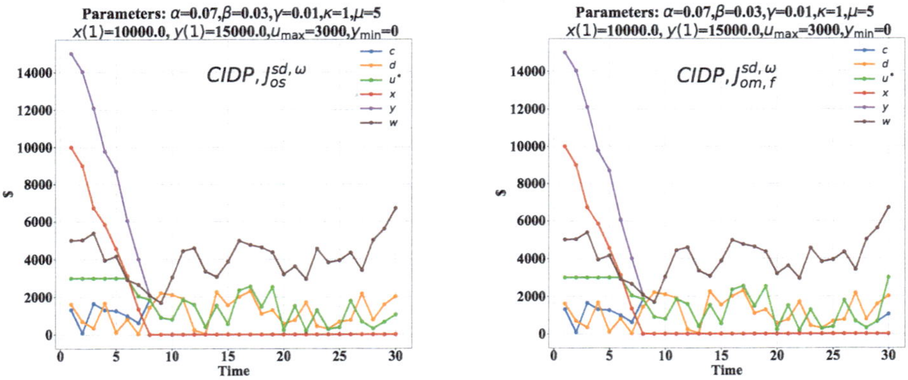

(a) One step ahead amortization payments (b) Omniscient amortization payments

Figure 3.5. *Amortization payments for Example* 9, *with parameters as in row* 9 *of Table* 3.2, *using* (a) *the one step ahead and* (b) *omniscient optimal controls. The one step ahead and omniscient strategies are identical, tracking the expenditure* c *(blue line) exactly after an initial transient.*

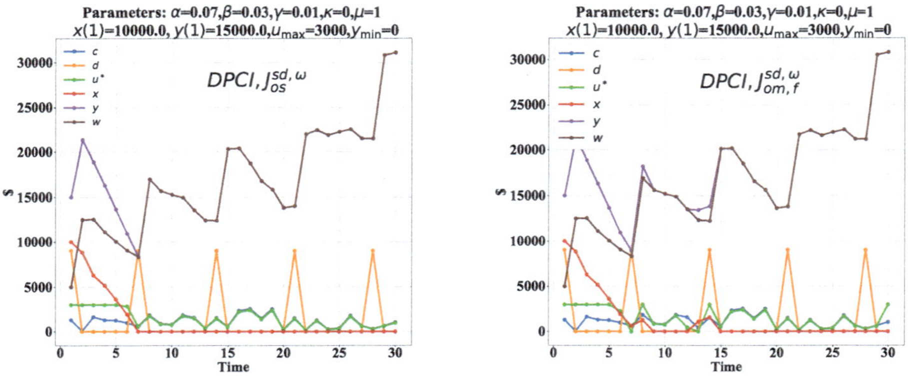

(a) One step ahead amortization payments (b) Omniscient amortization payments

Figure 3.6. *Amortization payments for Example* 10, *with parameters as in row* 5 *of Table* 3.2, *using* (a) *the one step ahead and* (b) *omniscient optimal controls, obtained by maximizing the indices* $J_{os}^{sd,\omega}$ *and* $J_{om,f}^{sd,\omega}$, *respectively. Observe that the amortization payments for the one step ahead and omniscient strategies are almost identical, both tracking the expenditure* c *(blue line) almost immediately after an initial transient.*

Example 10: Debt amortization, period 7 deposit sequence d_1 (DPCI model)

In order to compare the CIDP and DPCI models, Example 10 uses the DPCI model with the parameters of row 10 of Table 3.2 and with a periodic (weekly) deposit d_1 of 9000 units.

Discussion of numerical examples of OSAOC applied to the CIDP and DPCI models

The main lessons that can be learned from the numerical examples in this section are as follows:

1. For the CIDP model, the one step ahead optimal control, with weights chosen to amortize debt (i.e., $\kappa = 0, \mu = 1$) produces results identical to the omniscient solution, with weights chosen to maximize wealth (i.e., $\kappa = 1, \mu = 1$). This is remarkable, since the one step

ahead optimal control strategy, with debt amortization weight choice $\kappa = 0, \mu = 1$, does not use (unavailable) information about the future values of deposits or expenditures yet still achieves globally optimal (= omniscient) wealth maximization, in addition to zeroing the debt. On the other hand, the choice $\kappa = 0, \mu = 1$ is not a good one for the omniscient index, since it does not correspond to wealth maximization: this can be seen in rows 1, 4, 7 (CIDP), and 10 (DPCI) of Table 3.3. On the other hand, the choice $\kappa = 1, \mu = 1$ for wealth maximization does not work for the one step ahead index, since it results in zero control action for the CIDP model as shown in section 3.3.1, and the result is that, for this choice of index, the debt grows exponentially, as does the investment account balance, with a larger growth for the former, because of the higher interest rate. This can be seen in rows 2, 5, and 8 of Table 3.3. Finally, for the examples above, the choice of weights $\kappa = 1, \mu = 5$ results in debt amortization as well as wealth maximization for both the one step ahead strategy and the omniscient solution. However, for other parameter values, the choice of weights may require tuning, with a larger value of μ (for example) in order to ensure simultaneous debt amortization and wealth maximization. In this context, the choice of weights $\kappa = 0, \mu = 1$ for the one step ahead strategy is the best, since it requires no tuning for different parameters and always results in debt amortization (by design) and could also result in wealth maximization.

2. The final wealth values attained are larger for the DPCI model in comparison with those obtained for the CIDP model when, as in the numerical example, the interest rate on the debt is considerably higher than that on the investment account. In this scenario, discounting an amortization payment from the debt balance first and then calculating interest on the remaining debt clearly leads to a slower growth of the debt over time. Compare rows 1, 2, and 3 of Table 3.3 with rows 10, 11, and 12.

3. The one step ahead optimal control approach can be used as a financial calculator that allows a manager to decide, for example, optimal transfers from investment accounts to amortize debts, as well as the amount and frequency of deposits that must be made into the investment account.

Table 3.3. *Variation of final debt and wealth as a function of the weighting parameters $\kappa_i, \mu_i, i = 1, 2$. Final values of debt and wealth are evaluated at $k = 30$ in order to avoid the turnpike effect for the omniscient solutions. Entries in boldface represent globally optimal values of final wealth. The negative values for final wealth $w(K_f)$ that occur in the last column (in rows 2, 5, and 8) illustrate the result in section* 3.3.1.

Example	κ	μ	Model	Demand d	Final debt, $x(K_f)$		Final wealth, $w(K_f)$	
					$J^{md}_{om,f}$	J^{md}_{os}	$J^{md}_{om,f}$	J^{md}_{os}
1	0	1	CIDP	d_1	0	0	27033	**27682**
2	1	1	CIDP	d_1	0	172779	**27682**	−64902
3	1	5	CIDP	d_1	0	0	**27682**	**27682**
4	0	1	CIDP	d_2	0	0	2632	**3268**
5	1	1	CIDP	d_2	0	172779	**3268**	−89315
6	1	5	CIDP	d_2	0	0	**3268**	**3268**
7	0	1	CIDP	d_3	0	0	6577	**6696**
8	1	1	CIDP	d_3	0	172779	**6696**	−85887
9	1	5	CIDP	d_3	0	0	**6696**	**6696**
10	0	1	DPCI	d_1	0	0	30779	**31077**
11	1	1	DPCI	d_1	0	0	**31077**	**31077**
12	1	5	DPCI	d_1	0	0	**31077**	**31077**

3.5 ▪ Multiple debts and multiple investment accounts

In this section we assume that each debt sequence $\{x_i(k)\}$ to be amortized, subject to interest rate α_i, is increased by a sequence of expenditures $\{c_i(k)\}$ made by its holder, who also operates investment accounts with balances $y_j(k)$, each of which has an associated interest rate of β_j, and from each of which transfers can be made to amortize the debts. Each transfer $u_{ij}(k) > 0$ out of an investment account is subject to a transaction cost, proportional to the amount being transferred (i.e., $\gamma_j u_{ij}(k)$), and there is a cash flow (of deposits $\{d_j(k)\}$) into the investment account.

The **CIDP model for multiple debts and investment accounts** is given by the following recurrences:

$$x_i(k+1) = (1+\alpha_i)x_i(k) - \sum_{j=1}^{n} u_{ij}(k) + c_i(k), \quad i = 1, 2, \ldots, m, \tag{3.17}$$

$$y_j(k+1) = (1+\beta_j)y_j(k) - \sum_{i=1}^{m} u_{ij}(k) - \gamma_j \sum_{i=1}^{m} u_{ij}(k) + d_j(k) \; j = 1, \ldots, n. \tag{3.18}$$

The **DPCI model for multiple debts and investment accounts** is given by the following recurrences:

$$x_i(k+1) = (1+\alpha_i)\left(x_i(k) - \sum_{j=1}^{n} u_{ij}(k)\right) + c_i(k), \quad i = 1, 2, \ldots, m, \tag{3.19}$$

$$y_j(k+1) = (1+\beta_j)\left(y_j(k) - \sum_{i=1}^{m} u_{ij}(k)\right) - \gamma_j \sum_{i=1}^{m} u_{ij}(k) + d_j(k) \; j = 1, \ldots, n. \tag{3.20}$$

Defining the amortization payment made on debt i as

$$u_i(k) := \sum_{j=1}^{n} u_{ij}(k), \; i = 1, \ldots, m. \tag{3.21}$$

It is assumed that there is an upper bound on amortization payments:

$$u_i(k) \leq u_{i,\max}, \; k = 1, \ldots, K_f; i = 1, \ldots, m. \tag{3.22}$$

Some managers may desire to impose upper bounds on how large the ith debt may become:

$$0 \leq x_i(k) \leq x_{i,\max}, \; k = 1, \ldots, K_f; i = 1, \ldots, m. \tag{3.23}$$

Lower bounds on the investment account balances can also be stipulated:

$$0 \leq y_{j,\min} \leq y_j(k), \; k = 1, \ldots, K_f; j = 1, \ldots, n. \tag{3.24}$$

Remark. As in the case of a single debt and a single investment account, the multiple debt, multiple investment account models (3.17) through (3.20) are the simplest of their class. Alternative models that compute interest on the investment account only after all transactions (deposits, transfers) are made, or that allow transfers between investment accounts subject to some limits and costs, can certainly be constructed. The important point to note is that the one step ahead optimal control approach can be applied to all these variants.

3.5.1 ▪ Performance indices for the multiple debt amortization problem with wealth maximization

Performance indices for the case of multiple debts will be denoted with the superscript md, ω. The natural extension of the indices adopted for a single debt and investment account are defined as follows. The weight vector ω is composed of the weights $\kappa_j, \mu_i, j = 1, \ldots, n, i = 1, \ldots, m$.

Weighted debt amortization with wealth maximization performance indices, to be maximized, are defined as follows:

$$J_{os}^{md,\omega}(k+1) := \sum_{j=1}^{n} \kappa_j y_j(k+1) - \sum_{i=1}^{m} \mu_i x_i(k+1), \tag{3.25}$$

$$J_{om,f}^{md,\omega} := \sum_{j=1}^{n} \kappa_j y_j(K_f+1) - \sum_{i=1}^{m} \mu_i x_i(K_f+1). \tag{3.26}$$

As in the single debt case, in order to accommodate the different debt amortization models and performance indices, the notation D is used for debt amortization dynamics, where $D =$ CIDP (equations (3.17)–(3.18)) or DPCI (equations (3.19)–(3.20)).

With these definitions in place, the **omniscient and one step ahead optimal control problems** for the **multiple debt amortization with wealth maximization problem** are written as the following linear programs:

$$\begin{aligned}
&\text{maximize} \quad J_{om,f}^{md,\omega} && (3.27)\\
&\text{subject to dynamics } D \text{ [equality constraints]}, k = 1, \ldots, K_f, && (3.28)\\
&\qquad (3.22), (3.23) \text{ [ineq. constraints, upper bounds]}, k = 1, \ldots, K_f, && (3.29)\\
&\qquad (3.24) \text{ [ineq. constraints, lower bounds]}, k = 1, \ldots, K_f; && (3.30)
\end{aligned}$$

$$\begin{aligned}
&\text{maximize} \quad J_{os}^{md,\omega}(k+1) && (3.31)\\
&\text{subject to dynamics } D \text{ [equality constraints at } k], && (3.32)\\
&\qquad (3.22), (3.23) \text{ [ineq. constraints, upper bounds at } k], && (3.33)\\
&\qquad (3.24) \text{ [ineq. constraints, lower bounds at } k]. && (3.34)
\end{aligned}$$

Remark. A multiobjective approach to the multiple debt, multiple investment account can also be taken, but is complicated by the fact that there are many more trade-offs possible and, as a result, the need for weights associated to each debt and each investment account separately. Thus the next section will only carry out a numerical investigation of the case of two investment accounts and two debts, in which there are already four weights, associated to each account and each debt, showing results for a few possible choices of weights.

3.5.2 ▪ Numerical examples of amortization of two debts, using two investment accounts

The illustrative examples in this section all use the parameters shown in Table 3.5 and the expenditure and deposit sequences with the characteristics shown in Table 3.4. For brevity, only the CIDP model is considered.

Table 3.4. *Expenditure and deposit sequence statistics and properties. The mean and standard deviation of the expenditure sequences are both larger than the corresponding values for the deposit sequences, which implies that debt amortization will involve withdrawals from the investment accounts, since, over time, the deposits will not compensate for the expenditures.*

	Mean	Standard deviation	Property
Expenditures c_1	565	311	Random
Expenditures c_2	501	288	Random
Deposits d_1	345	147	Random
Deposits d_2	320	231	Random

Table 3.5. *Parameter values for the numerical examples in section* 3.5.2.

α_1	α_2	β_1	β_2	γ_1	γ_2	$u_{1,\max}$
0.05	0.07	0.08	0.11	0.02	0.01	2500
$x_1(0)$	$x_{1,\min}$	$x_{1,\max}$	$y_1(0)$	$y_{1,\min}$	$y_{2,\min}$	$u_{2,\max}$
10000	1000	10000	15000	1000	1000	2500

Debt amortization: Weights $\kappa_i = 0$ and weights $\mu_j = 1$

The choice of $\kappa_1 = \kappa_2 = 0$ and $\mu_1 = \mu_2 = 1$ implies that the debt is being minimized at each step (when using $J_{os}^{md,\omega}$) or that the final debt (at the end of some specified planning horizon) is being minimized (when using $J_{om,f}^{md,\omega}$).

Debt amortization with wealth maximization by choice of weights

The previous two examples show that policies which drive the second investment account to low levels, by preferring amortization payment withdrawals from it, perform poorly in terms of final wealth. Using this hindsight, the third example uses the weights $\kappa_1 = 1$, $\kappa_2 = 5$, $\mu_1 = 10$, $\mu_2 = 10$, which correspond to maximizing investment account balances, giving priority to investment account 2, and assigning larger relative weights to debt amortization, so as to drive the debts to zero.

Appropriate choice of weights for debt amortization and wealth maximization

Although debt amortization has the connotation of zeroing the debt, it is also important, in many contexts, to maximize total wealth at the end of a planning period. This implies that choice of the weights κ_i, μ_i needs to be made carefully, and the numerical examples in this subsection provide some insight. In order to facilitate the discussion, the numerical results, for final debt and final wealth, achieved by the various indices are summarized in Table 3.6.

Table 3.6 illustrates the following points:

1. Rows 1 and 2 of Table 3.6 (see Figs. 3.7 through 3.10) illustrate that, when the index chosen corresponds exclusively to debt amortization, both the one step ahead optimal and omniscient optimal control approaches achieve the desired goal of zeroing the final debt. However, *in terms of final wealth*, the one step ahead policy performs better than its omniscient counterpart, achieving a little more than double the value of the latter. This is not surprising mathematically, since the performance index maximized corresponds to final debt and not to final wealth. But it is interesting that the simple choice of one step ahead debt minimization also results in a high value of final wealth. As always, the omniscient

Table 3.6. *Variation of final total debt and wealth as a function of the weighting parameters $\kappa_i, \mu_i, i = 1, 2$. Boldface numbers in rows 2 and 7 are the best values (over all weight combinations) of final debt and final wealth.*

Row	Index	κ_1	κ_2	μ_1	μ_2	Final debt	Final wealth	Comments
1	$J^{md,\omega}_{om,f}$	0	0	1	1	0	93011	$x_1, x_2 \downarrow 0, y_2 \downarrow y_{2,\min}$
2	$J^{md,\omega}_{os}$	0	0	1	1	**0**	**215305**	$x_1, x_2 \downarrow 0, y_1 \downarrow y_{1,\min}$
3	$J^{md,\omega}_{om,f}$	1	1	1	1	22703	322604	$y_1 \downarrow y_{1,\min}$
4	$J^{md,\omega}_{os}$	1	1	1	1	20000	160026	$y_1 \downarrow y_{1,\min}$
5	$J^{md,\omega}_{om,f}$	1	5	10	10	0	319202	$x_1, x_2 \downarrow 0, y_1 \downarrow y_{1,\min}$
6	$J^{md,\omega}_{os}$	1	5	10	10	0	194998	$x_1, x_2 \downarrow 0, y_1 \downarrow y_{1,\min}$
7	$J^{md,\omega}_{om,f}$	1	1	10	10	**0**	**319206**	$x_1, x_2 \downarrow 0, y_1 \downarrow y_{1,\min}$
8	$J^{md,\omega}_{os}$	1	1	10	10	0	92731	$x_1, x_2 \downarrow 0, y_2 \downarrow y_{2,\min}$

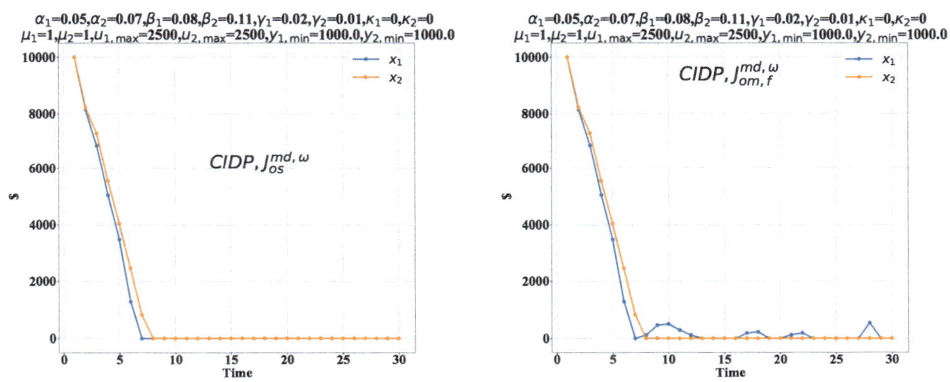

(a) Evolution of debts 1 and 2 under one step ahead policy, maximizing $J^{md,\omega}_{os}$.

(b) Evolution of debts 1 and 2: omniscient solution, maximizing $J^{md,\omega}_{om,f}$.

Figure 3.7. *Debt sequences 1 and 2 for the one step ahead optimal control and the omniscient solution are similar but not identical.*

solution requires knowledge of the expenditure and deposit sequences over the whole simulation horizon, whereas the one step ahead policy is implementable in real time, since it only requires knowledge of the current values of debts, expenditures, deposits, and investment account balances.

2. Rows 3 and 4 of Table 3.6 illustrate the practical difficulty of using final wealth as the performance index, since it results in a policy, for both indices, that maintains the debts at their initial levels. This happens because the deposits plus the withdrawals are equal to the interest corrected debt plus the expenditures. However, the one step ahead optimal and omniscient policies achieve this equality through different control sequences $u_{ij}(k)$. In this case, as expected, the omniscient solution attains a little more than double the final wealth attained by the one step ahead solution.

3. Comparing rows 1 and 2 with rows 3 through 6 of Table 3.6 leads to the intuitive conclusion that higher values of final wealth are achieved when debt amortization withdrawals are made from the investment account with lower interest rate (y_1). Rows 5 and 6 show the effect of using this hindsight, choosing a larger weight κ_2 for investment account 2, relative

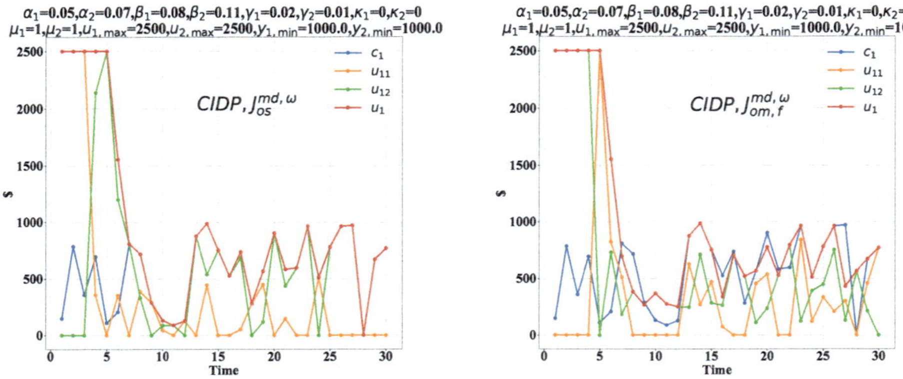

(a) One step ahead amortization payments for debt 1, maximizing $J_{os}^{md,\omega}$.

(b) Omniscient amortization payments for debt 1, maximizing $J_{om,f}^{md,\omega}$.

Figure 3.8. *Amortization payments for debt 1 using the one step ahead optimal control and the omniscient solution obtained by maximizing the indices $J_{os}^{md,\omega}$ and $J_{om,f}^{md,\omega}$, respectively. The total amortization payment $u_1 = u_{11} + u_{12}$ (red line), for the one step ahead strategy, tracks the expenditure c_1 (blue line), after an initial period at $u_{1,\max}$.*

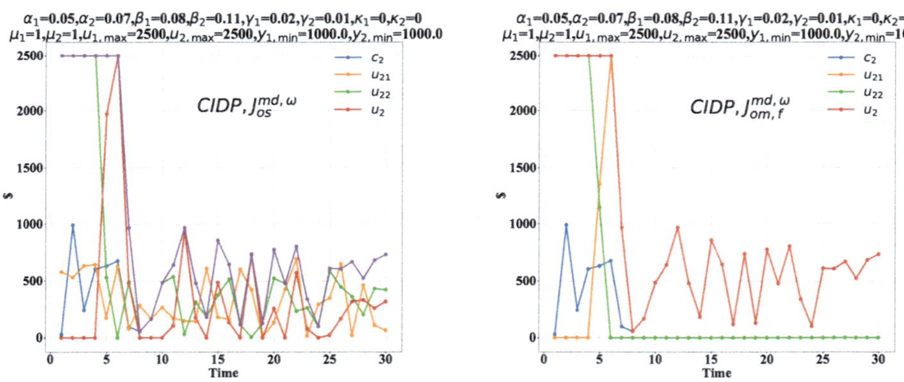

(a) One step ahead amortization payments for debt 2, maximizing $J_{os}^{md,\omega}$.

(b) Omniscient amortization payments for debt 2, maximizing $J_{om,f}^{md,\omega}$.

Figure 3.9. *Amortization payments for debt 2 using the one step ahead optimal control and the omniscient solution obtained by maximizing the indices $J_{os}^{md,\omega}$ and $J_{om,f}^{md,\omega}$, respectively. The total amortization payment $u_1 = u_{11} + u_{12}$ (red line), for the omniscient strategy, tracks the expenditure c_1 (blue line), after an initial period at $u_{1,\max}$.*

to κ_1 for account 1, and also obliging the debts to go to zero, by choosing larger weights μ_i for the debts (relative to the weights κ_j). The result, shown in Figs. 3.11 through 3.14, is that the final wealth attained by the omniscient solution improves (with respect to row 1), while that obtained by the one step ahead optimal control worsens slightly (with respect to row 2).

4. Row 7 of Table 3.6 shows that, for the omniscient approach, there is no significant advantage to increasing the weights μ_i of the debts. Row 8 compared with row 6 shows that tuning of weights can make a significant difference for the one step ahead case. However,

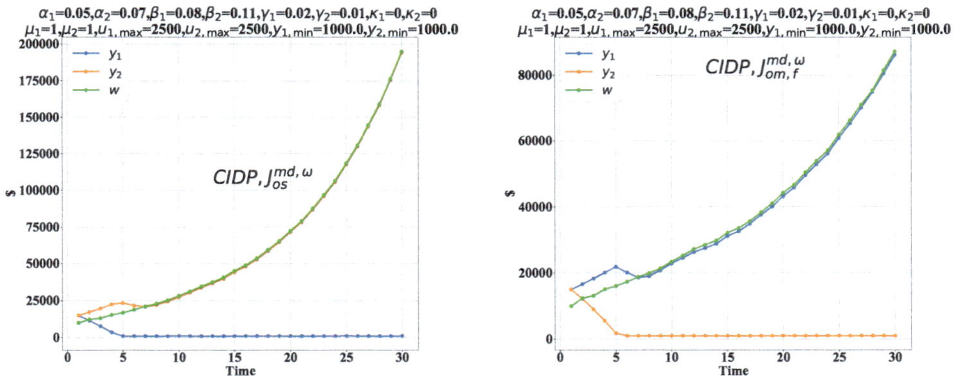

(a) Investment account 1 and 2 balances under one step ahead policy, maximizing $J_{os}^{md,\omega}$.

(b) Investment account 1 and 2 balances: omniscient solution, maximizing $J_{om,f}^{md,\omega}$.

Figure 3.10. *Difference in the evolution of investment account* 1 *and* 2 *balances and wealth for the one step ahead optimal control* (a) *and omniscient solution* (b). *The one step ahead policy takes investment account* 1 *to a minimum balance (*\$1000*), and the omniscient solution takes investment account* 2 *to the minimum balance.*

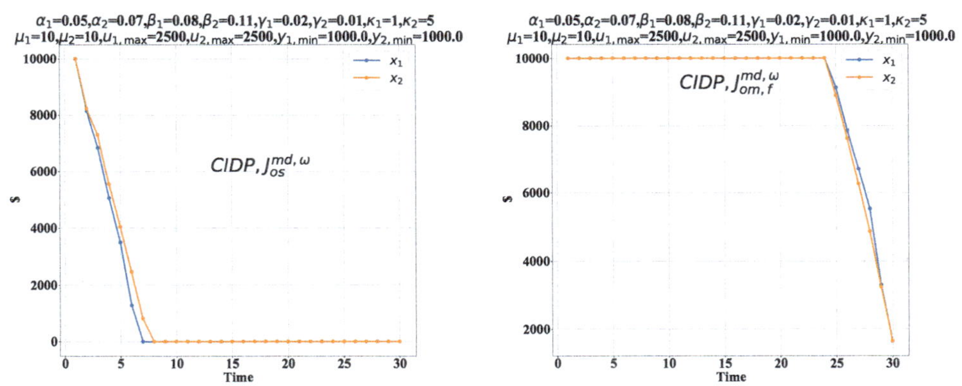

(a) Evolution of debts 1 and 2 under one step ahead policy, maximizing $J_{os}^{md,\omega}$.

(b) Evolution of debts 1 and 2 under omniscient policy, maximizing $J_{om,f}^{md,\omega}$.

Figure 3.11. *Debts* 1 *and* 2 *for the one step ahead optimal control and the omniscient solution. The omniscient solution maintains both debts at their upper bound of* 10,000 *units until* $k = 24$, *a few instants before the end of the simulation horizon of* 30 *units.*

comparing row 6 with row 2, we see the debt amortization choice (row 2) is clearly superior to the other choices of weights for the one step ahead approach.

5. A fair comparison between the one step ahead and omniscient approaches can be made by looking at the final wealth attained in row 2 (for the one step ahead case) and row 7 (for the omniscient case), since the final debts achieved are zero in all cases. This allows the conclusion that, for the example studied in this section, one step ahead optimal debt amortization (row 2) can attain 67.4% (= 215305/319206) of the omniscient optimal value of final wealth, noting as usual that the omniscient optimal control is not implementable in practice.

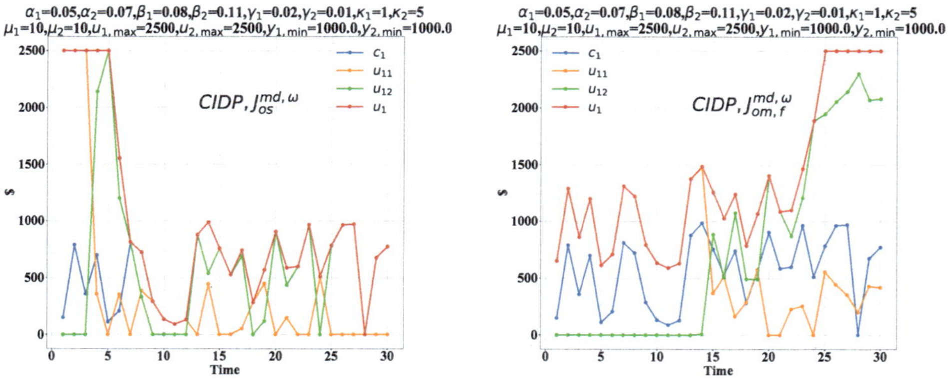

(a) One step ahead amortization payments for debt 1, maximizing $J_{os}^{md,\omega}$.

(b) Omniscient amortization payments for debt 1, maximizing $J_{om,f}^{md,\omega}$.

Figure 3.12. *Amortization payments for debt* 1 *using the one step ahead optimal control and the omniscient solution, obtained by maximizing the indices* $J_{os}^{md,\omega}$ *and* $J_{om,f}^{md,\omega}$*, respectively. Observe that the total amortization payment* $u_2 = u_{21} + u_{22}$ *(the purple line), for the one step ahead policy, tracks the expenditure* c_2 *(blue line) after an initial segment of payments, until* $k = 5$*, at the upper bound. The omniscient solution tracks the expenditure with a positive offset, maintaining debt* 1 *at its upper bound* $x_{2,\max}$*, until* $k = 23$*, after which it increases payment level to the upper bound, in order to zero final debt.*

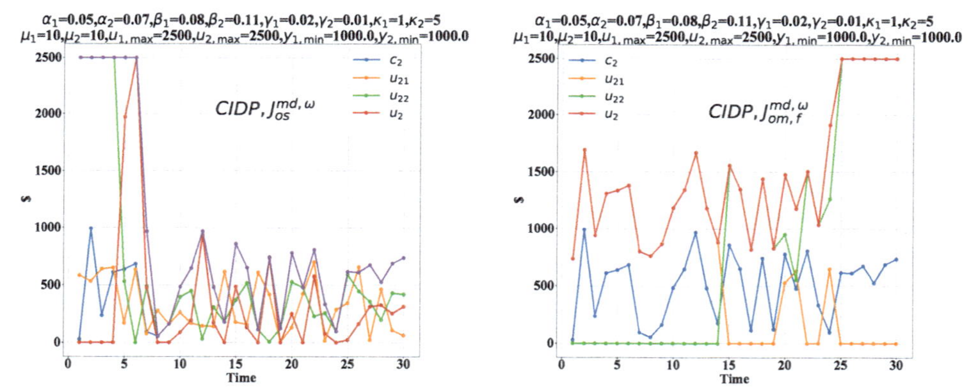

(a) One step ahead amortization payments for debt 2, maximizing $J_{os}^{md,\omega}$.

(b) Omniscient amortization payments for debt 2, maximizing $J_{om,f}^{md,\omega}$.

Figure 3.13. *Amortization payments for debt* 2 *using the one step ahead optimal control and the omniscient solution, obtained by maximizing the indices* $J_{os}^{md,\omega}$ *and* $J_{om,f}^{md,\omega}$*, respectively. Observe that the total amortization payment* $u_2 = u_{21} + u_{22}$ *(the purple line), for the one step ahead policy, tracks the expenditure* c_2 *(blue line) after an initial segment of payments, until* $k = 7$*, at the upper bound. The omniscient solution tracks the expenditure with a positive offset, maintaining debt* 2 *at its upper bound* $x_{2,\max}$*, until* $k = 23$*, after which it increases payment level to the upper bound, in order to zero final debt.*

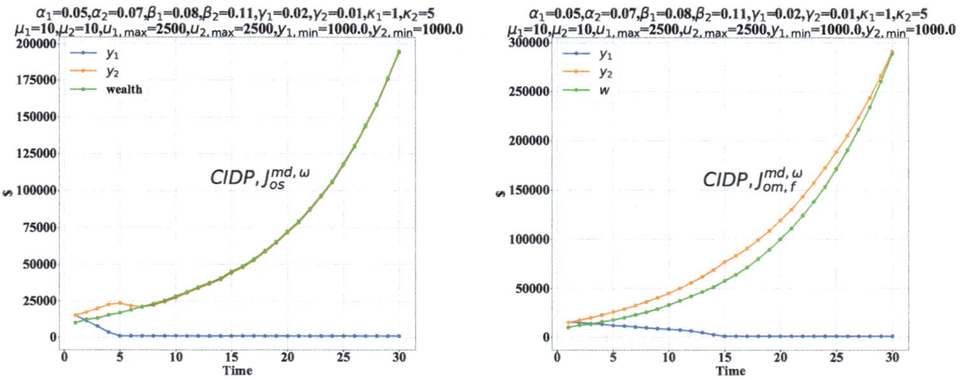

(a) Investment account 1 and 2 balances under one step ahead policy, maximizing $J_{os}^{md,\omega}$.

(b) Investment account 1 and 2 balances under omniscient policy, maximizing $J_{om,f}^{md,\omega}$.

Figure 3.14. *Evolution of investment account* 1 *and* 2 *balances and wealth for the one step ahead optimal policy (left panel) and omniscient solution (right panel) is different; although both take investment account* 1 *to minimum balance* (\$1000)*, they do so at different rates.*

6. The overall conclusion is that the one step ahead index with the debt amortization choice of weights (namely, $\kappa_i = 0$, $\mu_j = 1$, for all i, j) is a good candidate for real time debt management. In fact, in scenarios in which there are multiple debts and multiple investment accounts, it may be the only practical choice, in the absence of intuition with regard to a good choice of weights.

3.6 ▪ Chapter summary

This chapter showed how the debt amortization problem can be formulated as an optimization problem, with a natural linear performance index, which is the total debt at any given instant. A straightforward generalization to a weighted linear performance index allows simultaneous optimization of wealth (to be maximized) and debt (to be minimized or driven to zero), by a suitable choice of weights. This means that the omniscient and one step ahead optimal control problems are both linear programming problems. This permits application to problems of larger size in which there are multiple investment accounts and multiple debts to be amortized, with different constraints on the size of the amortization payments corresponding to each of the debts, different transaction costs on transfers from each investment account, different minimum balances for each investment account, and different upper bounds on each debt amortization payment. An important conclusion is that the one step ahead strategy that seeks to zero the debt at each step is an implementable policy that, in addition to maintaining the debt at zero after an initial transient, also achieves final wealth that is a reasonably high fraction of the wealth that could be achieved by an omniscient (but unimplementable) policy.

Notes and references

The debt amortization problem presented in this chapter is a generalization of the credit card debt problem proposed by Chong and Żak [CŻ13, p. 479 ff.], and solved by them using an omniscient approach (in the terminology of this book), with a quadratic objective function, based on the popular Linear Quadratic Regulator (LQR) control approach. It should be noted that, in the omniscient case, the approach used in [CŻ13, p. 479 ff.] cannot incorporate constraints on debt, amortization payments, and investment account balances.

Multiobjective optimization is introduced at a theoretical level in [Yan14] and, from the point of view of evolutionary algorithms, in [Deb01].

The turnpike effect. Under quite general assumptions, the optimal solutions of a given omniscient optimal control problem are composed of three segments. The first and last segments are transients lasting a relatively short time, while the middle segment is exponentially close to the optimal steady state solution of an associated static optimal control problem. This property was established for finite-dimensional optimal control problems in the economics literature by the authors of [DSS58, Chap. 12, sect. 12-2-10], who wrote that the optimal solution is

> exactly like a turnpike[1] paralleled by a network of minor roads. There is a fastest route between any two points; and if origin and destination are close together and far from the turnpike, the best route may not touch the turnpike. But if origin and destination are far enough apart, it will always pay to get on to the turnpike and cover distance at the best rate of travel, even if this means adding a little mileage at either end.

Since then, this property has been referred to as the turnpike effect or phenomenon. For omniscient optimal control problems, in several examples in the subsequent chapters of this book, the turnpike effect is noticeable. For more on the turnpike effect, see [TZ15; Zas17] and references therein.

[1]Toll roads, especially on the east coast of the United States of America, are often called turnpikes; the term turnpike originated from pikes, which were long sticks that blocked passage until the fare was paid and the pike turned at a toll house (or toll booth in current terminology).

Chapter 4

The cash balance problem

This chapter discusses the application of the one step ahead optimal control approach to models of the cash balance problem. While managing cash flows, both deposits and withdrawals, into current accounts with low interest rates, managers aim to make judicious transfers *from* investment accounts to make negative current account balances positive, or transfer excess positive balances in the current accounts *to* investment accounts, in order to obtain better returns. All transfers between accounts are subject to transaction costs, always deducted from current accounts. Determining the best way to make these transfers, given an unknown future cash flow sequence, is known as the cash balance problem. In this chapter, performance indices are defined, and maximization of an index for the next instant (day) by a suitable choice of cash transfers that satisfy desired constraints on account balances defines the basic one step ahead optimal control problem. It is shown that this one step ahead optimal control can be written as a mixed integer linear program of small size, leading to an implementable real time strategy.

4.1 ▪ Description of the cash balance problem

Every firm and financial institution needs to have a cash current account in order to meet its daily transaction requirements. The cash balance needs to be large enough to meet these requirements, but there is also an incentive to maintain a balance that is not much larger than this, since extra cash can earn larger returns in, for example, an investment account or securities. In many situations, it is necessary to keep the balance nonnegative, or above a certain minimum balance, to avoid interest imposed on overdrafts, or penalties incurred due to possible delays in meeting cash demands whenever the cash balance becomes too low or negative. There are two mechanisms for changing cash balance: withdrawing cash from an investment account to increase cash balance, or transferring cash to an investment account. Any change (increase or decrease) of the level of cash in a current account, through a transfer between accounts, involves a transaction cost that is usually proportional to the size of the change. Finally, daily cash flows are not completely predictable, although some transactions are preprogrammed (date and amount are known in advance). The goal of the account manager is, for example, to maximize the total wealth (sum of assets in cash and investment accounts), subject to some restrictions, for example, maintaining nonnegativity of cash and investment accounts, given the stochastic inflows and outflows of cash. In order to solve this optimization problem, it is necessary to calculate a policy that determines when and how much to transfer from a cash to an investment account or vice versa, and this is the subject of this chapter.

The classical Miller–Orr cash balance policy [MO66], proposed more than five decades ago, is still popular in the corporate sector (see [MNS15] and references therein). Miller and Orr assumed the cash inflows and outflows to be symmetric (i.e., positive and negative with the same probability and normalized to ± 1) and thus modeled cash demand as a Bernoulli process. They proposed a three level threshold type controller, which allows the current account balance (denoted x) to fluctuate freely between two predetermined lower (z_L) and upper (z_H) levels and then used the well-developed theory of such processes (random walks) to derive formulas for z_L, z, z_H, where z is a desired reference level between z_L and z_H. The three level method is further discussed in section 4.3.3.

In the Miller–Orr strategy, transfers to (resp., from) the investment account are triggered whenever the current account balance exceeds (resp., falls below) the upper (resp., lower) level. The intuition behind this strategy of cash balance control is that, under the assumption that the return on the investment account is higher than that on the current account, it is advantageous to minimize loss of investment opportunities due to excessive current account balance. In section 4.3.3, a Miller–Orr type policy is regarded as a threshold-based feedback control strategy. By considering the threshold levels as parameters to be optimized, the Miller–Orr type policy is brought into the optimization and control perspective adopted in this book.

This chapter takes the deterministic discrete-time model and the optimal control formulation proposed in [ST70] (also see [ST00]) as a starting point, allowing the cash flow demand to be stochastic, but without making specific assumptions about its distribution. In [ST70], assuming that the entire cash demand over a given horizon is known, the discrete-time maximum principle is used to solve the optimal control problem, obtaining a bang-bang solution in terms of the adjoint variables. This optimal control problem is referred to as the omniscient optimal control problem, since it requires knowledge of the cash demand over the whole planning horizon.

It is shown that the omniscient optimal control problem, using the model in [ST70], can be formulated as a mixed integer linear programming problem. This chapter then uses the one step ahead optimal control approach and shows that it leads to a simple feedback controller which is implementable in real time and does not require prior knowledge or forecasting of the cash demand (inflows and outflows over time). The performance of the one step ahead optimal controller, measured by a suitable index, is compared with that of the omniscient controller, which, although not implementable in practice, serves as a globally optimal benchmark.

4.2 ▪ The generalized cash balance problem

This section presents a model for a generalized version of the cash balance problem in which, at instant k, a manager has multiple current accounts with balances $x_i(k), i = 1, \ldots, N$, each of which receives debits (resp., deposits), $d_i(k) > 0$ (resp., < 0), referred to collectively as cash demands, as well as multiple investment accounts with balances $y_j(k), j = 1, \ldots, M$. A transfer between investment account j and current account i is denoted u_{ij} and is positive if it is from j to i and negative otherwise. Each such transfer incurs a transaction cost $\gamma_i |u_{ij}(k)|$, where γ_i is the transaction cost coefficient associated with current account i. Interest rates are α_i for the ith current account and β_j for the jth investment account. It is assumed that transaction cost free transfers are possible between current accounts i and m, which is expressed mathematically as $c_{im}(k)+c_{mi}(k) = 0$; thus if $c_{im}(k)$ is positive, then $c_{mi}(k)$ must be negative in the same amount, and vice versa. This is a reasonable assumption, since interest rates on current accounts are usually very low (if not zero), and thus there is usually no penalty or cost in transferring from one current account to another. Lower and upper bounds $x_{i,\min}, x_{i,\max}$ are imposed on the current account balances and the investment accounts subjected to a minimum balance requirement of $y_{j,\min}$. Figure 4.1 shows a representation of the description above in terms of a graph.

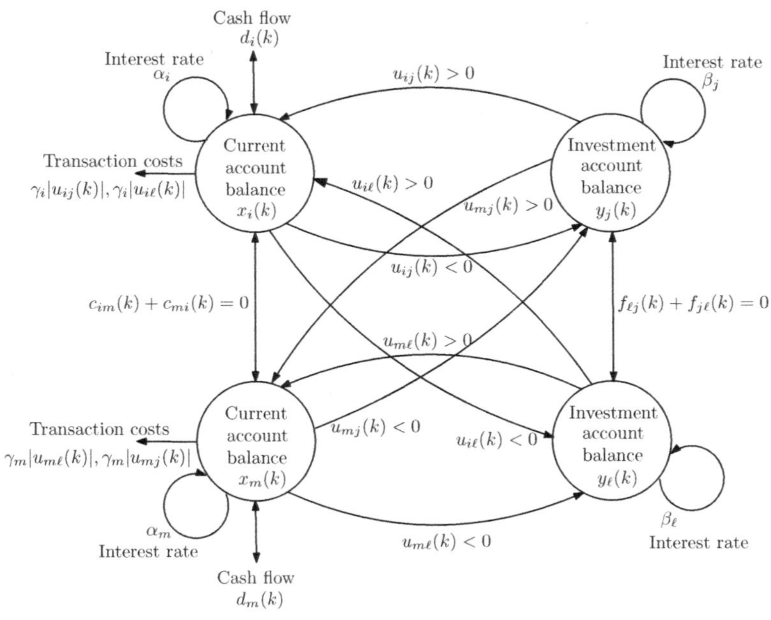

Figure 4.1. *Representation of the dynamics of cash balance, with multiple current accounts, each with its own demand sequence and multiple investment accounts. Arrows represent possible movements between accounts, and arrows feeding back to the nodes they originate from represent the effect of interest rates. The graph shows two of the N (resp., M) current (resp., investment) accounts.*

Thus the **generalized cash balance** dynamics can be represented by the following **discrete dynamical system**, with constraints on its states:

$$x_i(k+1) = (1+\alpha_i)x_i(k) + \sum_{j=1}^{M} u_{ij}(k) - \sum_{j=1}^{M} \gamma_i|u_{ij}(k)| - d_i(k) + \sum_{m\neq i} c_{im}(k) \;\forall i, \quad (4.1)$$

$$y_j(k+1) = (1+\beta_j)y_j(k) - \sum_{i=1}^{N} u_{ij}(k) \;\forall j, \quad (4.2)$$

$$0 = c_{im}(k) + c_{mi}(k) \;\forall i \;\forall m, \quad (4.3)$$

$$0 < x_{i,\min} \leq x_i(k) \leq x_{i,\max} \;\forall i, \quad (4.4)$$

$$0 < y_{j,\min} \leq y_j(k) \;\forall j. \quad (4.5)$$

Total wealth, $w(k)$, is expressed as

$$w(k) = \sum_{i=1}^{N} x_i(k) + \sum_{j=1}^{M} y_j(k). \quad (4.6)$$

If transaction cost free transfers between investment accounts j and ℓ are possible, this can be expressed by adding the constraint $f_{\ell j}(k) + f_{j\ell}(k) = 0$, and the corresponding term $\sum_{j\neq\ell} f_{\ell j}(k)$ added to the right-hand side of (4.2), but this will not be done in this book.

4.2.1 ▪ Performance indices for the generalized cash balance problem

The following **weighted performance indices**, to be **maximized**, are proposed for the optimal control of cash balance:

$$J_{os}^{\omega}(k+1) := \sum_j \kappa_j y_j(k+1) - \sum_i \mu_i x_i(k+1), \tag{4.7}$$

$$J_{om}^{\omega} := \sum_j \kappa_j y_j(K_f+1) - \sum_i \mu_i x_i(K_f+1) = J_{os}^{\omega}(K_f+1). \tag{4.8}$$

The choice of weights κ_j, μ_i permits the manager to achieve a balance between maximizing the investment account balances and minimizing the current account balances. The subscripts os and om refer, respectively, to the one step ahead and omniscient cases. The vector of all weights κ_j, μ_i is denoted ω, and the following choices of weights have the indicated interpretations:

- $\kappa_j = 1$ for all j and $\mu_i = -1$ for all i correspond to the maximization of total wealth $w(k)$, subject to the specified constraints.

- $\kappa_j = 1$ for all j and $\mu_i = 1$ for all i correspond to maximizing the sum of investment account balances and simultaneously minimizing the sum of current account balances, subject to the specified constraints.

- $\kappa_j = 0$ for all j and $\mu_i = 1$ correspond to minimizing the sum of current account balances subject to the specified constraints.

If, instead of specifying upper and lower bounds on the current account balances as in (4.4), it is desired to stipulate a certain reference level $x_{i,ref}$ for the ith current account balance, then an appropriate performance index, to be maximized, for the one step ahead optimal control problem is as follows:

$$J_{os}^{\omega,r}(k+1) := \sum_j \kappa_j y_j(k+1) - \sum_i \mu_i x_i(k+1) - \sum_i \nu_i \left(x_i(k+1) - x_{i,ref}\right)^2, \tag{4.9}$$

where the nonnegative weights ν_i determine the relative importance of the current account balances tracking the specified reference levels, and the superscript r indicates that reference values $x_{i,ref}$ for the current account balances are specified. The performance index (4.9) is quadratic and can be used in the context of risk aversion by cash managers, since the maintenance of a reference for the current account balance is a precautionary measure that reduces the risk of overdraft. The latter has associated charges which can be exorbitant. In this book, however, the linear performance indices (4.7) and (4.8) will be used, since they are computationally simpler and, since they impose only lower and upper bounds, more flexible than the imposition of reference levels, and are akin to the Miller–Orr approach.

4.3 ▪ Cash balance as a linear programming problem

Given the data $x_i(k), y_j(k), d_i(k)$ for all i, j at time k, the one step ahead optimal control problem (abbreviated OSA, OSAO) is that of maximizing the performance index $J_{os}^{\omega}(k+1)$, at time $k+1$, by a suitable choice of the transfers $u_{ij}(k), c_{im}(k)$, subject to the dynamics (4.1), (4.2) and the constraints (4.4)–(4.5). Since the dynamics (4.1), (4.2) can be viewed as equality constraints, the one step ahead optimal control problem is seen to be a mathematical programming problem, namely, that of maximizing an objective function (performance index) subject to equality and inequality constraints. More specifically, all constraints as well as the objective function are linear, except for (4.1), which is piecewise linear. A standard trick in optimization permits the rewriting of (4.1) in linear form, thus making the one step optimal control problem a mixed integer linear program. For each i, j, defining the two nonnegative functions,

$$
\begin{aligned}
u_{ij}^+(k) &:= u_{ij}(k) \quad \text{if } u_{ij}(k) \geq 0, \quad 0, \quad \text{otherwise,} \\
u_{ij}^-(k) &:= -u_{ij}(k) \quad \text{if } u_{ij}(k) \leq 0, \quad 0, \quad \text{otherwise,}
\end{aligned}
$$

the functions $u_{ij}(\cdot), |u_{ij}(\cdot)|$ can be written as follows:

$$
u_{ij}(k) = u_{ij}^+(k) - u_{ij}^-(k) \quad \forall k, \tag{4.10}
$$

$$
|u_{ij}(k)| = u_{ij}^+(k) + u_{ij}^-(k) \quad \forall k, \tag{4.11}
$$

$$
\text{provided that } u_{ij}^+(k) u_{ij}^-(k) = 0 \quad \forall k. \tag{4.12}
$$

The quadratic constraint (4.12) can be modeled as the two mutually exclusive logical statements

$$
\text{if } u_{ij}^+(k) > 0, \text{then } u_{ij}^-(k) = 0, \tag{4.13}
$$

$$
\text{or (exclusive) if } u_{ij}^-(k) > 0, \text{ then } u_{ij}^+(k) = 0. \tag{4.14}
$$

In order to use the so-called "big M" trick [Wil06], the binary variables $\delta_{ij,1}(k)$, $\delta_{ij,2}(k)$ (i.e., $\delta_{ij,m}(k) \in \{0, 1\}, m = 1, 2$, for all pairs i, j), and an upper bound M for $u_{ij}^+(k), u_{ij}^-(k)$ are introduced. The logical statements can then be written as the following equivalent algebraic linear constraints:

$$
u_{ij}^+(k) \leq M\delta_{ij,1}(k), \tag{4.15}
$$

$$
u_{ij}^-(k) \leq M\delta_{ij,2}(k), \tag{4.16}
$$

$$
\delta_{ij,1}(k) + \delta_{ij,2}(k) = 1. \tag{4.17}
$$

Substituting (4.10), (4.11) into (4.1), (4.2) yields

$$
\begin{aligned}
x_i(k+1) = (1 + \alpha_i)x_i(k) + \sum_{j=1}^{M}(u_{ij}^+(k) - u_{ij}^-(k)) - \sum_{j=1}^{M}\gamma_i(u_{ij}^+(k) + u_{ij}^-(k)) \\
- d_i(k) + \sum_{m \neq i} c_{im}(k) \, \forall i,
\end{aligned} \tag{4.18}
$$

$$
y_j(k+1) = (1 + \beta_j)y_j(k) - \sum_{i=1}^{N}(u_{ij}^+(k) - u_{ij}^-(k)) \, \forall j, \tag{4.19}
$$

$$
0 = c_{im}(k) + c_{mi}(k) \, \forall i, \forall m, \tag{4.20}
$$

$$
0 < x_{i,\min} \leq x_i(k) \leq x_{i,\max} \, \forall i, \tag{4.21}
$$

$$
0 < y_{j,\min} \leq y_j(k) \, \forall j. \tag{4.22}
$$

Equations (4.18), (4.19) are now linear equality constraints in the decision variables $u_{ij}^+(k), u_{ij}^-(k)$.

From the development above, **one step ahead optimal control of cash balance** can be written as the following **mixed integer linear program**:

$$\begin{array}{l}\text{maximize } J^{\omega}_{os}(k+1)\\ \text{by choice of controls } u^{+}_{ij}(k), u^{-}_{ij}(k) \geq 0, \text{ given } x_i(k), y_j(k), d_i(k)\ \forall i,j,\\ \text{and choice of the binary variables } \delta_{ij,1}(k)+\delta_{ij,2}(k)\ \forall k,\\ \text{subject to the linear equality constraints (dynamics) (4.18), (4.19),}\\ \text{linear equality constraints (intra-account transfers) (4.20),}\\ \text{linear inequality constraints (big M upper bounds) (4.15), (4.16),}\\ \text{linear equality constraints (exclusive OR constraints on binary variables) (4.17),}\\ \text{and box constraints on account balances (4.21), (4.22).}\end{array} \qquad (4.23)$$

It also follows that the **hypothetical omniscient optimal control of cash balance**, given the cash demand, $d(k)$, over a planning horizon $[1, K_f]$, can be found by solving the following **mixed integer linear program**:

$$\begin{array}{l}\text{maximize } J^{\omega}_{om}(K_f+1)\\ \text{by choice of controls } u^{+}_{ij}(k), u^{-}_{ij}(k) \geq 0 \text{ given } x_i(1), y_j(1), \text{and } d_i(k)\ \forall i,j,k,\\ \text{and choice of the binary variables } \delta_{ij,1}(k)+\delta_{ij,2}(k)\ \forall i,j,k,\\ \text{subject to the linear dynamics (equality constraints) (4.18), (4.19) } \forall k,\\ \text{linear equality constraints (intra-account transfers) (4.20) } \forall i,m,k,\\ \text{linear inequality constraints (big M upper bounds) (4.15), (4.16) } \forall i,j,k,\\ \text{linear equality constraints (exclusive OR constraints on binary variables) (4.17) } \forall i,j,k,\\ \text{and box constraints on account balances (4.21), (4.22) } \forall k, \forall i, \forall j.\end{array} \qquad (4.24)$$

It should be noted that the feasibility of the linear programs (4.23) and (4.24) depends on the initial current and investment accounts being large enough to meet the average demand levels.

The omniscient approach is referred to as hypothetical, since it assumes knowledge of the cash demand over the entire horizon in order to compute the optimal cash transfer sequence. In control terminology, it is also referred to as *open-loop*, since no feedback of state or output variables is involved. In contrast, the one step ahead optimal control approach is feedback control, since the effect of the control at instant k on state variables affects the computation at instant $k+1$. The next section, which discusses the case when the current cash demand $d(k)$ is not known, shows the feedback structure of the proposed controller explicitly.

4.3.1 ▪ One step ahead optimal control using estimates of current demands

If the current demands $d_i(k), i = 1, \ldots, N$, at time k are not known, the one step ahead method can be easily modified to use demand estimates $\hat{d}_i(k), i = 1, \ldots, N$, at time k, as shown in Fig. 4.2.

In terms of the linear programming formulation (4.23), the only change is to replace $d_i(k)$ by $\hat{d}_i(k)$ and then use the scheme in Fig. 4.2. Other important observations in this context are as follows:

- if it assumed that all transfers between accounts are end-of-the-day operations, as in [SM+20]; then it is perfectly reasonable to assume that the current demand $d(k)$ is known, i.e., $\hat{d}(k) = d(k)$, and this will be done in the next section, as well as in numerical examples, where indicated;

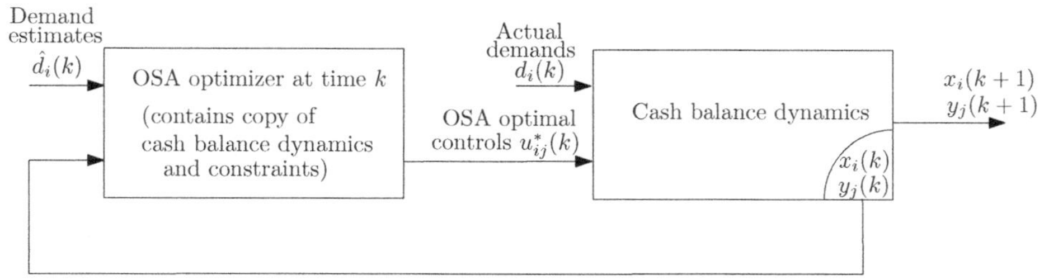

Figure 4.2. *A block diagram representation of one step ahead optimal control, showing feedback. The demand estimates $\hat{d}_i(k), i = 1, \ldots, N$, at time k are used in the one step ahead optimization routine, which also has knowledge of the current balances $x_i(k), y_j(k)$ through feedback. The computed optimal controls $u^*_{ij}(k)$ are then applied to the accounts on which the actual demands $d_i(k), i = 1, \ldots, N$, at time k are incident, producing the updated balances $x_i(k+1), y_j(k+1)$.*

- if there are delays involved in transfers between investment account and current accounts [SM+20], this can easily be incorporated into the proposed approach by augmenting the control vector;
- cash flows with known due dates, as discussed in [SM87], can easily be incorporated into our formulation. For example, minimum cash balance constraints that will meet positive demands on the given due dates can be imposed. For negative demands (deposits into current accounts) which occur on known dates, corresponding constraints on the controls for that account on the given day, namely, that they should be less than or equal to the corresponding deposits (which are negative values), ensure that deposits will not remain idle in the current accounts.

4.3.2 ▪ Analytical solution of a simple version of the one step ahead optimal control problem for cash balance

This section examines the simple case $M = N = 1$, for which the cash balance dynamics and constraints (4.1)–(4.5) simplify to

$$x(k+1) = (1+\alpha)x(k) + u(k) - d(k) - \gamma|u(k)|, \quad k = 1, \ldots, K_f, \tag{4.25}$$

$$y(k+1) = (1+\beta)y(k) - u(k), \quad k = 1, \ldots, K_f, \tag{4.26}$$

$$x_{\min} \le x(k) \le x_{\max} \quad \forall k, \tag{4.27}$$

$$y_{\min} \le y(k) \quad \forall k. \tag{4.28}$$

In order to gain some insight, this section solves the one step ahead optimal control problem analytically, temporarily ignoring the lower bound $y_{\min}$ and the upper bound $x_{\max}$. The first important observation is that the choice of weights $\kappa = 1$, $\mu = -1$ for the one step ahead performance index (corresponding to the one step ahead wealth maximization $J^{\omega}_{os}(k+1) = x(k+1) + y(k+1)$) leads to the optimal one step ahead control $u^*(k) = 0$. This is easily seen by adding (4.25) to (4.26), yielding

$$J^{\omega}_{os}(k+1) = x(k+1) + y(k+1) = (1+\alpha)x(k) + (1+\beta)y(k) - d(k) - \gamma|u(k)| \tag{4.29}$$

and showing that the optimal value of the control, that maximizes J^{ω}_{os}, is zero. Thus, throughout this chapter, for the one step ahead optimal control problem, the performance index will be assumed to have the weights $\kappa = 0$, $\mu = 1$. Observe that, in this case, one step ahead optimization reduces to the problem of minimizing the cash balance at step $k+1$. Assuming that the current account balance $x(k) \geq x_{\min}$, the transfer $u(k)$ should be chosen to make $x(k+1) = x_{\min}$. Such a strategy, in loose analogy with a similar feedback control strategy used in discrete-time systems, can also be referred to as *deadbeat control*. This amounts to setting the right-hand side of the state equation (4.1) to $x_{\min}$, yielding

$$(1+\alpha)x(k) + u(k) - d(k) - \gamma|u(k)| = x_{\min} \quad \forall k \tag{4.30}$$

which can be rearranged as

$$u(k) - \gamma|u(k)| = x_{\min} + d(k) - (1+\alpha)x(k), \tag{4.31}$$

which, in turn, can be solved for u by considering the possible signs of the right-hand side, to give the following explicit formula for the one step ahead optimal control u:

$$u(k) = \begin{cases} \frac{x_{\min}+d(k)-(1+\alpha)x(k)}{(1-\gamma)} & \text{if } x_{\min} + d(k) - (1+\alpha)x(k) > 0, \\ \frac{x_{\min}+d(k)-(1+\alpha)x(k)}{(1+\gamma)} & \text{if } x_{\min} + d(k) - (1+\alpha)x(k) < 0. \end{cases} \tag{4.32}$$

From the nature of the control, it is easy to see that the upper bound $x_{\max}$ is unnecessary, since the one step ahead control will keep the current account balance clamped at $x_{\min}$. The lower bound $y_{\min}$ is satisfied if the initial investment account balance is large enough to account for necessary transfers, recalling that average demand is negative (i.e., a firm's cash inflow exceeds outflow). The one step ahead optimal control (4.32) can be rewritten to make it clear that it is a feedback controller:

$$u(k) = \begin{cases} \beta_1(x_{\min} + d(k)) + \gamma_1 x(k) & \text{if } x_{\min} + d(k) - (1+\alpha)x(k) > 0, \\ \beta_2(x_{\min} + d(k)) + \gamma_2 x(k) & \text{if } x_{\min} + d(k) - (1+\alpha)x(k) < 0, \end{cases} \tag{4.33}$$

where $\beta_1 = \frac{1}{1-\gamma}, \gamma_1 = -\frac{1+\alpha}{1-\gamma}, \beta_2 = \frac{1}{1+\gamma}, \gamma_2 = -\frac{1+\alpha}{1+\gamma}$.

Note that the equivalent expressions (4.32) and (4.33) can be regarded as bang-bang type control, based on one component ($x(k)$) of the current state vector, the current demand $d(k)$, and the lower bound $x_{\min}$. The term bang-bang refers to the fact that the control switches between values which are affine functions of $x(k)$.

A notable feature of the control (4.32) is that it is simple and clearly implementable online, since it only uses the current demand and current account balance. Note that since the cash demand $d(k)$ at time k is a known quantity, the one step ahead optimal control is affine in the state variable $x(k)$. Deriving an analytic formula for the optimal control is more intricate when constraints are present, or in the case of multiple current and investment accounts, but one step ahead optimal controls can still be easily found using linear programming tools, and this is the preferred approach in this chapter, and, more generally, in this book.

4.3.3 ▪ Optimization and control perspective on the three level strategy

This section presents the classical cash balance strategy proposed by [MO66] from the optimization and control perspective of this book. Miller and Orr assumed the cash inflows and outflows to be symmetric (i.e., positive and negative with the same probability and normalized to ± 1) and thus modeled cash demand as a Bernoulli process. They proposed a three level threshold type controller, where the three levels are denoted z_L, z, z_H and satisfy $z_L < z < z_H$. The idea is to allow the current account balance (denoted by x) to fluctuate freely between the lower (z_L) and upper (z_H) levels or thresholds. Transfers to (resp., from) the investment account are triggered whenever the current account balance exceeds (resp., falls below) the upper (resp., lower) level and the amount transferred is determined by the middle or reference level z, as specified below. Since the cash flow is assumed to have a Bernoulli distribution, formulas for z_L, z, z_H are derived from random walk theory. Finally, since this chapter will consider the strategy described above in the context of the generalized Sethi–Thompson cash balance model, it will be referred to as a *three level strategy*, in order to differentiate it from the Miller–Orr strategy originally described in [MO66]. It should be noted that the simple three level strategy generalizes, in a straightforward manner, only to the case in which $M = 1$, i.e., there is only one investment account and, in addition, there are no intra-account transfers, i.e., $c_{im}(k) = 0\ \forall i, m, k$.

Under these simplifying assumptions, the subscript j can be dropped in the generalized model (4.1)–(4.5), since $M = 1$. Then, in control terminology, the three level strategy is a feedback control, $u_i(k)$, with a dead zone $[z_{iL}, z_{iH}]$, that is defined as follows:

$$u_i(k) = \begin{cases} z_i - x_i(k) & \text{if } x_i(k) \geq z_{iH}, \\ 0 & \text{if } z_{iL} \leq x_i(k) \leq z_{iH}, \\ z_i - x_i(k) & \text{if } x_i(k) \leq z_{iL}. \end{cases} \tag{4.34}$$

Substituting the control (4.34) into the dynamics (4.25)–(4.26) leads to the following set, for $i = 1,\ldots, N$, of pairs of difference equations that describe the closed-loop system, for each of the possibilities for the state $x_i(k)$:

$$x_i(k+1) = (1+\alpha_i)x_i(k) - d_i(k) \quad \text{if } x_i(k) \in (z_{iL}, z_{iH}), \tag{4.35}$$

$$y(k+1) = (1+\beta)y(k) \quad \text{if } x_i(k) \in (z_{iL}, z_{iH}), \tag{4.36}$$

$$x_i(k+1) = \alpha_i x_i(k) + z_i - d_i(k) - \gamma|x_i(k) - z_i| \quad \text{if } x_i(k) \notin (z_{iL}, z_{iH}), \tag{4.37}$$

$$y(k+1) = (1+\beta)y(k) + \sum_i (x_i(k) - z) \quad \text{if } x_i(k) \notin (z_{iL}, z_{iH}). \tag{4.38}$$

Next, we have a performance index, similar to the one used by Miller and Orr. It is denoted J^{mo} and accumulates transaction cost and opportunity cost, for the ith current account, denoted $t_i(k)$ and $o_i(k)$, respectively. The latter is assumed to be given by the interest that would have been earned if the current account balance had been put in the investment account. Since the Sethi–Thompson model is used in this book, a transaction cost proportional to the transfer is used instead of the constant transaction cost used in [MO66]. This leads to the following definition of a Miller–Orr like performance index, to be minimized:

$$\begin{aligned} o_i(k+1) &= o_i(k) + (\beta - \alpha_i)x_i(k), \\ t_i(k+1) &= t_i(k) + \textstyle\sum_{i=1}^N \gamma_i|u_i(k)|, \\ J_i^{mo}(k+1) &= o_i(k+1) + t_i(k+1), \\ J^{mo}(k+1) &= \textstyle\sum_{i=1}^N J_i^{mo}(k+1). \end{aligned} \tag{4.39}$$

Miller and Orr [MO66] assume that the manager seeks to minimize the performance index under some "policy of simple form," which is taken to be the three-parameter (z_L, z, z_H) policy described above (for the case $N = M = 1$). Under the hypothesis of a Bernoulli cash demand, they derive optimal parameter values z_L^*, z^*, z_H^* that minimize the expected value of the sum of transaction and opportunity costs. If the cash demand distribution is not Bernoulli, then a three level controller can still be used, but the values derived by Miller and Orr will no longer be optimal in general and will need to be tuned in some suitable manner. Some possible approaches are described briefly in the next section. There is evidently a complementary relationship between the indices J^{mo} and J^{ω}_{os}, because minimizing transaction and opportunity costs has the effect of maximizing wealth.

4.3.4 ▪ Optimal three level control of cash balance

The formulas derived in the original Miller–Orr paper for z_{iL}, z, z_{iH} are only valid for Bernoulli demands and constant transaction costs. Thus, if it is desired to maintain a three level control policy, then, for the omniscient case, with a known demand, the levels can be determined by solving the optimal control problem defined below.

Given the demand over the entire planning horizon, the **omniscient optimal control of cash balance with lower and upper thresholds** z_{iL}, z_{iH} **and reference level** z_i, which are the parameters or "controls" to be determined, is as follows:

$$\begin{array}{l} \text{minimize } J^{mo}(K_f+1) \\ \text{by choice of threshold parameters } z_{iL}, z_{iH}, \text{ and } z_i \in (z_{iL}, z_{iH}), \\ \text{subject to the dynamics (4.35)–(4.38)} \quad \forall k, \\ \text{and minimum balance constraints } 0 \leq x_{i,\min} \leq x(k) \quad \forall i, k. \end{array} \tag{4.40}$$

Due to the logic of switching from one control to another, depending on a threshold, the transcription into a mathematical programming problem requires the introduction of logical (binary) variables and leads to a mixed integer linear programming problem. Furthermore, even if this is done, *the optimal solution* z^*_{iL}, z^*, z^*_{iH} *is only valid for the particular demand utilized in the optimization procedure.* This makes it clear that the one step ahead optimal formulation (4.23) circumvents the problem of having to know the entire demand a priori and, in addition, maintains the idea of a band or zone in which the current account balance is allowed to fluctuate. Observe that the one step ahead optimal version of (4.40) could be defined, yielding optimal values of $z^*_L(k), z^*(k), z^*_H(k)$ that would, in general, vary at each instant k. Although such an idea has been used in [GM07; SM19], in practice, most managers are more comfortable with fixed thresholds, as found in the majority of papers and textbooks in the area of cash management.

An omniscient version of a Miller–Orr type problem that can be transcribed as a linear program can also be defined. The idea is to keep the upper and lower bounds on the current account balance, eliminate the middle or reference level, and replace the performance index $J^{\omega}_{om,f}$ by J^{mo}, so that the control sequence is determined by optimization, instead of imposing the threshold control (4.34).

4.4 ▪ Numerical examples of the generalized cash balance problem

This section contains some numerical examples of the generalized cash balance problem, for different choices of weights and objective functions, in order to illustrate different aspects of its solution. It starts with the case of one current and one investment account. In order to compare the performances of different strategies, it is important to keep in mind the difference between a bound imposed in an optimization strategy and the thresholds z_{iL}, z_{iH} used in the three level strategy. The former is a constraint that cannot be violated by any feasible solution of the optimization problem, whilst thresholds can be violated; when they are, the three level policy is designed so as to drive the current account balance back into the operating band between lower and upper bounds. However, the return to the operating band depends on the cash demand and is not necessarily immediate. Thus, the thresholds used in the three level formulation may be thought of as soft upper and lower bounds, which can be violated momentarily, since the control action then acts to return the current account balance to the operating band. Given that negative cash balances result in much higher penalty costs in comparison with holding costs for cash balances [SM20], it is important to note that the operating bands, and especially the lower bounds, in the three level strategy must be chosen in such a way that nonnegativity of the current account cash balances is ensured, and this is not easy to achieve for unknown cash demands. Since the indices used in the different optimization strategies are not necessarily identical, there should be a common performance metric, evaluated in the same way for all strategies. Finally, given the stochastic nature of the cash demand, it is essential to compare average performance over a set of demands, randomly generated from some distribution.

In view of these considerations, the following decisions were taken in the numerical experiments reported below:

1. In the Miller–Orr strategies, the lower threshold parameters z_{iL} are adjusted so that, for the whole set of demands used in the performance evaluation, the current account balances do not become negative. Observe that this confers an (unfair) advantage to the Miller–Orr strategies when compared with optimization strategies which use the same lower bound (i.e., $x_{i,\min} = z_{iL} > 0$), since the former may violate it and even become negative (overdraft), but the latter will respect it. The lower and upper bounds for the current account balance in (4.27) are chosen to be equal to the lower and upper thresholds for the Miller–Orr control policy (4.34), i.e., $x_{i,\min} = z_{iL}$ and $x_{i,\max} = z_{iH}$.

2. The wealth gain for a single demand is defined as the increase in wealth over the entire horizon divided by the initial wealth, i.e.,

$$\begin{array}{l} \text{wealth gain for a single demand} := \frac{w(K_f)-w(1)}{w(1)}, \\ \text{where } w(k) = \sum_i x_i(k) + \sum_j y_j(k). \end{array} \tag{4.41}$$

   The common performance metric is taken to be the *average wealth gain over the set of demands*.

3. The cash demand distributions were taken to be Bernoulli (equiprobable ± 1, as proposed in [MO66]), normal, uniform, and midinterval change from uniform to normal.

4. For each demand distribution, results are reported for two cases: (a) the current demand $d(k)$ is known, and (b) when the current demand $d(k)$ is unknown and the estimate $\hat{d}(k)$ is used instead.

4.4.1 ▪ Numerical example with two current accounts and one investment account

As indicated in the previous section, comparison of the proposed one step ahead controller with a three level controller is only possible in the case $M = 1$ and, for illustrative purposes, it will be assumed that $N = 2$. Note that the limitation $M = 1$ is imposed by the three level strategy, not by the proposed OSA method, which is applicable for all positive integers M and N.

For ease of reference, the model and performance index are recalled here:

$$\begin{aligned} x_1(k+1) &= (1+\alpha_1)x_1(k) + u_1(k) - d_1(k) - \gamma_1|u_1(k)| - c_{12}(k), \\ x_2(k+1) &= (1+\alpha_2)x_2(k) + u_2(k) - d_2(k) - \gamma_2|u_2(k)| + c_{12}(k), \\ y(k+1) &= (1+\beta)y(k) - u_1(k) - u_2(k). \end{aligned} \tag{4.42}$$

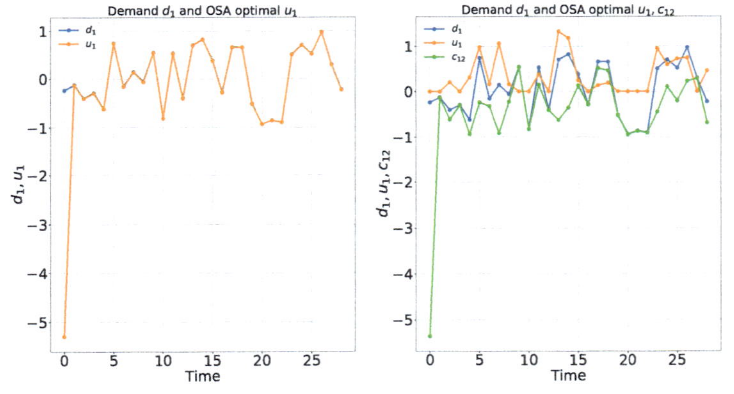

Figure 4.3. *(Left panel) One step ahead optimal transfer sequences u_1 and demand d_1. No intra-account transfers, $c_{12} \equiv 0$. (Right panel) One step ahead optimal transfer sequences u_1, demand d_1, and intra-account transfers c_{12}.*

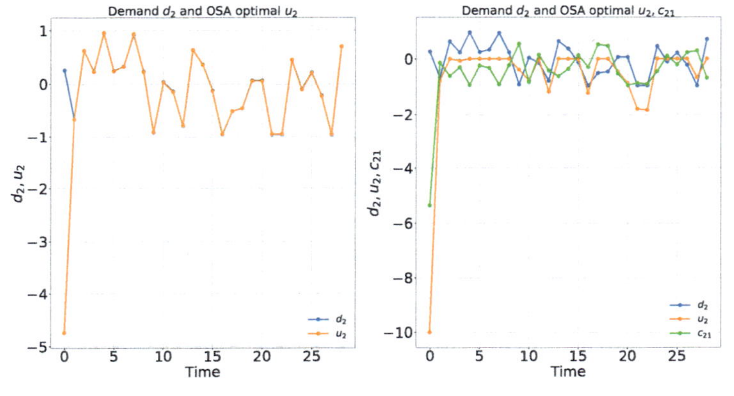

Figure 4.4. *(Left panel) One step ahead optimal transfer sequences u_2 and demand d_2. No intra-account transfers, $c_{12} \equiv 0$. (Right panel) One step ahead optimal transfer sequences u_2, demand d_2, and intra-account transfers c_{21}.*

The performance index can be expressed concisely as

$$J_*^{\omega}(k+1) = \kappa y(k+1) - \mu_1 x_1(k+1) - \mu_2 x_2(k+1) \tag{4.43}$$

and is to be maximized by choice of the decision variables (controls). As explained in sect. 4.3.2, if $* = os$ (the OSA index), the weights are chosen as $\kappa = 0, \mu_1 = \mu_2 = 1$, and the decision variables at instant k are the optimal transfers $u_i(k), i = 1, 2, c_{ij}(k)$. If $* = om$, the omniscient index is defined by choosing $k = K_f$, $\kappa = 1, \mu_1 = \mu_2 = -1$, and the decision variables are the sequences of optimal transfers $\{u_i(k)\}_{k=1}^{K_f}, i = 1, 2, \{c_{im}(k)\}_{k=1}^{K_f}$. If intracurrent account transfers are not allowed, then $c_{im}(k) \equiv 0$.

The data for the numerical examples are as follows: $\alpha_1 = \alpha_2 = 0.01$, $\beta = 0.04$, $\gamma_1 = 0.01$, $\gamma_2 = 0.02$. Initial cash account balances are $x_1(1) = x_2(1) = 6$; initial investment account balance is $y = 6$.

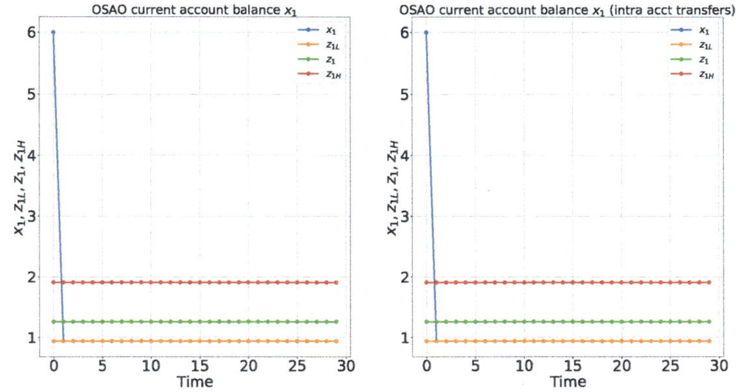

Figure 4.5. *(Left panel) One step ahead optimal current account balance x_1 and bounds. No intra-account transfers, $c_{12} \equiv 0$. (Right panel) One step ahead optimal current account balance x_1, demand d_1, when intra-account transfers c_{12} not allowed.*

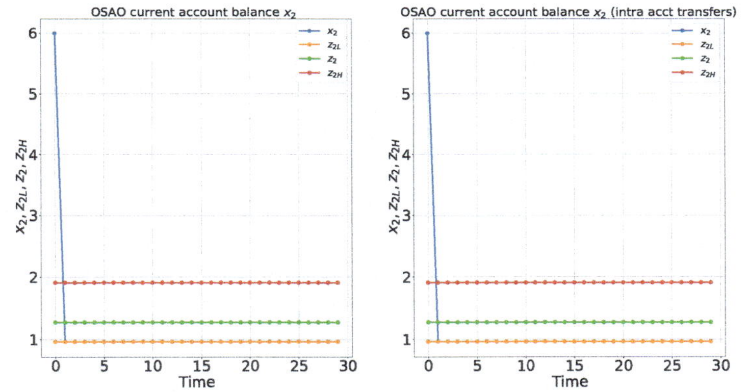

Figure 4.6. *(Left panel) One step ahead optimal current account balance x_2 and bounds. No intra-account transfers, $c_{21} \equiv 0$. (Right panel) One step ahead optimal current account balance x_2, demand d_2, when intra-account transfers c_{21}, are allowed.*

Cash demand 30-day sequences, uniformly distributed with mean values 0.025 and -0.054, are as follows:

$$\begin{aligned}
&d_1 = [-0.2346, -0.1229, -0.3993, -0.2908, -0.6182, 0.7403, -0.1529, 0.1459,\\
&-0.0562, 0.5464, -0.8178, 0.5315, -0.4000, 0.7024, 0.8213, 0.3795, -0.2766, 0.6585,\\
&0.6556, -0.5148, -0.9366, -0.8588, -0.8967, 0.5069, 0.7014, 0.5180, 0.9718, 0.2957,\\
&-0.2248, -0.6137],\\
&d_2 = [0.2602, -0.6652, 0.6206, 0.2360, 0.9448, 0.2478, 0.3307, 0.9242, 0.2334,\\
&-0.9193, 0.0418, -0.1381, -0.7846, 0.6339, 0.3646, -0.1211, -0.9557, -0.5063,\\
&-0.4520, 0.0667, 0.0645, -0.9570, -0.9555, 0.4512, -0.0986, 0.2131, -0.2184,\\
&-0.9624, 0.6952, -0.2288].
\end{aligned} \tag{4.44}$$

The results of the numerical experiments are shown in Figs. 4.3 through 4.12. Some remarks on this numerical experiment are as follows:

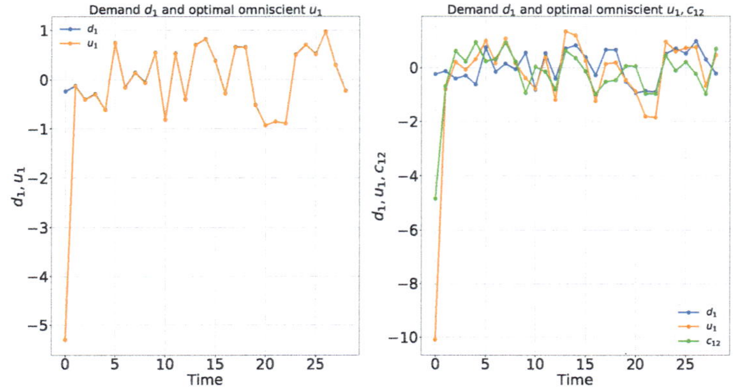

Figure 4.7. *(Left panel) Omniscient optimal transfer sequences u_1 and demand d_1. No intra-account transfers, $c_{12} \equiv 0$. (Right panel) Omniscient optimal transfer sequences u_1, demand d_1, and intra-account transfers c_{12}.*

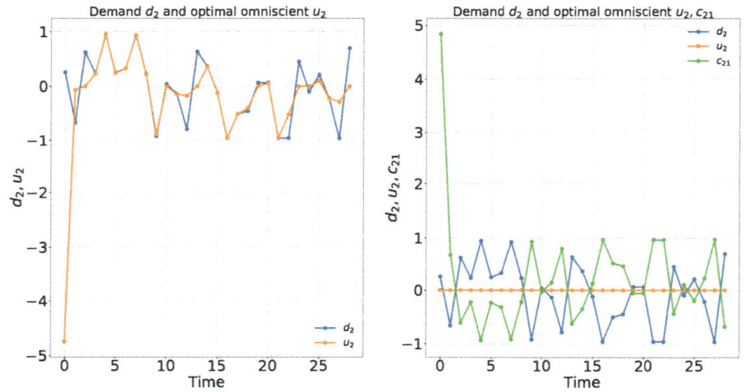

Figure 4.8. *(Left panel) Omniscient optimal transfer sequences u_2 and demand d_2. No intra-account transfers, $c_{12} \equiv 0$. (Right panel) Omniscient optimal transfer sequences u_2, demand d_2, and intra-account transfers c_{21}.*

- The one step ahead optimal strategy is to drive the current account balances to their lower bounds (Figs. 4.5 and 4.6). This is achieved (when $c_{12} \equiv 0$) by tracking the demand (Figs. 4.3(left) and 4.4(left)), but, when intracurrent account transfers are allowed ($c_{12} \not\equiv 0$), by a more complex strategy which takes advantage of excess balance in either one of the current accounts to meet excess demand in the other (Figs. 4.3(right) and 4.4(right)).

- The omniscient (globally) optimal solution, without intracurrent account transfers, has behavior similar to the one step ahead optimal controller (Fig. 4.7(left)), although demand tracking is no longer exact (Fig. 4.8(left)), and, indeed, Fig. 4.10(left) shows that the omniscient strategy does not make the current account balances equal to their lower bounds at all instants. With intracurrent account transfers permitted, in this example, the omniscient sequence zeros the control input u_2 essentially by "mirroring" the demand sequence d_2 (i.e., transferring it to current account 1) (Fig. 4.8(right)).

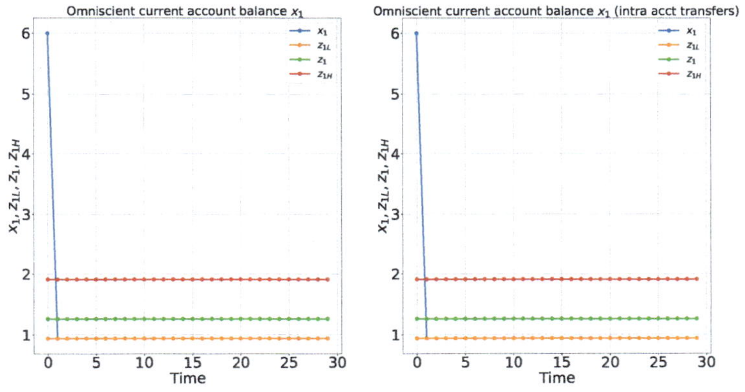

Figure 4.9. *(Left panel) Omniscient optimal current account balance x_1 and bounds. No intra-account transfers, $c_{12} \equiv 0$. (Right panel) Omniscient optimal current account balance x_1, demand d_1, when intra-account transfers c_{12} not allowed.*

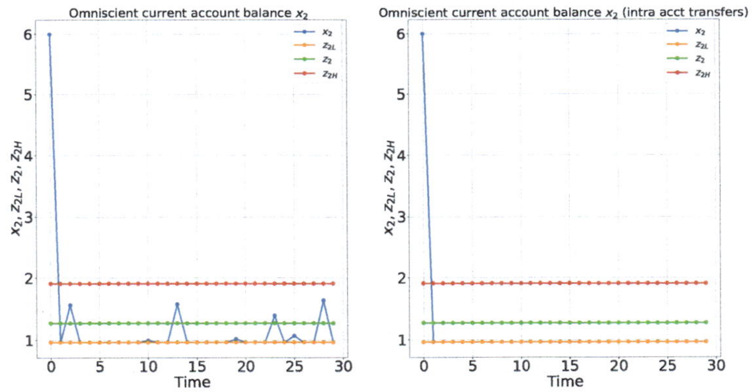

Figure 4.10. *(Left panel) Omniscient optimal current account balance x_2 and bounds. No intra-account transfers, $c_{21} \equiv 0$. (Right panel) Omniscient optimal current account balance x_2, demand d_2, when intra-account transfers c_{21} are allowed.*

- The three level controller based on the current demand produces a transfer sequence that approximately tracks the demand, with a delay of 1 time unit (Fig. 4.11) and, after being tuned to achieve nonnegativity of current account balances (which cannot be guaranteed analytically, only probabilistically [i.e., in a Monte Carlo sense]), keeps the current account balances approximately within the stipulated upper and lower bounds, although repeated violations can be seen in Fig. 4.12.

4.4.2 ▪ Numerical examples of average performance for single cash and single investment account

The parameters are chosen as follows: $x(1) = y(1) = 40$, $\alpha = 0.01$, $\beta = 0.04$, $\gamma = 0.02$, $K_f = 30$, and the average performance was computed over a test set of 30 randomly generated demands. The fixed levels z_L, z, z_H of the three level strategy were tuned using a training set of 30 demands in order to maintain the nonnegativity of the account balances. Tuning of the

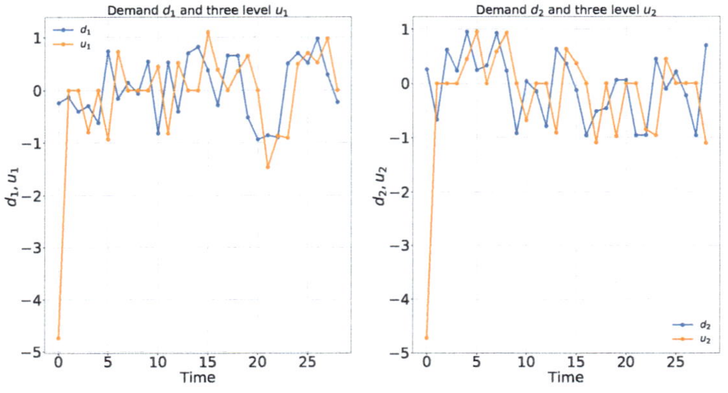

Figure 4.11. *Three level controller transfer and demand sequences: (Left panel)* u_1, d_1 *and (Right panel)* u_2, d_2.

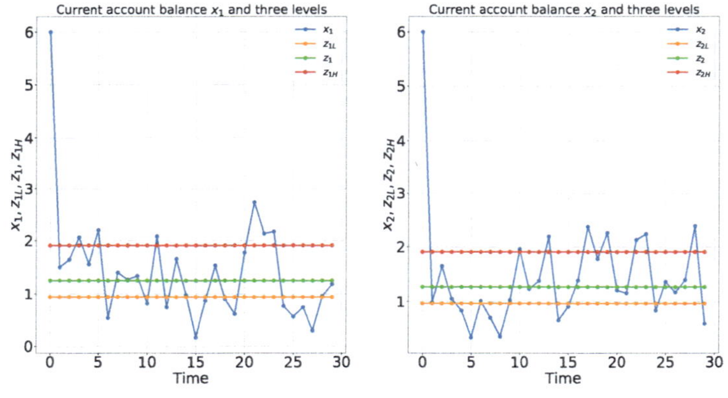

Figure 4.12. *Three level controller current account balances: (Left panel)* x_1 *and (Right panel)* x_2.

three levels or thresholds of the three level controller is necessary to maintain nonnegativity of the current account balance and needs knowledge of the demand distribution, or records of past demand data, as well as additional computational effort.

The following policies are compared: (i) the one step ahead optimal control obtained using J^{ω}_{os} with weights chosen as $\kappa = 0$, $\mu = 1$; (ii) the three level policy (4.34) with the optimal parameters tuned using a training set, fixing z_L; (iii) the omniscient optimal control obtained using J^{ω}_{om}; and (iv) the omniscient optimal control obtained using J^{mo}. The latter two strategies are included merely as a globally optimal benchmarks, even though they are not implementable, since they use knowledge of the entire demand and for J^{ω}_{om} the weights used are $\kappa = 1$ and $\mu = -1$, corresponding to maximization of final wealth.

The variation of average wealth gains as a function of the 30 randomly distributed demands is presented in Figs. 4.13 and 4.14.

4.4.3 ▪ Average performance with current demand unknown

This section assumes that the current demand $d(k)$ is unknown and, for the one step ahead optimal strategy, uses the simplest estimator $\hat{d}(k) = d(k-1)$ of the unknown current demand.

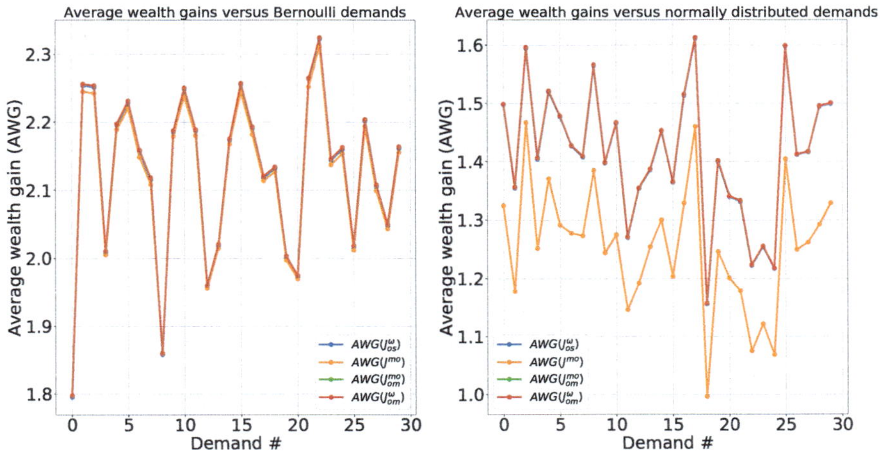

Figure 4.13. *Average wealth gains versus (left panel) Bernoulli demands and (right panel) normally distributed demands.*

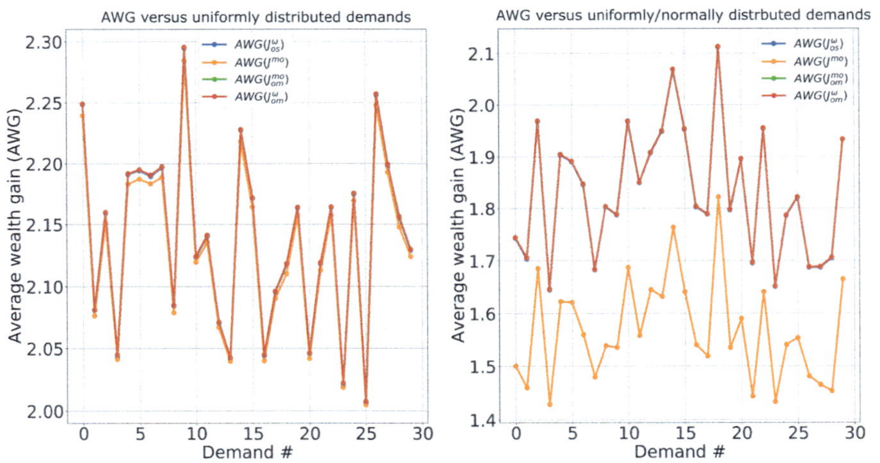

Figure 4.14. *Average wealth gains versus (left panel) uniformly distributed demands and (right panel) uniformly and normally distributed demands.*

Remarks on the numerical examples

- If the cash demand distribution is known to be binomial or uniform, then it is possible to use a set of synthetic demands with the same distribution in order to tune the three level controller to achieve a performance that is almost identical to the proposed one step ahead optimal controller. Indeed, both controllers achieve performance levels very close to omniscient global optimal (Figs. 4.13(left) and 4.14(left)).

- If the cash demand is normally distributed, the proposed one step ahead optimal controller continues to achieve a performance that is almost identical to omniscient global optimal (Fig. 4.13(right)). However, the three level controller exhibits a discernible drop in performance level (see Fig. 4.13(right)). A similar, but more pronounced drop in performance occurs when the cash demand distribution switches from uniform to normal in the middle of the evaluation horizon (see Fig. 4.14(right)).

- When the current demand $d(k)$ is known, the proposed OSAO method requires no tuning at all, and the lower bound for the current account balance can be taken as zero without violating nonnegativity. This is not true of the Miller–Orr controller, which requires tuning to ensure nonnegativity of the current account balance.

- When the current demands $d_i(k)$ are unknown, the simple estimate $\hat{d}(k) = d(k-1)$ works well in this example, without the use of more elaborate estimation schemes (such as those proposed in [HCI16; OT12; SM+17]). However, in this case, it may be necessary to impose a lower bound on the current account balance, essentially in order to ensure a viable solution to the one step ahead optimization problem. This lower bound can be found empirically by increasing from a small value until feasibility of the one step ahead linear program is achieved. In contrast, the three level strategy, which does not explicitly use the current cash demand, needs careful adjustment of its three levels in order to ensure nonnegativity of the current account balance, and, besides the fact that the entire demand needs to be known in order to do this, there is also no simple linear program formulation of the problem of computing these levels.

- Finally, it should be pointed out that, in the context of the cash balance problem, the assumption that the current demands $d_i(k)$ are known merely corresponds to the assumption that all transfers between accounts are made at the end of the day instead of being made at the beginning of the day, and this may be reasonable in many cases.

4.5 ▪ Average performance of one step ahead optimal strategies

This section compares the average performance of the one step ahead optimal (OSAO) strategies, **n**o **i**ntra-account and **w**ith **i**ntra-account (abbreviated NI and WI, respectively) transfers, in terms of average wealth gain over a 30-day horizon. Results for the globally optimal theoretical omniscient solutions are presented as well in order to serve as benchmarks. The four algorithms compared are abbreviated as OS_NI, OS_WI, OM_NI, and OM_WI. The experiments are designed as follows.

1. A grid is set up in the current account-investment account space. For each pair (N_{CA},N_{IA}), where $N_{CA}, N_{IA} \in \{2,4,6,8,10\}$ (i.e., for each of 25 grid points), a set of 20 cash demands of 30 days duration is generated. The connection graph of the current and investment accounts is assumed to be complete, i.e., transfers between all accounts of both types are permitted.

2. Average wealth gains and their standard deviations (shown as error whiskers in the grouped bar plots) are computed for each grid point and the results plotted as grouped bar charts (one for each even number of investment accounts, as the even number of current accounts varies on the horizontal axis).

3. The demands are taken to be normally distributed, with zero mean; the minimum current account cash balances are stipulated to all be zero; the upper bounds on cash balances (for the big M estimates) were all taken to be equal and twice as large as the initial conditions. The initial conditions were taken to be equal to five units in all the accounts.

4. The alpha, beta, and gamma parameters were generated from normal distributions with mean 2 and standard deviation 1, accepting only nonnegative values, with the generated values then being divided by 2000 for alpha, 200 for beta, and 4000 for gamma, i.e., the current account interest rates (resp., transaction cost rates) are taken to be 10 (resp., 20) times smaller than the investment account interest rates, which are closer to reality than the exaggerated values chosen (merely for illustrative purposes) in sect. 4.4.

5. For the one step ahead algorithms, all the kappa values are chosen equal to zero and the mu values equal to one, whereas the omniscient solutions maximize total final wealth (i.e., all kappa values equal to one and all mu values equal to -1 in (4.8).

6. For each experiment, the absolute average wealth gains and their standard deviations, over a set of 20 randomly generated demands, are reported for each of the four methods: one step ahead optimal, no intracurrent account transfers; with intracurrent account transfers; omniscient solution, no intracurrent account transfers; and with intracurrent account transfers, abbreviated, respectively, in the grouped bar charts as OS_NI, OS_WI, OM_NI, and OM_WI. In addition, the average wealth gains of the one step ahead methods relative to the omniscient counterparts denominated relative average wealth gains, abbreviated as RG_NI and RG_WI, are also plotted as grouped bar charts.

4.5.1 ▪ Comparison for normally distributed demands with current demand known

This subsection shows the results of the experiments described at the beginning of the section for normally distributed demands with current demand known. The figures are organized as follows. In each, the horizontal axis represents the number of current accounts, taking the values 6, 8, and 10, and Fig. 4.15 for 6, Fig. 4.16 for 8, and, finally, Fig. 4.17 for 10 investment accounts, with the left panels showing the average wealth gain of each of the four methods and the right panels showing the relative average wealth gains (one step ahead optimal over omniscient optimal).

4.5.2 ▪ Comparison for normally distributed demands with current demand unknown

This subsection shows the results of the experiments described at the beginning of the section for normally distributed demands with current demand unknown. The figures are organized as follows: in each, the horizontal axis represents the number of current accounts, taking the values 6, 8, and 10, and Fig. 4.18 for 6, Fig. 4.19 for 8, and, finally, Fig. 4.20 for 10 investment accounts, with the left panels showing the average wealth gain of each of the four methods and the right panels showing the relative average wealth gains (one step ahead optimal over omniscient optimal).

4.5.3 ▪ Comparison for uniformly and Bernoulli distributed demands with current demand unknown

This subsection shows the results of the experiments described at the beginning of the section for uniformly distributed demands with current demand unknown. In Fig. 4.21, the horizontal axis represents the number of current accounts, taking the values 2, 4, 6, 8, and 10, for 10 investment accounts, with the left panel showing the average wealth gain of each of the four methods and the right panel showing the relative average wealth gains (one step ahead optimal over omniscient optimal). Figure 4.22 shows the analogous results for Bernoulli distributed demands.

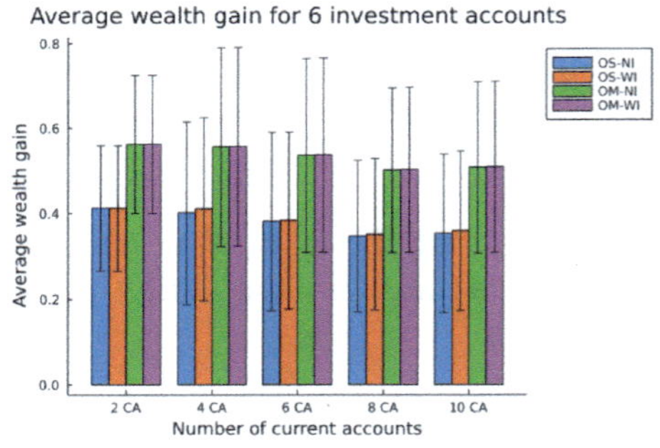

(a) Average wealth gain

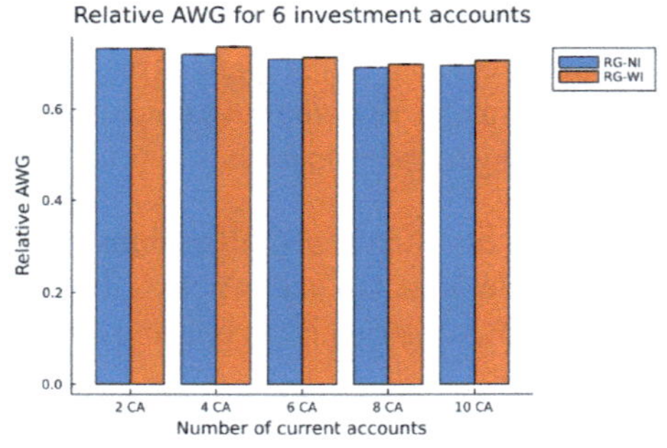

(b) Relative average wealth gain

Figure 4.15. (a) *Average wealth gains and* (b) *relative average wealth gains, varying the number of current accounts (horizontal axis) for normally distributed demands for six investment accounts.*

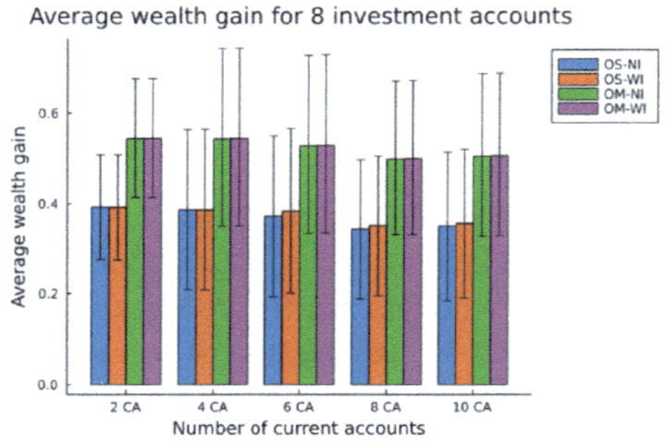

(a) Average wealth gain

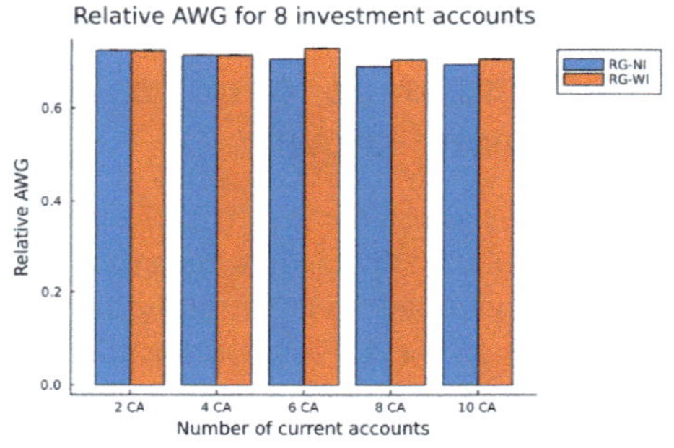

(b) Relative average wealth gain

Figure 4.16. (a) *Average wealth gains and* (b) *relative average wealth gains, varying the number of current accounts (horizontal axis) for normally distributed demands for eight investment accounts.*

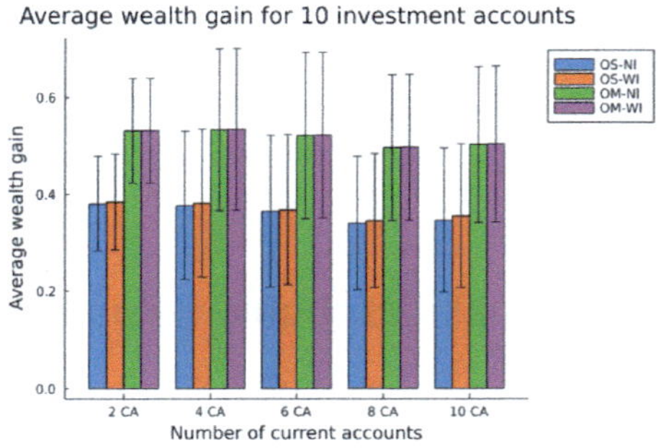

(a) Average wealth gain

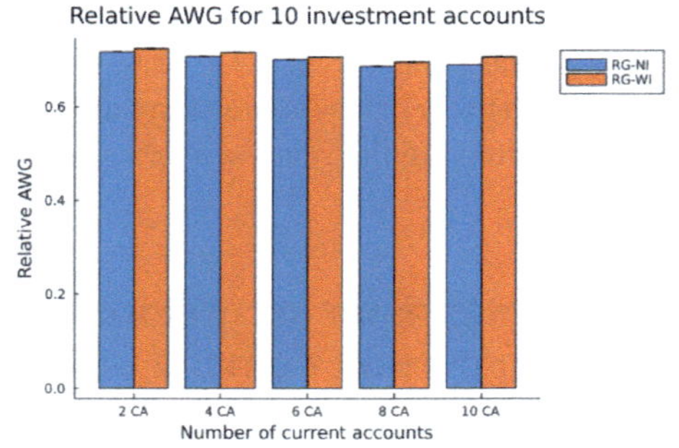

(b) Relative average wealth gain

Figure 4.17. (a) *Average wealth gains and* (b) *relative average wealth gains, varying the number of current accounts (horizontal axis) for normally distributed demands for 10 investment accounts.*

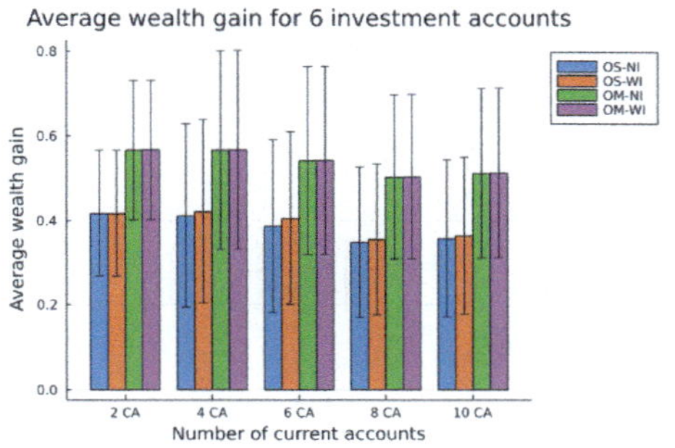

(a) Average wealth gain

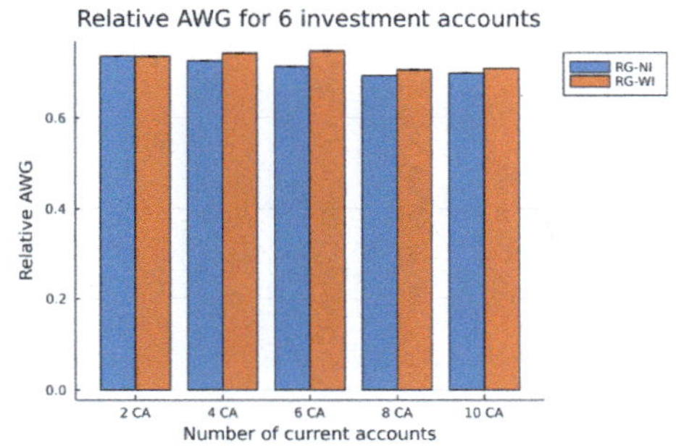

(b) Relative average wealth gain

Figure 4.18. (a) *Average wealth gains and* (b) *relative average wealth gains, varying the number of current accounts (horizontal axis) for normally distributed demands for six investment accounts.*

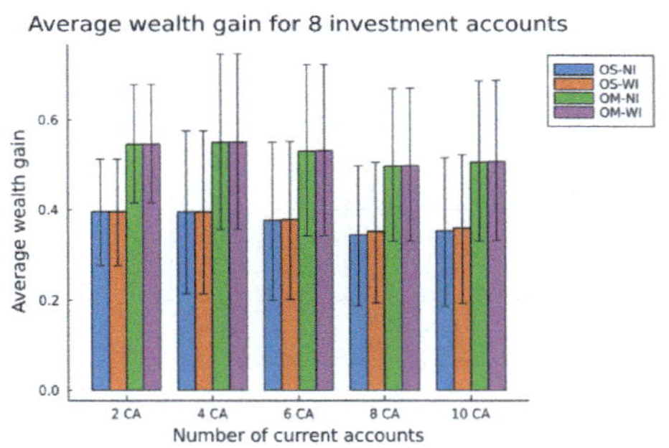

(a) Average wealth gain

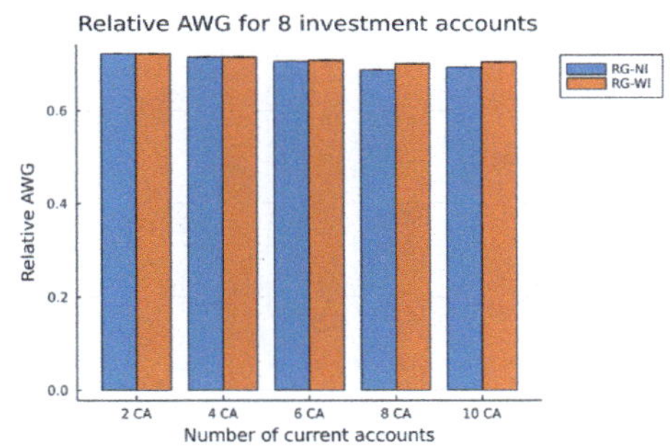

(b) Relative average wealth gain

Figure 4.19. (a) *Average wealth gains and* (b) *relative average wealth gains, varying the number of current accounts (horizontal axis) for normally distributed demands for eight investment accounts.*

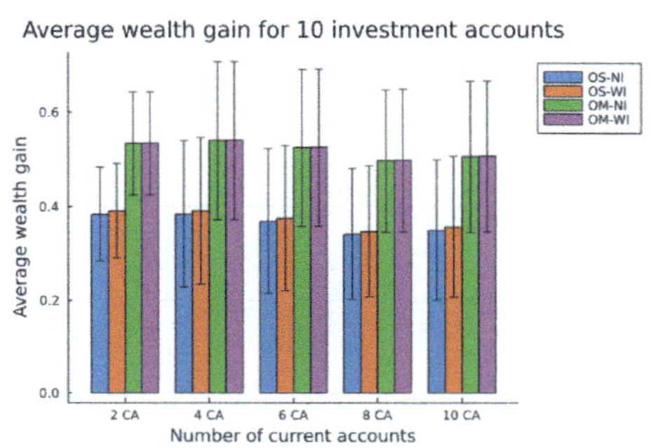

(a) Average wealth gain

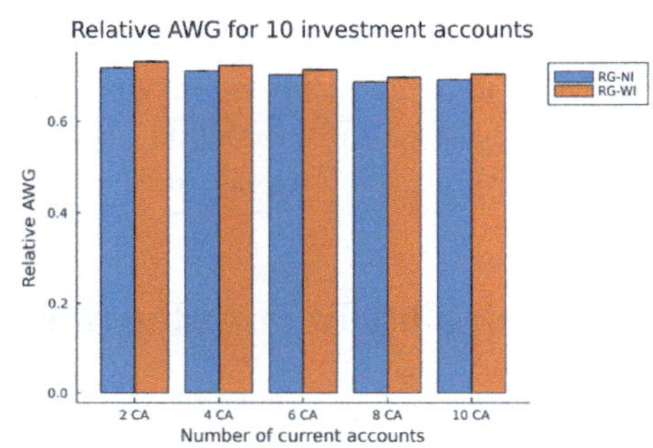

(b) Relative average wealth gain

Figure 4.20. (a) *Average wealth gains and* (b) *relative average wealth gains, varying the number of current accounts (horizontal axis) for normally distributed demands for* 10 *investment accounts.*

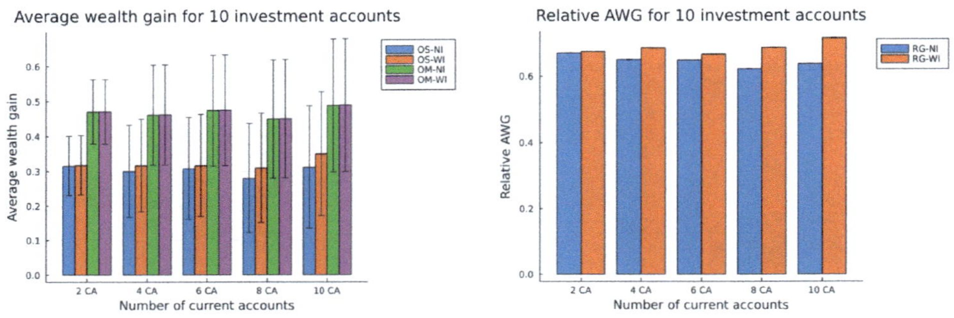

(a) Average wealth gain (b) Relative average wealth gain

Figure 4.21. *Case of uniformly distributed demands:* (a) *average wealth gains and* (b) *relative average wealth gains, varying the number of current accounts (horizontal axis) for uniformly distributed demands for* 10 *investment accounts.*

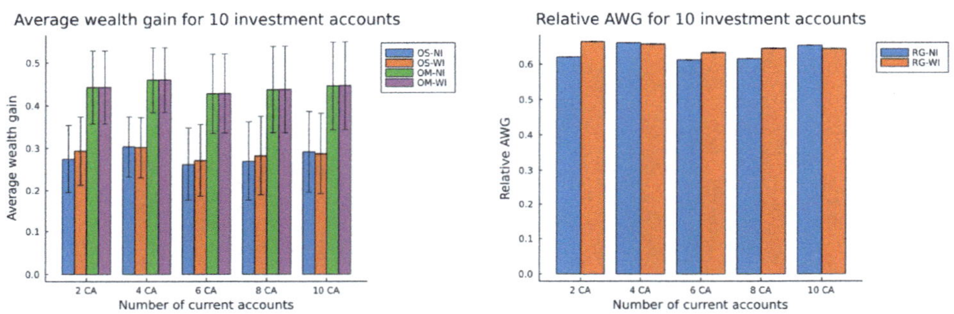

(a) Average wealth gain (b) Relative average wealth gain

Figure 4.22. *Case of Bernoulli distributed demands:* (a) *average wealth gains and* (b) *relative average wealth gains, varying the number of current accounts (horizontal axis) for Bernoulli distributed demands for* 10 *investment accounts.*

4.5.4 ▪ Average wealth gains: Case of high transaction costs

In this subsection, numerical examples show that, in the case of high transaction costs, it is advantageous to use intracurrent account transfers. The term high transaction costs refers to the fact that for Fig. 4.23, the transaction costs were chosen to be, on average, twice the investment account interest rates, and the demands normally distributed.

4.5.5 ▪ Scalability of one step ahead approaches

This subsection shows how the compute time and memory requirements scale with the number of accounts in the case of 10 current accounts and a varying number of investment accounts $(2, 4, 6, 8, \text{and } 10)$. The demands are assumed to be normal and the current day's demand assumed known, since this does not affect the compute times. The `BenchmarkTools` suite in Julia [Rev22] was used on each method. The command `@benchmark` from this suite runs the code being tested several times and produces the following statistics: min, max, median, average, and standard deviation of the compute times (Fig. 4.24(a)) as well as an estimate of the

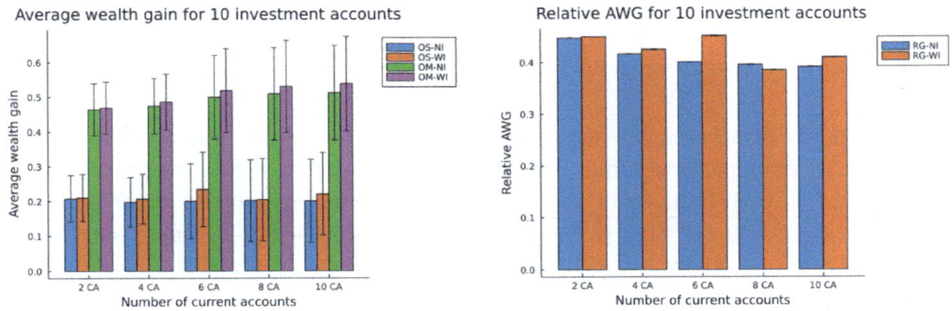

(a) Average wealth gain (b) Relative average wealth gain

Figure 4.23. *Case of high transaction costs:* (a) *average wealth gains and* (b) *relative average wealth gains, varying the number of current accounts (horizontal axis) for normally distributed demands and for* 10 *investment accounts.*

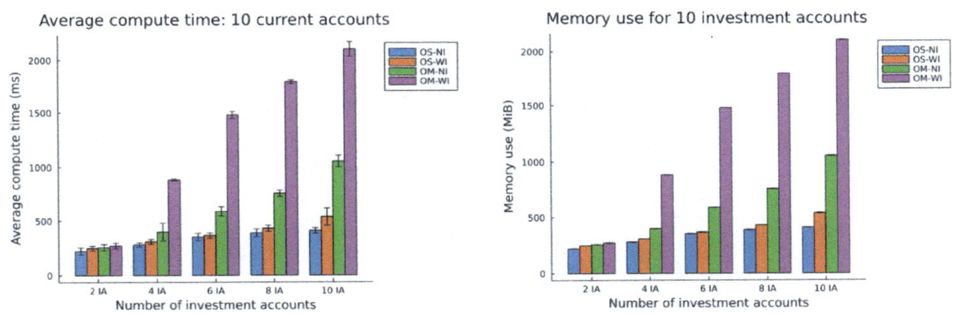

(a) Average compute time (b) Memory use

Figure 4.24. *Case of current accounts and the number of investment accounts (horizontal axis) varying, for normally distributed demands:* (a) *compute time plot (in milliseconds) and* (b) *memory use plot (in MiB).*

memory use (Fig. 4.24(b)). It should be noted that only the compute time is measured, not the compilation time.

4.5.6 ▪ Discussion of average performance for the cash balance problem

1. As expected the omniscient solutions are superior to the one step ahead optimal algorithms, and the hierarchy OSA_NI $\leq$ OSA_WI $\leq$ OM_NI $\leq$ OM_WI is respected, in terms of the average wealth gains. The difference between OM_NI and OM_WI is very small; however, for the one step ahead optimal approach, there is always an advantage, even though it may be small, in using intracurrent account transfers, which, we recall, are assumed to be free of transaction costs.

2. The variance of the average wealth gain (represented by the error whiskers in the grouped bar plots) reduces as the number of current and investment accounts increases in both cases (current day's demand known or unknown).

3. The behavior of the average wealth gain is very similar in both the known and unknown current demand cases. However, the variances are, expectedly, larger in the case when the current day's demand is unknown.

4. For normally distributed demands, over all combinations of the numbers of current and investment accounts, an absolute average wealth gain of at least 40% is achieved and a relative average wealth gain (with repect to the global omniscient maximum) of at least 70%, for both cases (current day's demand known or unknown). For Bernoulli and uniformly distributed demands, the average wealth gain is a little lower, around 30%, and the relative average wealth gain around 60% (with or without knowledge of the current day's demand). This can be considered to be very satisfactory behavior for the proposed one step ahead optimal method, in light of its minimal requirements of information about the demand and its distribution.

5. For higher transaction costs, although absolute average wealth gains are evidently lower, using intracurrent account transfers increases the average wealth gain with respect to the cases when no intracurrent account transfers are allowed.

6. From the time and memory plots in Fig. 4.24, it seems that the implementable one step ahead optimal methods have linear increases in time and memory requirements, when the number of current accounts is held fixed and the number of investment accounts increases. A similar conclusion was reached in the symmetrical case (not shown here), when the number of investment accounts is held fixed and the number of current accounts increases. On the other hand, Fig. 4.24 also shows that the average compute times for the hypothetical omniscient optimal control appear to increase exponentially. The bar plots of the omniscient methods are, of course, just shown to underscore the scalability of the proposed one step ahead optimal schemes.

4.6 ▪ Chapter summary

In this chapter, the classical cash balance problem of finite horizon cash management, formulated as an optimal control problem, was then rewritten as a mixed integer linear program, leading to a one step ahead optimal control scheme, and also a mixed integer linear program (of much smaller dimension). The main consequence of this was the proposal of a simple and implementable one step ahead optimal controller, **without any knowledge of stochastic cash demand distribution**. This distribution-free one step ahead optimal control approach was shown to be easily extended to cases with multiple cash and investment accounts, taking into account both wealth maximization and risk minimization, by an appropriate choice of the one step ahead objective function and the constraints. When the current demand is unknown and the previous day's demand is used as its simple estimator, performance of the one step ahead algorithm is reduced, with respect to the case in which the current day's demand is known. Although the average wealth gain is still positive, for small numbers of current and investment accounts, the variances may be large enough to annul the gain. However, as the number of accounts increases, the average wealth gains tend to increase and the variances reduce considerably, showing the usefulness of the proposed method. Thus the proposed method can also be used as a "flight simulator" by an account manager, who can use typical or past demands to decide how many and which current accounts should be involved in the management process, as well as to decide the actual cash management policy (i.e., the transfers to be made) in real time.

Notes and references

The early papers [Bau52; RTJ65; ST70] treated deterministic models of the optimal cash balance problem, while the celebrated paper [MO66] considered a stochastic cash balance problem with fixed transactions costs (i.e., independent of the amount of funds transferred) and with the stochastic changes in the cash balance generated by a Bernoulli process. Subsequently, some authors [BPY05; CSL09; HW01; LT14; Nea70] also consider the stochastic cash balance problem as a cost minimization problem faced by a firm that has to decide how much cash to hold in order to meet its transaction requirements for a given planning horizon. At the beginning of each time period, given the current requirements, the firm makes decisions about the right amount of cash to hold. The objective of the firm is to find a policy for holding cash so as to minimize the total expected (possibly discounted) cost over the entire planning horizon. The cash balance problem has also been approached as a special type of inventory control problem [Bau52] and, indeed, can also be used to model several other important applications not related to cash, such as stochastic inventory management (see, for example, [FL07]).

Liu and Xin [LX08] use the terminology online to refer to OSAC and offline to omniscient control and propose a method based on the Sleator–Tarjan paging algorithm. Vörösmarty and Dobos [VD13] show that zero current account balance is omniscient optimal via an algebraic proof. Moraes et al. [MN13; MN14; MNS15], in a series of papers, investigate optimization of the Miller–Orr algorithm using evolutionary optimization, including the case of multiple assets. Orlova [Orl19] uses a dynamic programming approach to the cash balance problem. Salas-Molina, Pla-Santamaria, and Rodriguez-Aguilar [SMPSRA18; SMRAPS20] investigate the applicability of multiobjective and stochastic goal programming optimization of cash balance strategies. Pekkarinen [Pek17] studies the problem of lower bounds on interest rates in order to maintain viability of the cash balance problem. In [SM19], a general piecewise linear transfer cost function is also dealt with in an optimization framework introducing binary variables and using mixed integer linear programming to design cash management policies, although the main focus is on the fitting of random cash management models to data.

The form of the feedback and deadbeat controllers suggests connections with the disturbance affine controllers proposed for scalar systems in [BIP10].

Chapter 5
Dynamic trading

Trading refers to the activity of buying and selling shares or stocks, currencies, etc., on financial markets. Typically, a broker acts as an intermediary between the trader and the buyers and sellers who make up the financial market and charges a commission for his services. In this chapter, a simple model of the trading problem is set up in order to show how the one step ahead optimal control approach is applied to it. The basic question addressed in this chapter can be formulated as follows: given an initial capital that can be used to buy assets, as well as certain initial quantities of assets, how does the trader with this initial composition of capital and assets manage his holdings, as asset prices vary in time? Another way to phrase the question is, at any given instant, since future asset prices are unknown, what decision making procedure should guide the trader in buying and selling assets?

5.1 ▪ Description of the dynamic trading problem

In its most basic form, the trading problem for an investor with a certain initial amount of cash and assets (stocks, bonds, etc.) can be stated as follows. Given that asset prices fluctuate in accordance with the market, what strategy should the investor use to maximize assets in the short term? A set of assets is called a portfolio, and the essence of successful trading is to choose an appropriate portfolio so that the trading algorithm guides decisions to buy and sell the assets belonging to this portfolio in a way that maximizes the total wealth at the end of the trading period.

The specification of a short horizon usually distinguishes the trading problem from the investment problem, which looks at long-term profit and deals with the choice of a portfolio, given statistical information such as mean return and standard deviation of each candidate asset. In the trading problem, in contrast, the investor makes short-term or even real time decisions to buy or sell assets, as price and other relevant information becomes available. Of course, even in the short-term case, uncertainty in future prices leads to uncertainty in the expected return, usually referred to as risk.

Trading has been extensively studied in the literature, and approaches have been classified into the broad categories of quantitative, fundamental, and technical. The first category makes heavy use of statistical and probabilistic models of price series and other relevant variables, while the second studies financial characteristics of the firms whose stock is being traded as well as behavioral characteristics of financial agents (buyers, sellers, etc.). The third category of technical trading can be loosely described as the forecasting of asset prices by the study of past prices and related summary statistics in order to guide the trading process. The approach taken in this chapter is related to the first category, in the sense that it involves algorithmic procedures, based on the general one step ahead optimal control methodology of the book. It is also weakly related to the third category of technical trading, in the sense that the proposed procedure uses a predictor of price at the next (future) instant, and exemplifies it by using the simple moving average, without being tied to this specific predictor.

The term asset is used in this chapter to refer to a product that can be traded (i.e., bought or sold). The term product, in turn, encompasses a variety of things such as commodities, bonds, or shares. Asset prices vary and thus, if one invests in a certain asset and holds it over a period of time, the return on the asset is given by the difference between the selling and buying prices times the quantity of the asset held, less any transaction costs. At any given time, the future variation of asset prices is unknown, so the return could be either positive (profit, when selling price is higher than buying price) or, inversely, negative (loss). It will also be assumed in this chapter, for simplicity, that the trading algorithm works with a prespecified set of assets or portfolio. Thus, at each instant in the trading horizon, the choices are to buy assets within this portfolio, to the extent permitted by the investment account balance and transaction costs, or to sell assets from this portfolio which are held at the instant in question.

Suppose that, at time k, an investor holds quantity $q_i(k)$ of asset i and a given quantity of cash, $c(k)$, in the investment account. Asset i has price $p_i(k)$ at time k and can be sold and converted into cash at this price. In the reverse direction, the investor can buy assets with cash, at their current prices, converting cash into assets. Cash is held in an investment account that accumulates interest at a given rate. Withdrawals from this account to buy assets are subject to a transaction cost that is proportional to the amount withdrawn. Given asset price series which vary with time according to the market, the simplest version of the dynamic trading problem, over a given horizon, is that of determining the sequence of asset and cash holdings, at each instant in this horizon, that will lead to the maximization of the total wealth (cash plus cash value of assets held at the end of the horizon). The investor is only aware of past and current prices at the time they have to make each decision over the trading horizon. The first step in this chapter is to apply the one step ahead optimization approach to this problem. For illustrative purposes, the one step ahead approach is compared with the omniscient one, where the latter assumes that the asset prices are known over the entire trading horizon. Subsequently, some more realistic metrics are used to evaluate the performance of the one step ahead approach.

5.1.1 ▪ Mathematical model of dynamic trading

Let $q_i(k)$ be the quantity of asset i that the investor possesses at instant k, and let $c(k)$ be the capital available for investment. At instant k, the investor can buy a quantity $b_i(k)$ or sell a quantity $s_i(k)$ of the ith asset, at the current price $p_i(k)$. Suppose that the cash account has an interest rate of α and that movement to or from the cash account involves a transaction cost proportional to the amount of cash moved, with proportionality constant γ.

In the notation just established, the **dynamics of the trading process** can be written as follows:.

$$q_i(k+1) = q_i(k) + b_i(k) - s_i(k), i = 1, \ldots, n, \tag{5.1}$$

$$c(k+1) = (1+\alpha)c(k) - \sum_{i=1}^{n} p_i(k)(b_i(k) - s_i(k)) - \gamma \sum_{i=1}^{n} p_i(k)(b_i(k) + s_i(k)), \tag{5.2}$$

where the variables should satisfy the following constraints, for $i = 1, \dots, n$ and for $k = 1, 2, \dots$:

$$p_i(k)b_i(k) \le c(k), \tag{5.3}$$
$$s_i(k) \le q_i(k), \tag{5.4}$$
$$q_i(k) \ge 0, \tag{5.5}$$
$$c(k) \ge 0, \tag{5.6}$$
$$b_i(k) \ge 0, \tag{5.7}$$
$$s_i(k) \ge 0. \tag{5.8}$$

The dynamics (5.1) represents an update of the ith asset quantity after buying and selling occur. The dynamics (5.2) represents an update of the cash holding after interest, buying, and selling of the n assets and the associated transaction costs. The constraint (5.3) limits the investor to buying assets within his available cash budget: in other words, no cash loans are permitted. The constraint (5.4) prevents the investor from selling more of asset i than they possess, i.e., no shorting is permitted for any i. The remaining four constraints are the natural nonnegativity constraints on the variables that have been so defined.

It will be convenient to write the portfolio dynamics in more compact vector form, and to do this we define the *asset or portfolio vector* $\mathbf{q}(k) = (q_1(k), \dots, q_n(k))$, and the associated buying and selling vectors $\mathbf{b}(k)$ and $\mathbf{s}(k)$. The portfolio dynamics can then be written compactly as follows:

$$\mathbf{q}(k+1) = \mathbf{q}(k) + \mathbf{b}(k) - \mathbf{s}(k), \tag{5.9}$$
$$c(k+1) = (1+\alpha)c(k) - \mathbf{p}(k)^\mathsf{T}(\mathbf{b}(k) - \mathbf{s}(k)) - \gamma\mathbf{p}(k)^\mathsf{T}(\mathbf{b}(k) + \mathbf{s}(k)). \tag{5.10}$$

The constraints are written compactly as follows, for $k = 1, 2, \dots$:

$$\mathbf{p}(k)^\mathsf{T}\mathbf{b}(k) \le c(k), \tag{5.11}$$
$$\mathbf{s}(k) \le \mathbf{q}(k), \tag{5.12}$$
$$\mathbf{q}(k) \ge \mathbf{0}, \tag{5.13}$$
$$c(k) \ge 0, \tag{5.14}$$
$$\mathbf{b}(k) \ge \mathbf{0}, \tag{5.15}$$
$$\mathbf{s}(k) \ge \mathbf{0}. \tag{5.16}$$

Remark. Note that, in general, for each asset i, only one action, buying or selling, will take place, i.e., either $b_i(k) > 0$ and $s_i(k) = 0$, or $b_i(k) = 0$ and $s_i(k) > 0$. However, this complementarity condition, simply expressed as $\mathbf{b}^\mathsf{T}\mathbf{s} = 0$, is not imposed or required. The observant reader will also note the similarity to the treatment of cash balance dynamics in Chapter 4, since a single decision variable vector $\mathbf{u}(k)$ could be defined as $\mathbf{b}(k) - \mathbf{s}(k)$, in which case the vector $\mathbf{b}(k) + \mathbf{s}(k)$ occurring in (5.10) could be written as $|\mathbf{u}(k)|$, where the absolute value is applied componentwise to the vector $\mathbf{u}(k)$.

5.1.2 ▪ Performance indices for the dynamic trading problem

The total wealth at instant k of a given n-asset portfolio, made up of the asset vector $\mathbf{q}(k)$, with its corresponding price vector $\mathbf{p}(k)$, and investment account balance $c(k)$ is defined as

$$w(k) = c(k) + \mathbf{p}(k)^\mathsf{T}\mathbf{q}(k). \tag{5.17}$$

Over a given trading horizon $[1, K_f]$, the percentage gain of the trading policy is defined as follows:

$$\text{percentage gain of trading policy} = \frac{w(K_f) - w(1)}{w(1)} \times 100\%. \tag{5.18}$$

A negative gain is, of course, a loss.

In the omniscient scenario, the price series $p_i(k)$ is known for each asset i over the entire horizon $[1, K_f + 1]$.

Since it is desired to maximize total wealth at the end of the horizon, the obvious **performance index for the omniscient case** is

$$J^{tr}_{om,f} = \mathbf{p}(K_f + 1)^\mathsf{T}\mathbf{q}(K_f + 1) + c(K_f + 1), \tag{5.19}$$

where the superscript tr refers to trading and the subscripts om and f refer to the omniscient case and the fact that the index equals the final wealth.

The obvious problem that arises when it is desired to pass from the omniscient formulation to the one step ahead version is the lack of knowledge, at instant k, of the price series vector $\mathbf{p}(k+1)$. This is circumvented as follows.

Assume that an estimate $\hat{\mathbf{p}}(k+1)$, constructed from knowledge only of $\mathbf{p}(m), m \leq k$, is available. Then the **one step ahead performance index** $J^{tr}_{os}(k+1)$ can be written as follows:

$$J^{tr}_{os}(k+1) := \hat{\mathbf{p}}(k+1)^\mathsf{T}\mathbf{q}(k+1) + c(k+1). \tag{5.20}$$

Initially, as in the previous chapters, the results obtained by following the one step ahead optimal strategy for a given period will be compared with the omniscient index attained over the same period. Later, less stringent and more realistic performance indices will be defined and used.

5.1.3 ▪ Omniscient optimal control formulation of the dynamic trading problem

In this chapter, the term omniscient refers to the fact that all asset prices over the entire trading horizon are assumed to be known. Thus, comparison of the omniscient problem with the one step ahead optimal control problem may be thought of as backtesting, in trading terminology, in which a trading algorithm is evaluated to see how well it would have done ex post. Backtesting assesses the viability of a trading algorithm by evaluating its return on historical data. The only difference is that, in the specific model problem described in section 5.1.1, the return of the one step ahead optimal trading algorithm can be compared to that of the globally optimal omniscient algorithm. This is to be compared with the usual practice in backtesting, which is to evaluate a trading algorithm in terms of the return or gain in wealth that it achieves relative to initial wealth.

The **omniscient optimal trading problem** is written as the following optimal control problem:

$$\begin{aligned}
&\text{Given } \mathbf{q}(1), c(1), \mathbf{p}(k), k = 1, \dots, K_f + 1,\\
&\text{maximize } J^{tr}_{om,f}(K_f + 1)\\
&\text{by choice of } \mathbf{b}(k), \mathbf{s}(k), k = 1, \dots, K_f,\\
&\text{subject to (5.9) through (5.16)}, k = 1, \dots, K_f.
\end{aligned} \tag{5.21}$$

Observe that the omniscient optimal control problem (5.21) has a linear objective function (5.19). Furthermore, the equality constraints (5.9), (5.10), as well as the inequality constraints (5.11) through (5.16), are all linear. Thus it can be formulated and solved as a linear program. The explicit formulation as a linear program is as follows.

Linear programming formulation of omniscient optimal trading problem

This section shows how the omniscient optimal control formulation of the portfolio problem can be rewritten as a linear programming problem, following the general method proposed in Canon, Cullum, and Polak [CCP70].

The optimal control problem (5.21) is written compactly by defining a state vector $\mathbf{x}(k)$ and a control vector $\mathbf{v}(k)$ as follows:

$$\mathbf{x}(k) := (\mathbf{q}(k), c(k)), \tag{5.22}$$

$$\mathbf{v}(k) := (\mathbf{b}(k), \mathbf{s}(k)). \tag{5.23}$$

The following matrices and vectors are also needed to complete the formulation:

$$\mathbf{A} := \begin{bmatrix} \mathbf{I} & \mathbf{0} \\ \mathbf{0} & 1+\alpha \end{bmatrix}, \tag{5.24}$$

$$\mathbf{B}(k) := \begin{bmatrix} \mathbf{I} & -\mathbf{I} \\ -(1+\gamma)\mathbf{p}(k)^{\mathsf{T}} & (1-\gamma)\mathbf{p}(k)^{\mathsf{T}} \end{bmatrix}, \tag{5.25}$$

$$\mathbf{H}_1(k) := \begin{bmatrix} \mathbf{p}(k)^{\mathsf{T}} & \mathbf{0} \\ \mathbf{0} & \mathbf{I} \end{bmatrix}, \tag{5.26}$$

$$\mathbf{H}_2 := \begin{bmatrix} \mathbf{0} & \mathbf{I} \\ \mathbf{I} & \mathbf{0} \end{bmatrix}, \tag{5.27}$$

$$\mathbf{m}(k)^{\mathsf{T}} := [\mathbf{p}(k)^{\mathsf{T}} \quad 1]. \tag{5.28}$$

In this notation, the performance index (5.19) is written as

$$J^{tr}_{om,f}(K_f+1) = \mathbf{m}(K_f+1)^{\mathsf{T}}\mathbf{x}(K_f+1). \tag{5.29}$$

The omniscient optimal control problem formulation above is now the problem of maximizing $J^{tr}_{om,f}(K_f+1)$ subject to the dynamics

$$\mathbf{x}(k+1) = \mathbf{A}\mathbf{x}(k) + \mathbf{B}(k)\mathbf{v}(k), \quad \mathbf{x}(1) = (\mathbf{q}(1), c(1)), \tag{5.30}$$

and the constraints

$$\mathbf{x}(k) \geq \mathbf{0} \text{ for all } k \geq 1, \quad \text{nonnegativity of states,} \tag{5.31}$$

$$\mathbf{v}(k) \geq \mathbf{0} \text{ for all } k \geq 1, \quad \text{nonnegativity of controls,} \tag{5.32}$$

$$\mathbf{H}_1(k)\mathbf{u}(k) \leq \mathbf{H}_2\mathbf{x}(k) \text{ for all } k \geq 1, \quad \text{no loans, no shorting constraint.} \tag{5.33}$$

Introducing the slack variable vector $\varepsilon(k) \geq 0$, the no loans, no shorting constraints (5.33) can be rewritten as the following equality constraint:

$$-\mathbf{H}_2(k)\mathbf{x}(k) + \mathbf{H}_1(k)\mathbf{v}(k) + \varepsilon(k) = \mathbf{0}, \quad k = 1, 2, \ldots. \tag{5.34}$$

Finally, define the decision vector $\mathbf{z}$, the vector $\mathbf{w}$, and the matrix $\mathbf{H}$ as follows:

$$\mathbf{z} := (\mathbf{x}(1), \mathbf{v}(1), \boldsymbol{\varepsilon}(1), \ldots, \mathbf{x}(K_f), \mathbf{v}(K_f), \boldsymbol{\varepsilon}(K_f), \mathbf{x}(K_f+1)), \tag{5.35}$$

$$\mathbf{w} := (\mathbf{0}, \mathbf{0}, \mathbf{0}, \ldots, \mathbf{m}(K_f+1)), \tag{5.36}$$

$$\mathbf{H} := \begin{bmatrix} \mathbf{A} & \mathbf{B} & \mathbf{0} & -\mathbf{I} & \mathbf{0} & \cdots & & \\ \mathbf{0} & \mathbf{0} & \mathbf{0} & \mathbf{A} & \mathbf{B} & \mathbf{0} & -\mathbf{I} & \cdots \\ \vdots & \vdots & \vdots & \vdots & \vdots & \vdots & \vdots & \cdots \\ -\mathbf{H}_2(1) & \mathbf{H}_1(1) & \mathbf{I} & \mathbf{0} & \cdots & & & \mathbf{0} \\ \vdots & \vdots & \vdots & \vdots & \vdots & \vdots & \vdots & \vdots \\ \mathbf{0} & \mathbf{0} & \mathbf{0} & \cdots & -\mathbf{H}_2(K_f) & \mathbf{H}_1(K_f) & \mathbf{I} & \mathbf{0} \\ \mathbf{0} & \cdots & & & & & & \mathbf{0} \end{bmatrix}. \tag{5.37}$$

The optimal control problem (5.21), rewritten in vector form in (5.30) through (5.33), can now be written as a standard form linear program,

$$\begin{aligned} &\text{maximize } \mathbf{w}^\mathsf{T}\mathbf{z} \\ &\text{subject to } \mathbf{H}\mathbf{z} = \mathbf{0} \\ &\text{and } \mathbf{z} \geq \mathbf{0}. \end{aligned} \tag{5.38}$$

Once again, as mentioned in Chapter 4, when using a modeling language such as JuMP in Julia, the formulation (5.21) is preferable, and it is unnecessary to set up the standard form LP (5.38).

5.1.4 ▪ One step ahead optimal control approach to dynamic trading

Substituting for the terms $\mathbf{q}(k+1), c(k+1)$ in (5.20) by the respective right-hand sides (5.9), (5.10) yields, after simplification,

$$\begin{aligned} J_{os}^{tr}(k+1) \quad := \quad & (1+\alpha)c(k) + \hat{\mathbf{p}}(k+1)^\mathsf{T}\mathbf{q}(k) \\ & + \Delta\mathbf{p}(k)^\mathsf{T}(\mathbf{b}(k) - \mathbf{s}(k)) - \gamma\mathbf{p}(k)^\mathsf{T}(\mathbf{b}(k) + \mathbf{s}(k)), \end{aligned} \tag{5.39}$$

where

$$\Delta\mathbf{p}(k) := \hat{\mathbf{p}}(k+1) - \mathbf{p}(k). \tag{5.40}$$

Note that when optimizing the posttrade index $J_{os}^{tr}(k+1)$ at instant k, the current cash and asset holdings, $c(k)$ and $\mathbf{q}(k)$, are known, and the future price vector estimate $\hat{\mathbf{p}}(k+1)$ is given, and it is desired to determine the optimal choices of the decision variables $\mathbf{b}(k)$ and $\mathbf{s}(k)$. Let the sum of the first two terms in (5.39) be denoted by $\hat{J}(k)$:

$$\hat{J}(k) := (1+\alpha)c(k) + \hat{\mathbf{p}}(k+1)^\mathsf{T}\mathbf{q}(k). \tag{5.41}$$

For the one step ahead optimization at instant k, the value of $\hat{J}(k)$ is a known constant (offset to the value of the objective function) and can be removed, since it will not affect the optimal values of the decision variables $\mathbf{b}(k)$ and $\mathbf{s}(k)$. Thus, the **one step ahead optimal dynamic trading problem** may be written as follows:

$$\begin{array}{l}\text{Given } \mathbf{q}(k), c(k), \hat{\mathbf{p}}(k+1),\\ \text{maximize } \Delta\mathbf{p}(k)^{\mathsf{T}}(\mathbf{b}(k)-\mathbf{s}(k))-\gamma\mathbf{p}(k)^{\mathsf{T}}(\mathbf{b}(k)+\mathbf{s}(k))\\ \text{by choice of } \mathbf{b}(k), \mathbf{s}(k),\\ \text{subject to (5.9) through (5.16).}\end{array} \tag{5.42}$$

Observe that, as with the omniscient problem, the objective function is linear in the decision variables $\mathbf{b}(k)$ and $\mathbf{s}(k)$, and the equality and inequality constraints are also linear, so that, once again, the one step ahead optimal control problem, as stated, can be formulated and solved as a linear program.

5.1.5 ▪ Dynamic trading for one asset: Analytic calculation of one step ahead optimal control

For a single asset and a single investment account, the dynamic trading problem is simple enough to admit a graphical analysis leading to its analytic solution. This section carries out this analysis, since it provides the background for more complex schemes to be presented later on. In this case, the trading dynamics can be written as follows:

$$q(k+1) = q(k) + u(k), \tag{5.43}$$

$$c(k+1) = (1+\alpha)c(k) - p(k)u(k) - \gamma p(k)|u(k)|, \tag{5.44}$$

where $u(k) := b(k) - s(k)$ and is positive when the trader buys $u(k)$ units of the asset and is negative when $u(k)$ units of the asset are sold at price $p(k)$ resulting in an increase, in the investment account, of $p(k)u(k)$ units of cash less the transaction cost $\gamma p(k)|u(k)|$. Also note that the constraints (5.11)–(5.16) can be expressed simply, in terms of $u(k)$, by requiring $q(k), c(k)$ to be nonnegative for all k.

The reduction of the two variables $b(k), s(k)$ to a single variable $u(k)$ simplifies the graphical analysis. The next step is to write the one step ahead performance index in a convenient form for graphical optimization and, in order to do this, notation is simplified by denoting $J(k+1)$ as J^+ and dropping the argument k, so that

$$J(k+1) =: J^+ = \hat{p}q^+ + c^+.$$

Using (5.43), (5.44) yields

$$\begin{aligned} J^+ &= \hat{p}(q+u) + (1+\alpha)c - pu - \gamma p|u| \\ &= \hat{p}q + (1+\alpha)c + p\left(\frac{\hat{p}-p}{p}u - \gamma|u|\right) \\ &= \hat{J} + p(\rho u - \gamma|u|), \end{aligned} \tag{5.45}$$

where

$$\hat{J} := \hat{p}q + (1+\alpha)c,$$

and

$$\rho := \frac{\hat{p}-p}{p} =: \frac{\Delta p}{p} \tag{5.46}$$

denotes the estimated relative price change (referred to as the current price) and is positive if the estimate (for the next instant) is larger than the current price and is negative otherwise.

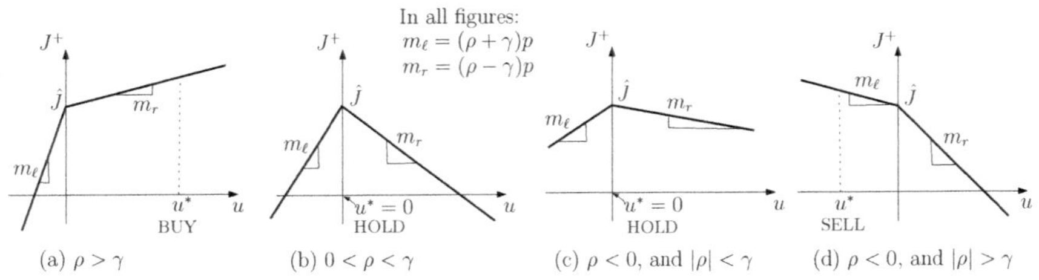

Figure 5.1. *Graphical solution of dynamic trading using one step ahead optimal approach.*

The right-hand side of (5.45) is now plotted as J^+ in Fig. 5.1, in the four possible cases, given that $p, \gamma > 0$: (a) $\rho > \gamma$, (b) $0 < \rho < \gamma$, (c) $\rho < 0$ and $|\rho| < \gamma$, and (d) $\rho < 0$ and $|\rho| > \gamma$.

From the four graphs in Fig. 5.1, and the constraints on buying and selling, it can be shown that

the **one step ahead optimal control at instant** k, $u^*(k)$, for the price estimate or predictor $\hat{p}$, can be written as follows:

$$u^*(k) = \begin{cases} \frac{(1+\alpha)c(k)}{(1+\gamma)p(k)} & \text{if } \rho > \gamma \text{ (BUY)}, \\ 0 \quad \text{if } 0 < \rho < \gamma \text{ (HOLD)}, \\ 0 \quad \text{if } \rho < 0, \text{ and } |\rho| < \gamma \text{ (HOLD)}, \\ q(k) \quad \text{if } \rho < 0, \text{ and } |\rho| > \gamma \text{ (SELL)}. \end{cases} \tag{5.47}$$

To exemplify this, the first expression on the right-hand side of (5.47) is explained. Since, in this case, $u^*(k) > 0$, the largest value that it can have must be such that the constraint $c(k+1) \geq 0$ becomes tight, i.e., $c(k+1) = 0$. From (5.44), this means that

$$(1+\alpha)c(k) - p(k)u(k) - \gamma p(k)u(k) = 0,$$

which yields the first expression on the right-hand side of (5.47). This one step ahead optimal control can be represented graphically (see Fig. 5.13(a)).

In control terminology, the one step ahead optimal control (5.47) would be referred to as a bang-bang control with a dead zone (the HOLD region in the ρ-γ space, in which the trader neither buys nor sells). The term bang-bang is used in optimal control to refer to switching between maximum and minimum controls permitted by the constraints.

In words, the one step ahead optimal control (5.47) can be described as follows:

- If the estimated relative decrease (ρ) of the current price is greater than the transaction cost coefficient (γ), then *buy* as much of the asset as the investment account balance permits, after paying transaction cost.

- If the estimated relative decrease of the current price is less than the transaction cost coefficient, then *hold* the asset.

- If the estimated relative increase (in modulus) of the current price is less than the transaction cost coefficient, then *hold* the asset.

- If the estimated relative increase (in modulus) of the current price is more than the transaction cost coefficient, then *sell* the total amount of the asset, with the proceeds of the sales less transaction cost going into the investment account.

If the price estimator $\hat{p}$ is taken to be the moving average over some window of past prices, then the classical "simple moving average" (SMA) philosophy is stated as follows [EP05] (also see [Pra10; ZZ09]):

- Buy when the current price crosses the moving average from below, i.e., $\hat{p} - p < 0$, which, on dividing throughout by p, becomes $\rho < 0$.

- Sell when the current price crosses the moving average from above, i.e., $\rho > 0$.

Observe that, for $\gamma = 0$, the one step ahead optimal control (5.47) is the opposite of the SMA philosophy. The word philosophy is used for SMA to emphasize that, in order to become a policy, it is necessary to specify the amount of the asset to be bought or sold in each situation, and this is the key feature that distinguishes different policies that all subscribe to the SMA philosophy and variants (see, for example, [AFFR08; BLL92; ZZ09]).

Finally, it is clear that this section actually presented the graphical solution of a linear program corresponding to the simple single asset, single investment account model. In the case of multiple assets and investment accounts, the use of linear programming and, more generally, mathematical programming software, is essential as will be seen in the next section.

5.1.6 ▪ Numerical examples of dynamic trading without risk reduction using one step ahead optimal control

This section starts with some simple illustrative examples of the one step ahead optimal approach applied to a single asset, single investment account. In this section and the next, the one step ahead optimal and omniscient optimal trading problems are implemented using the Optimization Toolbox of MATLAB and also using the CLP (Coin-OR linear programming) and Ipopt solvers in JuMP/Julia.

Example of a pulse in asset price

In this illustrative example, the asset price has a step increase (from 25 units to 35 units) at instant $k = 16$ and at $k = 22$ goes back down through a step decrease to its original value of 25 units. This is referred to as a pulse in the asset price.

Figures 5.2–5.4 are time plots, organized, clockwise from top left, as follows: asset price series and the moving average over the last five days, quantity q of the asset held, investment

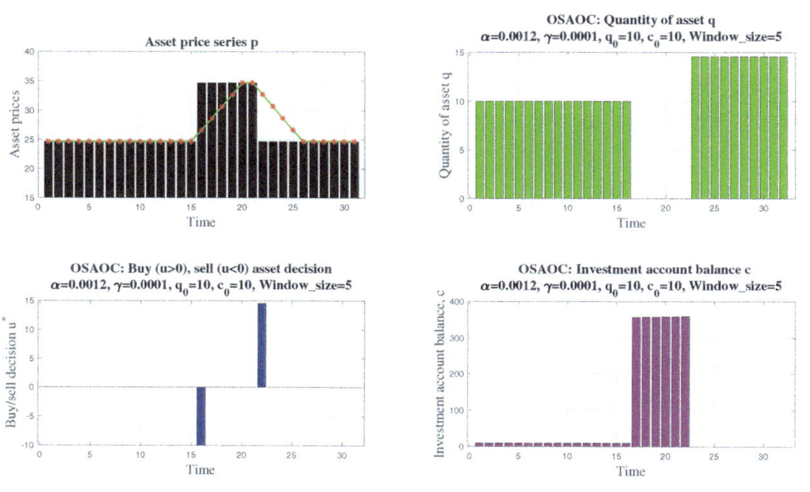

Figure 5.2. *Graphs showing the behavior over time of asset prices, asset holding, investment account balance, and trading decisions for the one step ahead optimal control.*

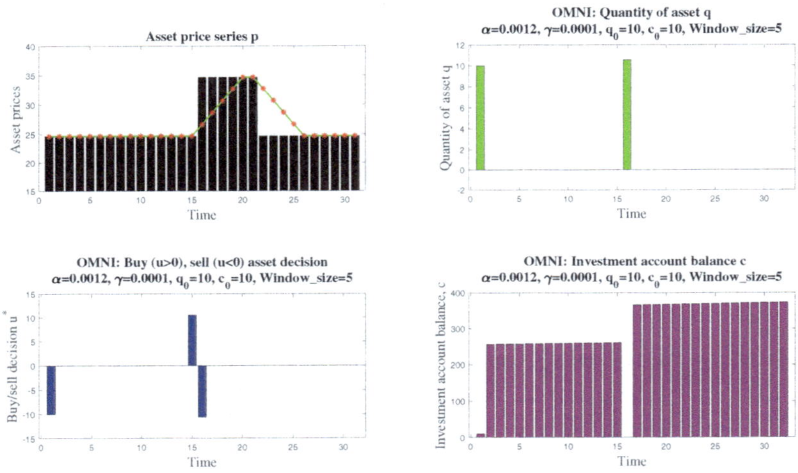

Figure 5.3. *Graphs showing the behavior over time of asset prices, asset holding, investment account balance, and trading decisions for the omniscient solution.*

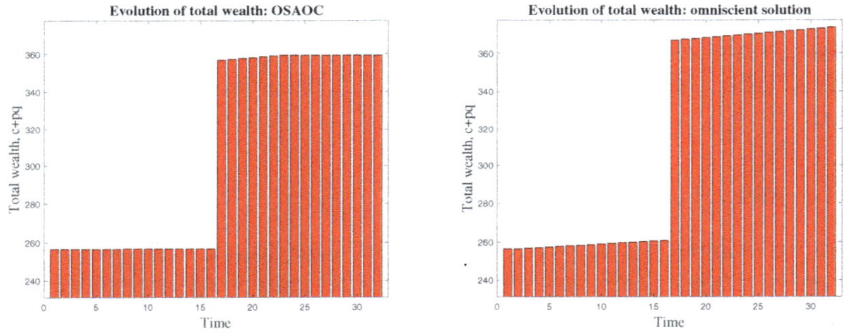

Figure 5.4. *Evolution of total wealth under the one step ahead optimal policy (left) and the omniscient solution (right) for a single asset with a pulse in its price.*

account balance c, one step ahead optimal buying and selling decisions for the asset. The top left subfigure, which depicts the asset price series, also contains a green curve joining the red dots, which represent the moving averages over the last 5 days.

Discussion of example of a single pulse in the asset price

For this example of a single pulse in the asset price, the one step ahead policy attains a final wealth of 359 units, as opposed to 373 units attained by the omniscient solution. In both cases, the initial wealth is 256.7 units. Thus, the one step ahead optimal policy produces a percentage gain (relative to initial wealth) of $(359-257)/257 = 39.6\%$, while the omniscient solution has a percentage gain of $(373-257)/257 = 45.1\%$. This represents an efficiency $\eta = (39.6/45.1) = 0.88$ of the one step policy, taking the omniscient solution gain as baseline. Observe that, even though the one step ahead optimal trading policy achieves a relatively high return compared to the omniscient solution, the buying and selling decisions are qualitatively very different. The one step ahead optimal policy, which is based on the difference between the moving average and the current price, liquidates the total amount of asset held at $k = 16$ immediately after the asset price exceeds the moving average. Conversely, at $k = 22$ when the asset price drops below the moving average, the total investment account balance, less the transaction cost, is converted into the equivalent quantity of the asset, which is then held until the end of the trading horizon. The omniscient solution, on the other hand, has foreknowledge of the rise and subsequent fall in the asset price, so it starts by converting the total asset less transaction cost to investment account balance, which accumulates interest. This means that a larger quantity of the asset can be bought back at the initial price at $k = 15$, just prior to the price increase and then all of it sold, immediately after the price rise, at $k = 16$, to once again accumulate interest in the investment account, and also be unaffected by the price drop at $k = 21$. The relatively small difference in the performances of the one step ahead optimal policy and the omniscient solution can be attributed to the fact that the overall asset price variation is quite small.

Example of a synthetic asset price sequence with bounded variation

The following example, graphed in Figs. 5.5, 5.6, and 5.7, compares the behavior of the one step ahead optimal trading with the omniscient solution for a synthetic asset price sequence, in which the price variation over the trading horizon is bounded.

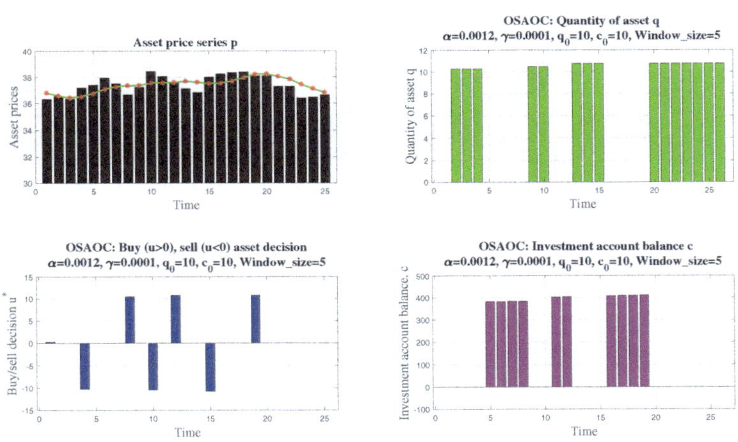

Figure 5.5. *Graphs showing the behavior over time of asset prices, asset holding, investment account balance, and trading decisions for the one step ahead optimal control.*

Discussion of example of bounded asset price variation

This example reinforces the observation made in the previous example, that small price variation leads to small overall trading gain. In this synthetic example, which is inspired by a real price series (synthetic only because its mean value was adjusted), the one step ahead policy attains a final wealth of 395 units, as opposed to 437 units attained by the omniscient solution. In both cases, the initial wealth is 373 units. Thus, the one step ahead optimal policy produces a percentage gain (relative to initial wealth) of $(395 - 373)/373 = 5.8\%$, while the omniscient solution has a percentage gain of $(437 - 373)/373 = 17.1\%$. This represents an efficiency $\eta = (5.8/17.1) = 0.34$ of the one step ahead optimal policy, taking the omniscient solution gain as baseline. The one step ahead policy percentage gain is in keeping with gains expected in real trading.

Once again, there are clear differences between the one step ahead policy and the omniscient solution. It is possible to see, studying the top and bottom left in Fig. 5.6, that the omniscient solution follows the general "buy low, sell high" policy, with buys occurring at lows at $k = 1, 3, 8, 14, 23$ and sells occurring at highs at $k = 2, 6, 10, 18$. In this example, both the one step

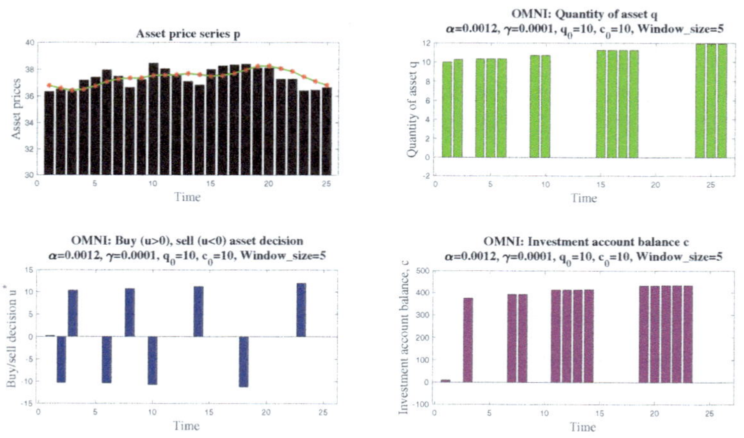

Figure 5.6. *Graphs showing the behavior over time of asset prices, asset holding, investment account balance, and trading decisions for the omniscient solution.*

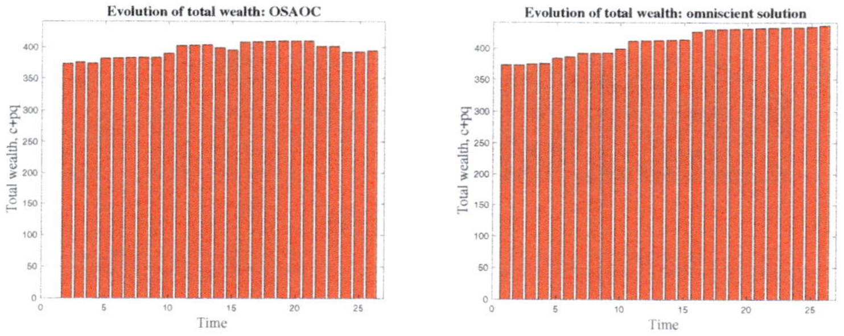

Figure 5.7. *Evolution of total wealth under the one step ahead optimal policy (left) and the omniscient solution (right) for a single asset with a synthetic price sequence with small variation.*

ahead policy and the omniscient solution end up holding only the asset and have zero balance in the investment account, at the end of the trading horizon. However, by virtue of its prescience, leading to trades at the "right" instants of price lows and highs, the omniscient solution is able to achieve a final quantity of assets slightly larger than the one obtained by the one step ahead optimal policy. Finally, in regard to requiring only nonnegativity of the investment account balance, it should be pointed out that, in both formulations (5.42) and (5.21), it is easy to include a minimum balance constraint and, if necessary, even a minimum or maximum quantity of asset holding, if this is deemed necessary by the trader.

5.1.7 ▪ Buying and selling two assets using one step ahead optimal trading

This section deals with an illustrative example of a two asset portfolio. The asset price sequences, which are taken from real datasets but selected to have roughly the same mean value, are used to illustrate the behavior of the one step ahead optimal trading policy. Once again, comparison of the dynamic behavior produced by the one step ahead and omniscient optimal solutions is compared in Figs. 5.8–5.11. Figure 5.12 compares the evolution of total wealth under the two policies.

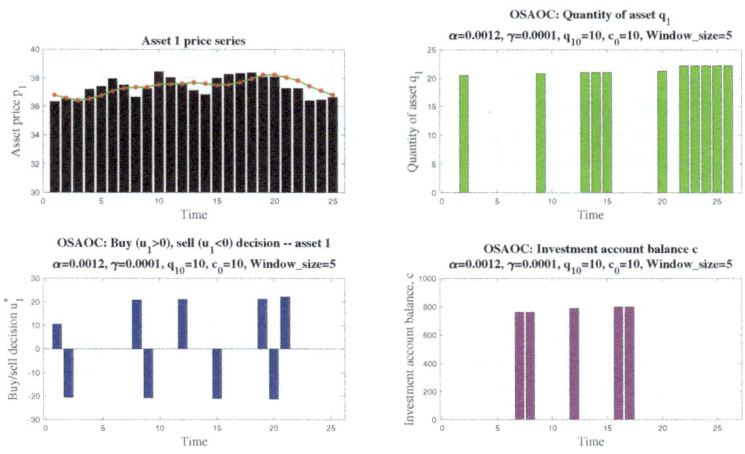

Figure 5.8. *Graphs showing the behavior over time of prices, asset holding, investment account balance, and trading decisions for asset* 1*, under one step ahead optimal trading.*

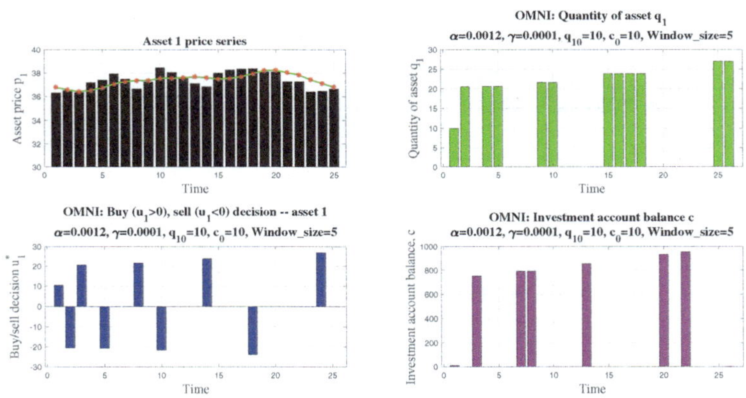

Figure 5.9. *Graphs showing the behavior over time of prices, asset holding, investment account balance, and trading decisions for asset* 1*, under omniscient trading.*

Discussion of example of two asset portfolio with bounded variation in asset prices

In this synthetic example, which is inspired by a real price series (synthetic only because its mean value was adjusted), the one step ahead policy attains a final wealth of 815 units, as opposed to 989 units attained by the omniscient solution. In both cases, the initial wealth is 745 units. Thus, the one step ahead optimal policy produces a percentage gain (relative to initial wealth) of $(815 - 745)/745 = 9.3\%$, while the omniscient solution has a percentage gain of $(989 - 745)/745 = 32.7\%$. This represents an efficiency $\eta = (9.3/32.7) = 0.28$ of the one step ahead optimal policy, taking the omniscient solution gain as baseline. The one step ahead policy percentage gain is in keeping with gains expected in real trading. In this case, both the one step ahead policy and the omniscient solution end up holding only asset 1, and completely liquidate both asset 2 and the investment account balance. However, there are clear differences between the one step ahead policy and the omniscient solution. The omniscient solution, as expected, buys low and sells high, and this is particularly evident when comparing the trading decisions. The one step ahead policy makes nine trades (Fig. 5.10), but because of its dependence on the

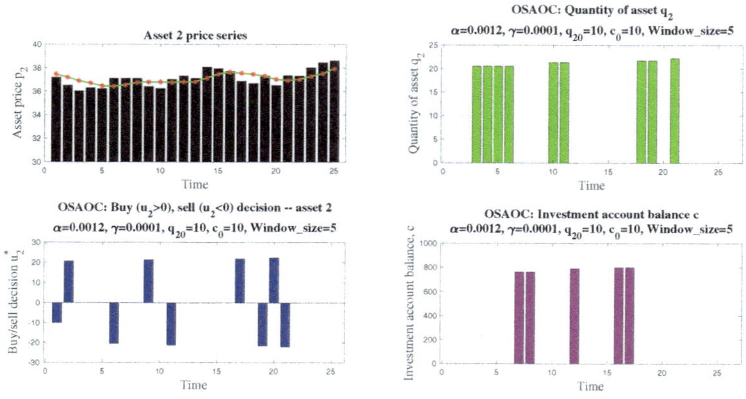

Figure 5.10. *Graphs showing the behavior over time of prices, asset holding, investment account balance, and trading decisions for asset 2, under one step ahead optimal trading.*

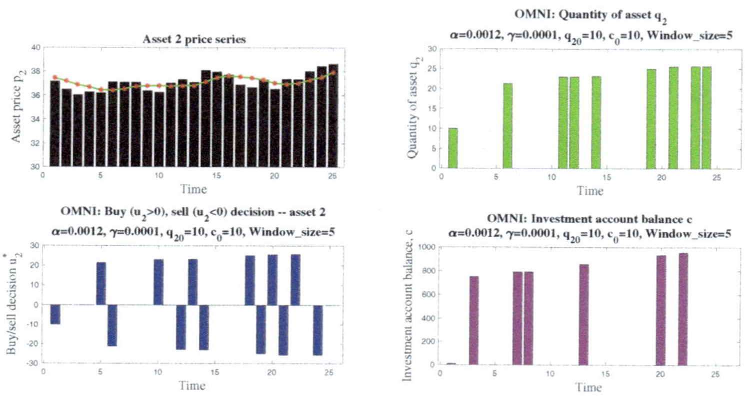

Figure 5.11. *Graphs showing the behavior over time of prices, asset holding, investment account balance, and trading decisions for asset 2, under omniscient trading.*

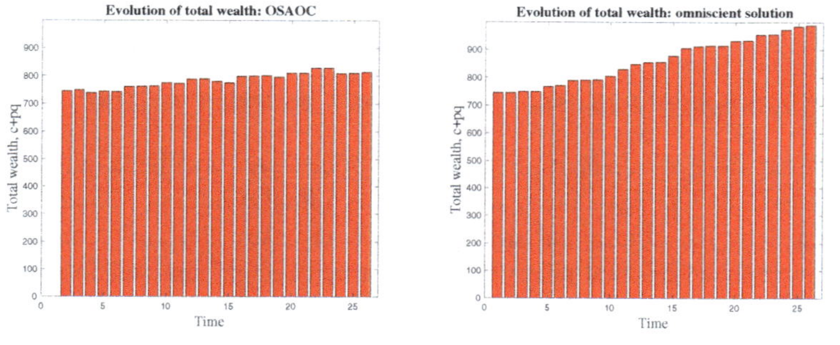

Figure 5.12. *Evolution of total wealth under the one step ahead optimal policy (left) and the omniscient solution (right) for a two asset portfolio, with price sequences showing bounded variation.*

(lagged) five (past) days moving average, it is not able to take advantage of all the lows and highs. The omniscient solution takes advantage, more frequently, of lows to buy asset 2 and highs to sell it, making a total of 13 trades (Fig. 5.11).

5.2 ▪ Strategies for risk reduction in dynamic trading

The one step ahead optimal trading strategy of the previous section is naive in the sense that the trade-off between return and risk has not been considered. In the classical Markowitz setup for portfolio design, using historic data on expected return and its standard deviation, interpreted as risk, the trade-off is considered by using an objective function combining the (linear) expected return and its (quadratic) variance. This leads to a (static) quadratic programming problem, the solution of which defines the optimal Markowitz portfolio. This section proposes the addition of some logic to the basic (and simple) one step ahead optimal scheme in such a way that return and risk can be traded off in the dynamic one step ahead trading scheme. In the jargon of trading, this logic is referred to as a trade trigger, which is a market condition, such as the rise or fall in the price of an asset, which triggers a sequence of trades. Trade triggers are used to automate certain types of trades, for example, buying or selling shares when the price crosses or reaches a certain value.

The most common measure of investment risk is the standard deviation of asset prices over a given window. Assets with a large standard deviation are considered to be more volatile, meaning that investor gains are large during upswings and, conversely, losses become large when markets swing down. Risk-averse investors usually prefer assets with range bounded price variations and consequently smaller standard deviations, since they are less volatile, meaning that expected losses have smaller probability. The expected values for upswings and downswings around the mean price of an asset are measured by the standard deviation. Since the mean asset price over a window in the past is already used in the one step ahead optimal trading rule derived in the previous section, the remaining task is to show how to incorporate information on the standard deviation in order to add risk reduction to the one step ahead optimal policy. Let $\hat{p}_i(k)$ (resp., $\sigma_i(k)$) denote the mean (resp., standard deviation) of the ith asset price over a window of past asset prices. Let σ_{th} be a prespecified (risk) threshold for the standard deviation.

The **simple risk reduction strategy** is to **add** the following **trade trigger to the one step ahead optimal trading policy** (5.47):

if $\sigma_i(k) \geq \sigma_{th}$ **and** $|\hat{p}_i(k) - p_i(k)| \geq \sigma_{th}$, **then** $u_i^*(k) = 0$.

The additional logic above, added to the one step ahead optimal dynamic trading policy (5.47), is a mean and standard deviation based triggering of interruption of one step ahead optimal trading and can be thought of as augmenting the dead zone of Fig. 5.13(a). Defining

$$\rho_i(k) := \frac{\hat{p}_i(k) - p_i(k)}{p_i(k)}, \tag{5.48}$$

the second condition can now be expressed as

$$\rho_i(k) < -\frac{\sigma_{th}}{p_i(k)} \quad \text{or} \quad \rho_i(k) > \frac{\sigma_{th}}{p_i(k)}. \tag{5.49}$$

Graphical representations of the trade trigger are shown in Fig. 5.13 in the ρ-γ plane at two points on the σ-axis: one below $\sigma_{\max}$ (left) and the other above it (right).

Observe that, by specifying a single risk threshold σ_{th} for all assets, it is critical to choose it carefully, with respect to the standard deviations of all assets making up the trader's portfolio. Clearly, if the threshold σ_{th} is chosen to be too small, very little buying and selling will occur and this, although safe (extremely risk averse), may be detrimental to overall gain over the trading period. Conversely, if threshold σ_{th} is chosen to be too large, excessive buying and selling will occur, leading to large transaction costs, also detrimental to overall gain, as well as to high exposure to risk.

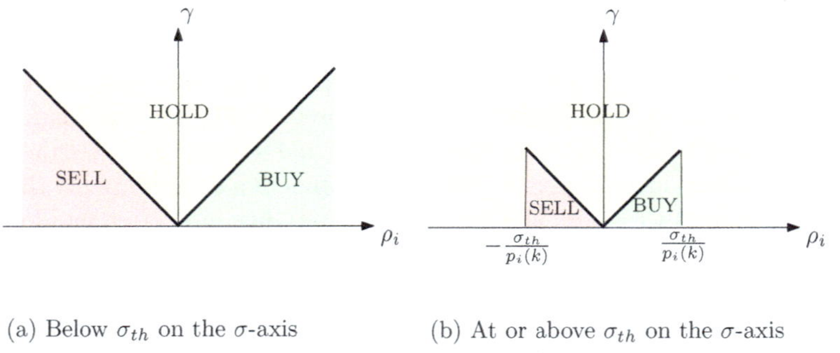

Figure 5.13. *The trade interruption trigger condition shown in the ρ-γ plane at two points on the σ-axis:* (a) *below and* (b) *above σ_{th}. In* (b) *on the right, the whole region, in light yellow, outside the selling (red) and buying (green) wedges is a hold region.*

It is worth repeating the general philosophy of this chapter, namely, that the one step ahead optimal policy is independent of the price predictor $\hat{p}(k)$, which could be chosen as the moving average or as the trader's favorite predictor and utilized with the proposed one step ahead optimal policy plus risk reduction trade trigger. A similar comment applies to the estimator of the standard deviation.

5.3 ▪ Numerical examples of dynamic trading with risk reduction

The previous section gave numerical examples of one step ahead optimal trading without risk reduction. This section contains two different examples of five asset portfolios: the datasets are taken from RapidAPI [Rap], and the risk reduction logic discussed in section 5.2 is used. Comparison of the final wealth at the end of a 30-day trading period with risk reduction is compared with that obtained using the one step ahead optimal policy without risk reduction. Each example presents a bar graph of the time evolution of asset prices and the days on which the asset price reaches a value for which the risk reduction logic is activated (inhibiting buying or selling of assets); the corresponding asset price bar is colored yellow.

5.3.1 ▪ Dynamic daily trading of portfolios of uncorrelated assets

This section presents two illustrative examples of trading involving two five-asset portfolios. The datasets, which correspond to real asset price series, are named AV COMPUTER 1 and AV Banks and were extracted from the site RapidAPI [Rap], where AV refers to Alpha Vantage.

Example 1: Five-asset portfolio from the AV COMPUTER 1 dataset

The dataset (AV COMPUTER 1) used for the numerical example in this section was taken from RapidAPI [Rap]: the price series of each of the 5 assets in shown in Fig. 5.14, and the windowed mean and standard deviation over a window of 5 days in the past, is shown in Fig. 5.15.

In the groups of Figs. 5.16–5.20, the top left subfigure in each group, which depicts the asset price series, also contains a green curve joining the red dots, which represent the moving averages over the last 5 days. The bottom right subfigure is identical in all 5 groups of four figures each, because it represents the single investment account that is used to buy any of the assets desired and receives the proceeds of any asset sales, after transaction costs are deducted.

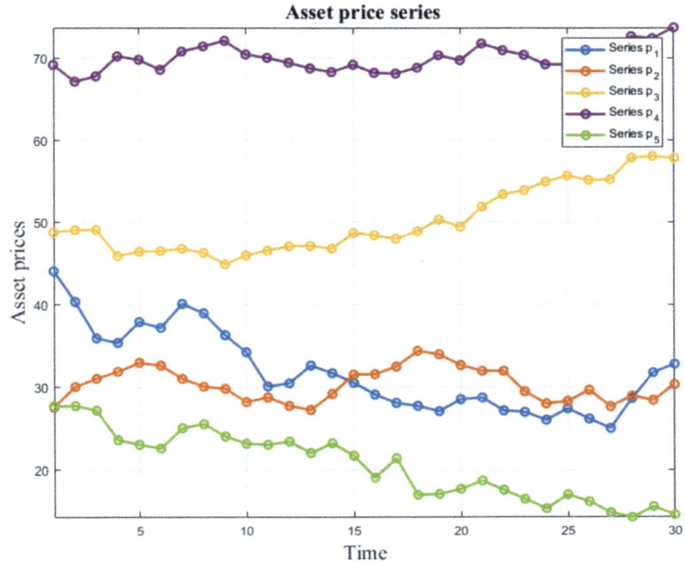

Figure 5.14. *Price series of* 5 *different assets over a* 30*-day period from the dataset AV COMPUTER* 1*, available from RapidAPI [Rap].*

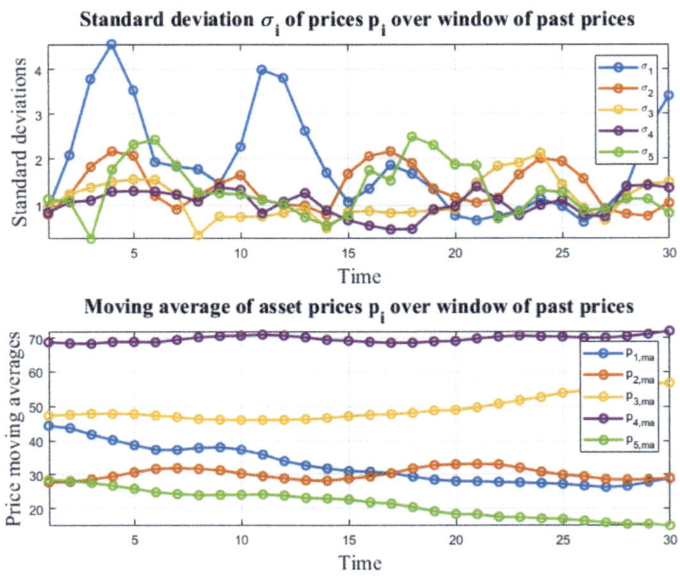

Figure 5.15. *The moving average and standard deviation calculated over a window using the last* 5 *days of each price series in Fig.* 5.14*.*

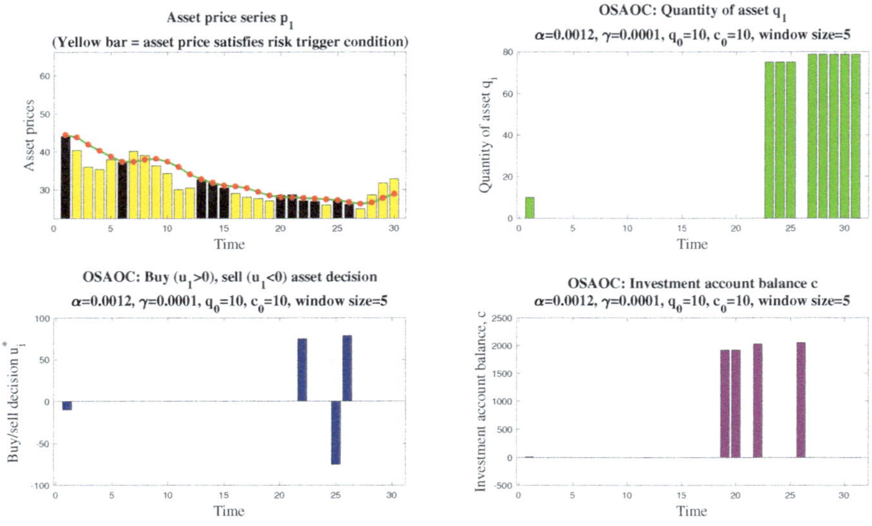

Figure 5.16. *Clockwise from top left: Asset* 1 *price series, quantity of asset* 1 *held over time, investment account balance over time, buying and selling decisions for asset* 1 *using one step ahead optimal trading with risk reduction.*

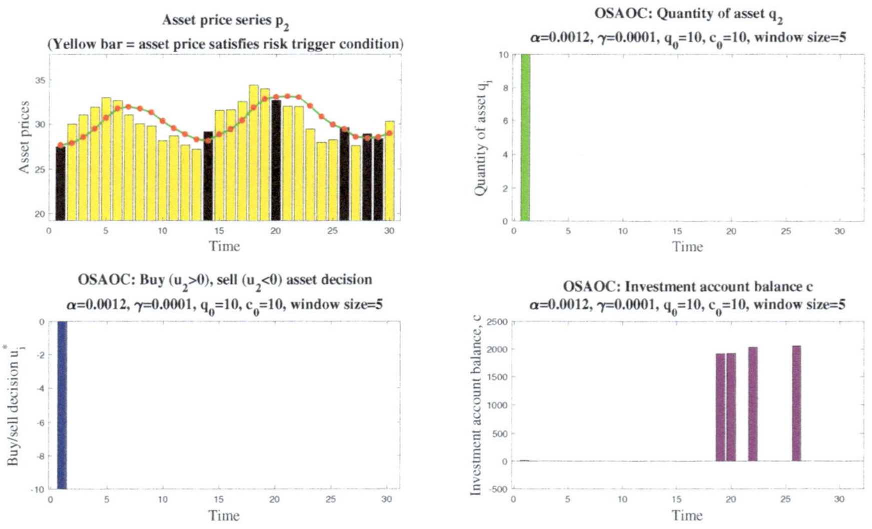

Figure 5.17. *Clockwise from top left: Asset* 2 *price series, quantity of asset* 2 *held over time, investment account balance over time, buying and selling decisions for asset* 2 *using one step ahead optimal trading with risk reduction.*

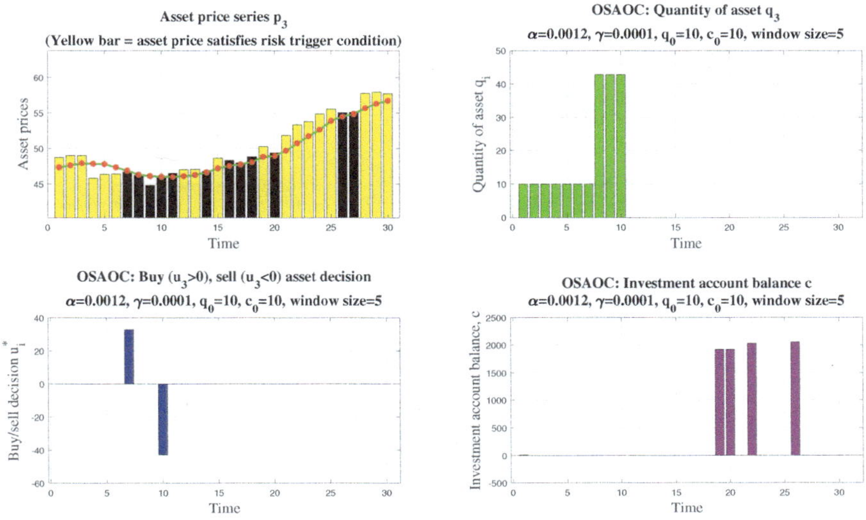

Figure 5.18. *Clockwise from top left: Asset 3 price series, quantity of asset 3 held over time, investment account balance over time, buying and selling decisions for asset 3 using one step ahead optimal trading with risk reduction.*

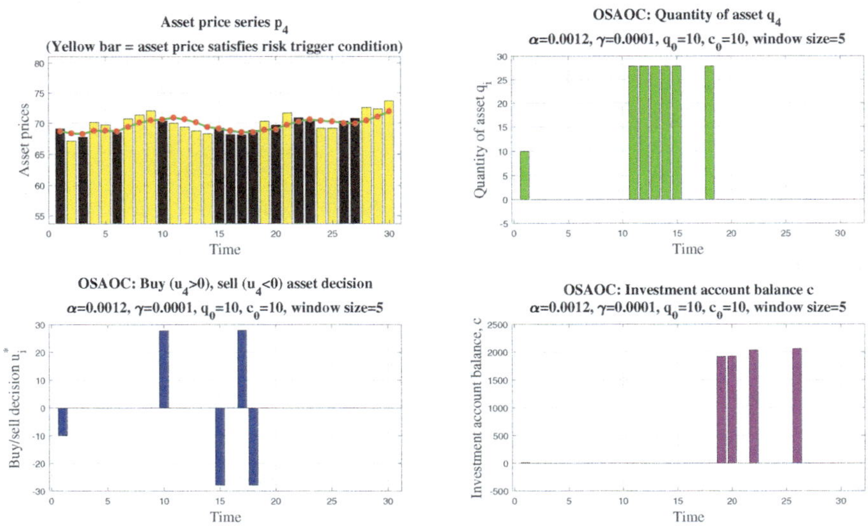

Figure 5.19. *Clockwise from top left: Asset 4 price series, quantity of asset 4 held over time, investment account balance over time, buying and selling decisions for asset 4 using one step ahead optimal trading with risk reduction.*

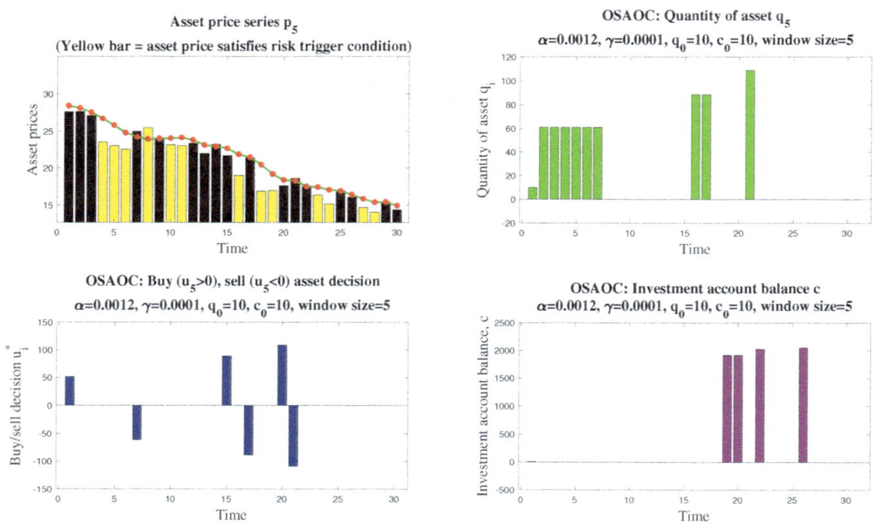

Figure 5.20. *Clockwise from top left: Asset* 5 *price series, quantity of asset* 5 *held over time, investment account balance over time, buying and selling decisions for asset* 5 *using one step ahead optimal trading with risk reduction.*

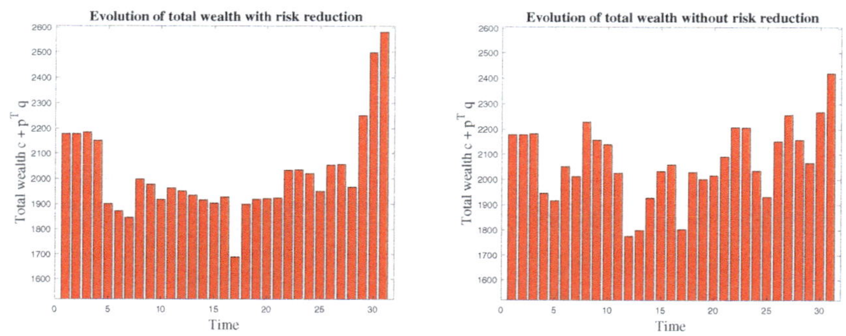

Figure 5.21. *Comparison of the evolution of total wealth using the one step ahead optimal scheme with risk trigger (left) and without risk trigger (right) for the* 5 *assets from the AV COMPUTER* 1 *dataset from RapidAPI [Rap].*

Figure 5.21 compares the evolution of total wealth under one step ahead optimal trading with and without risk reduction.

Discussion of AV COMPUTER 1 five asset portfolio example

In the groups of Figs. 5.16 to 5.20, the frequent occurrence of yellow bars in the top left graphs indicates that the risk trigger condition, that inhibits trading, is satisfied during a large part of the trading horizon, which causes a significant reduction in trading activity. In Fig. 5.21, the effect of the risk-averse behavior is seen to be justified, since the one step ahead optimal trading scheme with risk reduction ends up with a final wealth of 2581.4, whereas the same scheme without risk reduction achieves a final wealth of 2420.5, both starting from an initial wealth of 2179.8 units. This represents a gain of $(2581.4 - 2179.8)/2179.8 = 18.4\%$ for the one step ahead optimal trading algorithm with risk reduction, as opposed to a gain of $(2420.5 - 2179.8)/2179.8 = 11\%$ for the corresponding algorithm without risk reduction.

Example 2: Five asset portfolio from the AV Banks dataset

The dataset (AV Banks) used for the numerical example in this section was taken from RapidAPI [Rap]: the price series of each of the 5 assets in shown in Fig. 5.22, and the windowed mean and standard deviation over a window of 5 days in the past, is shown in Fig. 5.23.

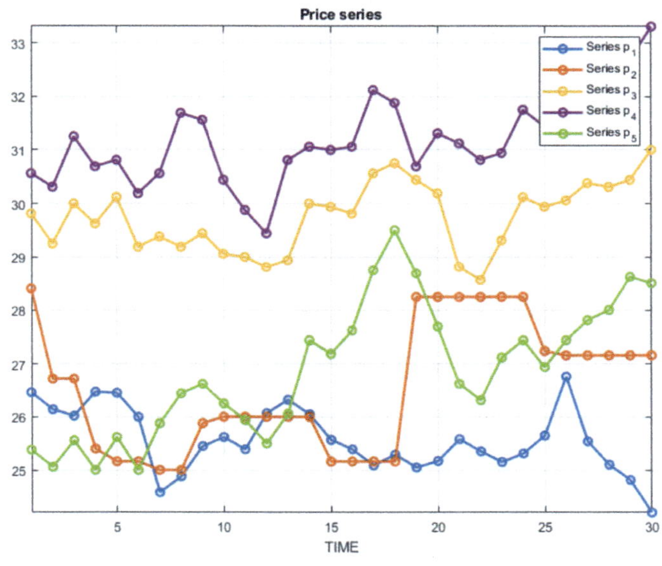

Figure 5.22. *Price series of a 30-day period from the dataset AV Banks, available from RapidAPI [Rap].*

In the groups of Figs. 5.24 to 5.28, the top left figure in each group, which depicts the asset price series, also contains a green curve joining the red dots, which represent the moving averages over the last 5 days. The bottom right figure is identical in all 5 groups of four figures each, because it represents the single investment account that is used to buy any of the assets and receives the proceeds of any asset sales, after transaction costs are deducted. Figure 5.29 compares the evolution of total wealth under one step ahead optimal trading with and without risk reduction.

Discussion of AV banks five asset portfolio example

In the groups of Figs. 5.16 to 5.20, the occurrence of yellow bars in the top left graphs indicates that the risk trigger condition, that inhibits trading, is satisfied during much less of the trading horizon than in the previous AV COMPUTER 1 example. This is reflected in the larger number of total trades (25), compared with the previous example (18). In Fig. 5.29, the effect of the risk reduction is seen to be justified, since the one step ahead optimal trading scheme with risk reduction ends up with a final wealth of 1509.5 units, while the scheme without risk reduction achieves a final wealth of 1388.6 units. Since the initial total wealth is 1416.1 units, this means that risk reduction is able to turn a loss (without it) of 1.9% into a gain of 6.6%.

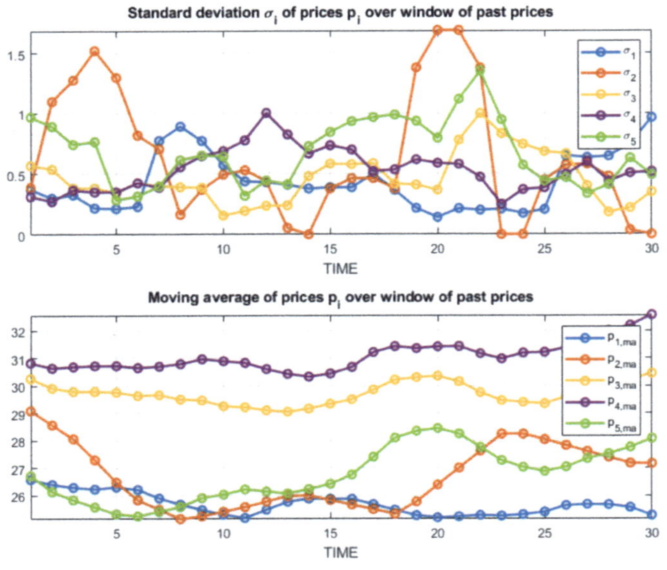

Figure 5.23. *The moving average and standard deviation calculated over a window using the last 5 days of each price series in Fig. 5.22.*

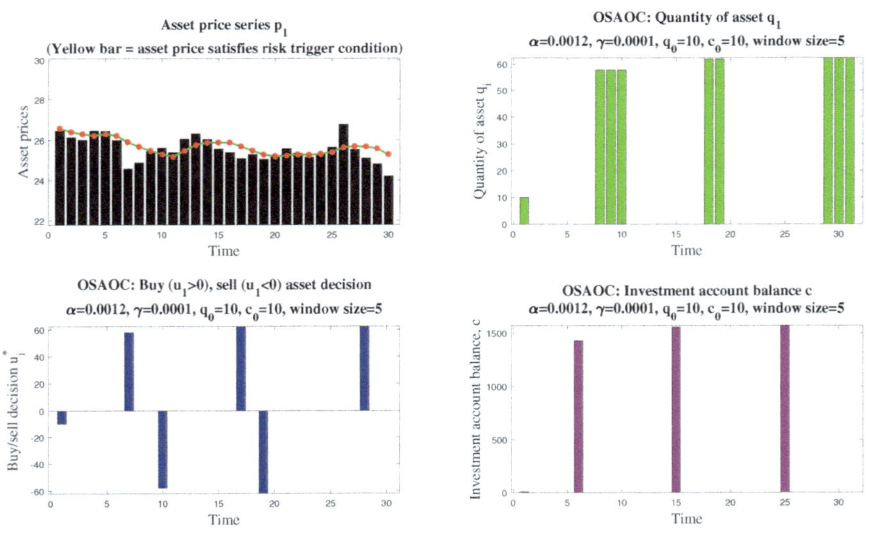

Figure 5.24. *Clockwise from top left: Asset 1 price series, quantity of asset 1 held over time, investment account balance over time, buying and selling decisions for asset 1 over time. The green curve with red dots in the top left figure represents the moving average of the price, over a window of the last 5 days.*

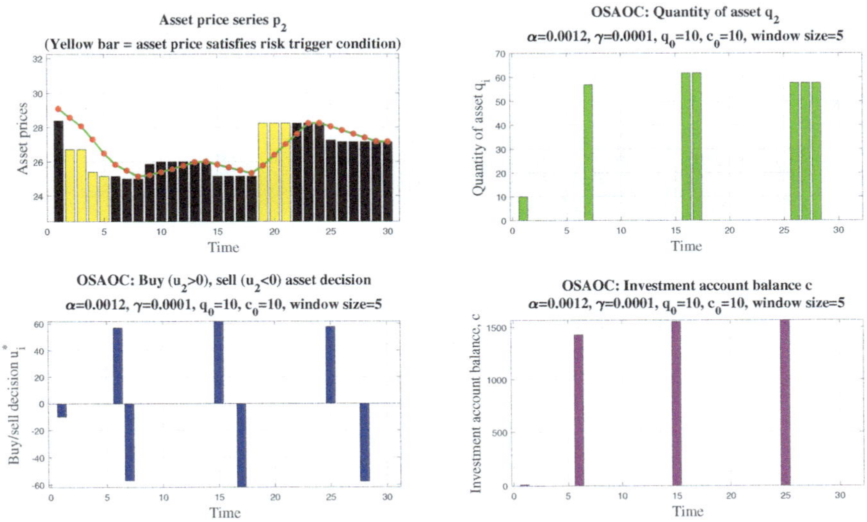

Figure 5.25. *Clockwise from top left: Asset* 2 *price series, quantity of asset* 2 *held over time, investment account balance over time, buying and selling decisions for asset* 2 *over time. The green curve with red dots in the top left figure represents the moving average of the price, over a window of the last* 5 *days.*

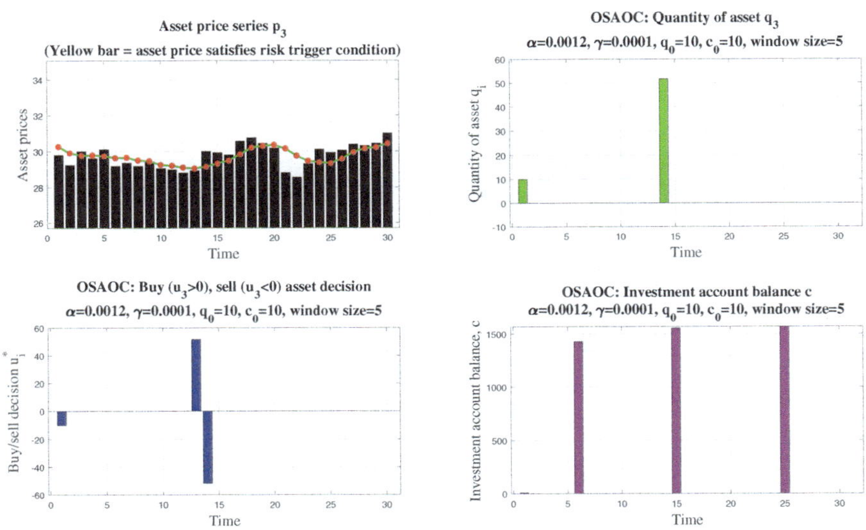

Figure 5.26. *Clockwise from top left: Asset* 3 *price series, quantity of asset* 3 *held over time, investment account balance over time, buying and selling decisions for asset* 3 *over time. The green curve with red dots in the top left figure represents the moving average of the price, over a window of the last* 5 *days.*

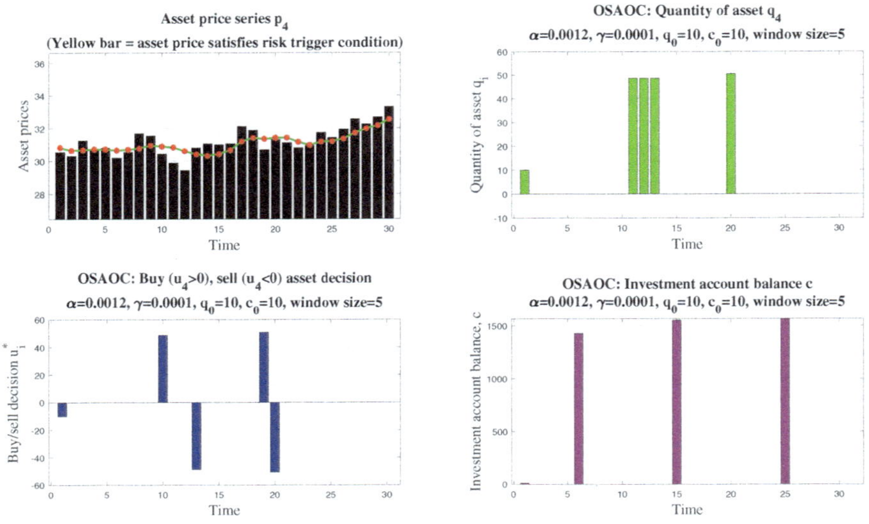

Figure 5.27. *Clockwise from top left: Asset 4 price series, quantity of asset 4 held over time, investment account balance over time, buying and selling decisions for asset 4 over time. The green curve with red dots in the top left figure represents the moving average of the price, over a window of the last 5 days.*

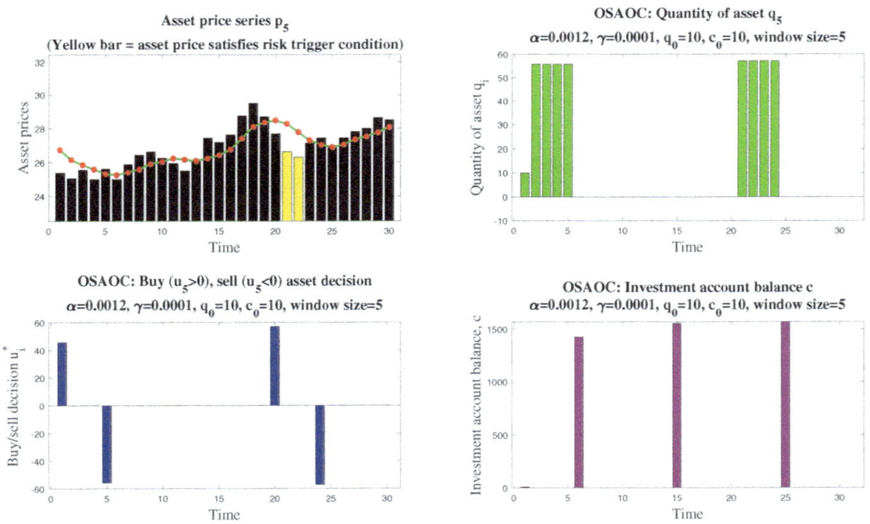

Figure 5.28. *Clockwise from top left: Asset 5 price series, quantity of asset 5 held over time, investment account balance over time, buying and selling decisions for asset 5 over time. The green curve with red dots in the top left figure represents the moving average of the price, over a window of the last 5 days.*

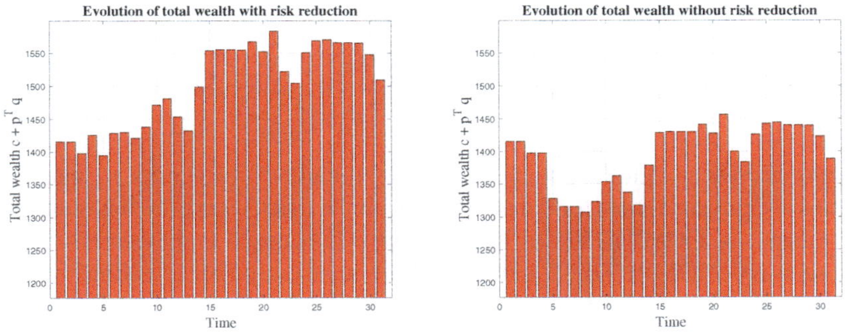

Figure 5.29. *Comparison of the evolution of total wealth using the one step ahead optimal scheme with risk trigger (left) and without risk trigger (right) for the* 5 *assets from the AV Banks dataset.*

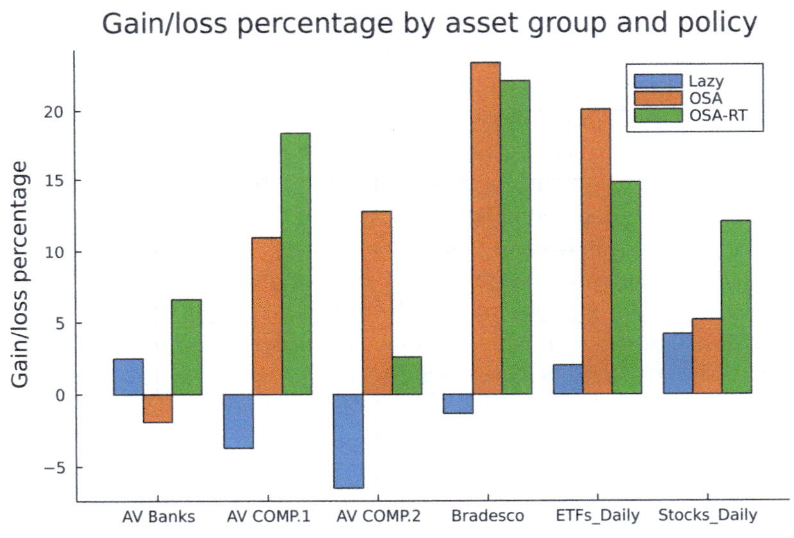

Figure 5.30. *Comparison of gain/loss percentages grouped by asset for the lazy trader, the one step ahead optimal control without risk trigger (OSA), and the one step ahead optimal control with risk trigger (OSA-RT).*

5.3.2 ▪ Comparison of the different approaches to optimal trading portfolios

This subsection compares the performance of the one step ahead optimal control approach with and without risk triggers to the lazy trader (i.e., one who neither buys nor sells assets for the whole trading period, so that his gains or losses depend only on the price variation between the initial and final instants of the trading period). Six datasets from RapidAPI [Rap], each comprising five assets taken from AV Banks, AV COMPUTER 1, AV COMPUTER 2, Bradesco, ETFs_Daily, and Stocks_Daily, are used in the comparison, shown in Fig. 5.30. The first two datasets, AV Banks and AV COMPUTER 1, were presented in detail in the previous section.

This is a preliminary comparison, since a more profound comparison would involve testing each approach over several periods and computing error bars on the gain/loss percentages for each approach. However, for this small sample, the results for which are shown in Fig. 5.30, certain observations are clear:

- The one step ahead optimal policy, with the risk trigger, outperforms the lazy trader, for all the assets considered. Without the risk trigger, the same holds, except for the asset AV Banks.
- The one step ahead optimal policies with and without the risk trigger are almost tied, with perhaps a slight advantage for the approach with the risk trigger which has three clear wins (AV Banks, AV COMPUTER 1, Stocks_Daily), as opposed to the others which have two clear wins (AV COMPUTER 2 and ETFs_Daily) and one small win (Bradesco). However, as just mentioned, a realistic comparison would involve statistical testing, more accurate models of transaction, and brokerage costs, etc.

5.4 ▪ Chapter summary

In keeping with the general philosophy of the book, the objective in this chapter was to illustrate that, once the basic model of wealth dynamics is established, one step ahead optimal control leads to a trading algorithm in the sense that it specifies a rule to buy or sell assets in a given portfolio, dependent on the evolution of their prices over time. The examples given in the previous section show that the proposed strategy performs reasonably well over datasets relating to different portfolios (banks, computers, ETFs, and stocks), for which asset prices are not too volatile. This is encouraging, but the usual caveats apply: more testing is required to calculate expected returns from the proposed policy for a larger number of portfolios, made up of assets whose prices may not be mean reverting, and so on.

Even though the examples indicate that the proposed strategy has potential for use in trading, it is not intended to be a recipe for direct use by a daily trader. In this respect, it is useful to recall Chan's affirmation [Cha13] that a scientific approach to algorithmic trading requires the algorithm user (trader) to carry out experiments to test hypotheses and predictions of the model. If the results obtained are poor for certain datasets, reasons for the failure should be sought and modifications to the hypotheses and models made, in order to start a new series of tests, with the testing and modification cycles continuing until the algorithm starts to become profitable. Finally, as also emphasized by Chan, the fact that additional judgement (subjective information) is sometimes required and incorporated into the trading process does not mean that developing quantitative rules, such as those of this chapter, is a futile exercise or that algorithmic traders are "dumber" than discretionary traders.

Notes and references

Luenberger [Lue98] gives a modern and authoritative presentation of investment science, including portfolio theory. For continuous-time models, Merton [Mer90] gives the classic treatment of finance, also including portfolio theory, extending the work in his celebrated paper [Mer69]. A companion paper by Samuelson [Sam69] treats the discrete-time case, using stochastic dynamic programming.

Portfolio optimization, as a long term problem in which expected returns and deviations of assets are assumed to be known, is a subject with a long and rich history, starting with the seminal papers of Markowitz [Mar52] and Samuelson [Sam69]. Myopic strategies are mentioned in Campbell and Viceira [CV02]. Mei, DeMiguel, and Nogales [MDN16] show that, for a certain class of optimization problems, myopia could cause large losses, but this could also occur with other nonanticipative policies.

The simple moving average (SMA) philosophy is based on the prediction of low and high prices, using a (lagging) moving average predictor. The word philosophy is used for SMA to emphasize that, in order to become a policy, it is necessary to specify the amount of the asset to be bought or sold in each situation, and this is the key feature that distinguishes different policies that all subscribe to the SMA philosophy and variants (see, for example, [AFFR08; BLL92; ZZ09]). Chan's book [Cha13] discusses several trading strategies that use moving averages in some form, as well as a wealth of practical details that need to be taken into account if a mathematical algorithm needs to progress from the realm of theory to that of practice.

A convex optimization based approach, with more complex models, including holding and transaction costs, is proposed in the excellent monograph [Boy+17]. Bemporad, Bellucci, and Gabbriellini [BBG14] present an approach related to the one in this chapter, but using more sophisticated discrete-time stochastic model predictive control and receding horizon optimization.

Chapter 6

The inventory control and management problem

This chapter formulates the inventory control and management problem for a single echelon supply chain as an omniscient optimal control problem, in which the demand is assumed to be known over the entire planning horizon and subsequently formulates the one step ahead optimal control version, which is realistic, in the sense that it does not make the assumption that future demand is known. In both optimal control formulations, the objective is to maximize economic value added, which is a comprehensive performance index commonly used in business management. This is to be contrasted with many purely control-inspired approaches, in which control objectives, such as regulation to a set point, are met, without any reference to economic objectives, such as profit maximization or cost minimization. It is in this context that the title of this chapter refers to both control and management of an inventory. Given the presence of delays in the supply chain dynamics, it is necessary to make a slight extension of the one step ahead approach and this is discussed in this chapter. In addition to the usual comparison of the one step ahead optimal and omniscient controllers, a comparison is also made with a classical controller, known as the (s, S) controller, where s and S refer to the low and high stock threshold levels used in deciding when to replenish stock.

6.1 ▪ Control-theoretic approaches to supply chain management

Ivanov et al. [Iva+18] in their recent survey write

> Modern production and logistics systems, supply chains, and Industry 4.0 networks are challenged by increased uncertainty and risks, multiple feedback cycles, and dynamics. Control theory is an interesting research avenue which contributes to further insights concerning the management of the given challenges in operations and supply chain management.

They also identify one of the main contributions of control theory as being the application of dynamic feedback control to production-inventory systems and point out that a wide range of control-theoretic tools have been used in this context, ranging from the classical PID control to model predictive control. We also point the reader to the recent survey [Lin+17] on control-theoretic approaches to the inventory control problem, since this chapter gives only a brief review.

An early idea for inventory control, that is still in use, was proposed by Arrow, Harris, and Marschak [AHM51] and, roughly speaking, consists of monitoring the inventory level and replenishing the stock, whenever it falls below a certain level. Since this control, usually referred to as (s, S) control, uses the stock or inventory level itself, it can be thought of as feedback control, based on the threshold levels s and S, as explained in section 6.4.2.

In the specific area of feedback control of inventory based on a state space model of its dynamics, most of the literature has been devoted to models that apply standard control ideas such as set point control or regulation, which involves choosing set points or targets, such as inventory level, for system variables. These approaches can be viewed as parametrized versions of several standard algorithms from the supply chain management literature, such as order-up-to-inventory control. A large class of such controllers is known by the acronym IOBPCS, which stands for inventory and order based production control system. Various prefixes, such as AP (for automatic pipeline) and MP (for matched parameter) identify variants of the basic IOBPCS scheme. Papers in this area also assume linear models and study the effect of the controller on the so called bullwhip effect (amplification of demand uncertainty observed in system variables) and on stability with regard to, for example, step changes in the demand; see, for example, [HBT07; LN19; LNS19].

The model predictive control (MPC) approach uses a model of the real plant, as well as past and current system data, to successively predict on some horizon; optimize some suitable performance index, on a (possibly different) horizon, using the predictions; and, finally, apply one or more of the computed optimal controls to the plant, before beginning a new predict-optimize-control sequence. For examples of this approach, see [WRK07] and references therein. If the performance index takes economic factors into account, the MPC approach is referred to as economic MPC and a recent example in the supply chain context is [SRM14].

This chapter uses the OSAOC approach that is related to the MPC approach; however, it uses only past and current values of the demand and system state, does not use a predictor, and uses a stage cost that is economic: it is the so-called economic value added (EVA) performance index, commonly used in the business and financial world [MH04]. A slight extension of the one step ahead optimal control idea is necessary on account of the lead time or delay present in the system and is used to optimize EVA using past demands, for just one step ahead of the current time, apply this optimal control to the system, update its state, and repeat the cycle of one step ahead optimization of EVA, until the end of the horizon. Note that the control scheme just described is set up to compute an ordering decision (or control) in real time, although it can also be used in a planning mode, for simulated demands.

6.2 ▪ A single echelon supply chain model

The single echelon supply chain model considered in this chapter can be thought of as a store, and this is, in fact, the context in [MH04], on which the model in this chapter is based. However, the model presented in this section is quite general and represents any single echelon supply chain, which essentially refers to a single source shipping a single *divisible* good, with a certain delay or lead time, to some location, which shall be referred to generically as a warehouse, in which there is a stock (inventory). Sales of this good, in response to a demand, are assumed to occur at the warehouse.

A single echelon supply chain thus has two main components: a delay between ordering and receiving, corresponding to a block named conveyor or pipeline and an accumulator, which receives the ordered good after the stipulated delay, corresponding to the warehouse (Fig. 6.1). It is assumed that there are capacity constraints, both on the warehouse and on shipping. Selling of the good occurs in accordance with the demand and it is assumed that all but the quantity w of the good (the amount in the safety stock) can be sold. Note that since it is assumed that the good is divisible, it is described by a real-valued variable, instead of an integer-valued variable. This is a reasonable approximation when the quantity of the good is large. The manager's objective is to choose an ordering sequence, in response to the demand, that maximizes cumulative profit

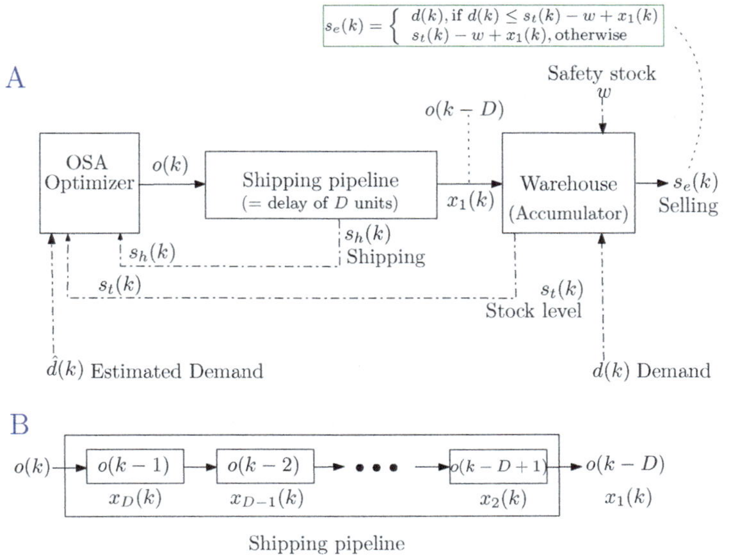

Figure 6.1. A: *Block diagram of a single echelon supply chain to define the inventory control problem, together with the one step ahead optimizer, showing how the overall scheme functions as a feedback controller. Continuous lines with arrows denote the flow of the good through the system, while dash-dotted lines show the flow of information regarding system variables. The optimizer finds the ordering that maximizes the economic value added,* $L(\cdot)$, *in accordance with* (6.35) *(one step ahead case) or* (6.32) *(omniscient case).* B: *The shipping pipeline in detail: it can be thought of as a conveyor, causing a delay of* D *units between ordering a certain quantity of the good and receiving it at the warehouse.*

over a given time horizon, assuming that there are costs and constraints associated with handling, shipping, storage, and stockouts. It is also assumed that there is no backordering; thus stockouts imply that customer demand is left unfulfilled, and the negative effect of this on sales is modeled by a high cost for lost sales. Finally, profits (= sales revenues minus costs) are discounted using a fixed interest rate and then added over the given horizon to obtain the cumulative profit, referred to as EVA [SSR01]. The notation used to formulate the mathematical model is summarized in Table 6.1.

The lead time or delay between ordering and receiving is written by introducing a string of D unit delays, which can be thought as a conveyor, as follows:

$$x_i(k+1) = x_{i+1}(k), \quad i = 1, \dots, D-1, \tag{6.1}$$

$$x_D(k+1) = o(k). \tag{6.2}$$

Thus the quantity of material in transit (i.e., being shipped) at time k, denoted by $s_h(k)$, can be written as

$$s_h(k) = \sum_{i=2}^{D} x_i(k), \tag{6.3}$$

while the quantity of material being received at the warehouse is $x_1(k)$, which is no longer considered as material being shipped, and corresponds to an order placed D time units in the past, so that ordering, denoted $o(k)$ is just $x_{D+1}(k)$.

Evolution of the stock level in the warehouse at time k is determined by the quantity of material being received ($x_1(k)$) plus the quantity currently in the warehouse $s_t(k)$ (setting aside a safety stock w not to be sold) less the quantity sold ($s_e(k)$) in response to the demand. The

Table 6.1. *Notation adopted to formulate the mathematical model.*

Symbol	Meaning
k	discrete-time counter.
$x_i(k)$	quantity of the good in the ith stage of shipping, $i = 1, \ldots, D$, where $i = 1$ corresponds to receiving.
D	delay between receiving and ordering.
$s_t(k)$	inventory (stock) level of warehouse at discrete-time instant k.
$d(k)$	customer demand at warehouse at time k.
$s_e(k)$	sales (selling) at time k.
p	price per unit of material sold.
w	quantity of the good in the safety stock.
$c_o(k)$	out-of-stock cost at time k.
$\alpha_o(k)$	out-of-stock cost per unit of demand not met at time k.
$c_h(k)$	handling cost at time k.
α_h	handling cost per unit of material handled.
$c_{st}(k)$	cost of maintaining stock level in warehouse at time k.
α_{st}	storage cost per unit of material stored.
$c_{sh}(k)$	shipping cost of material in transit.
α_{sh}	shipping cost per unit of material being shipped.
$c_t(k)$	total cost at time k.
$d_p(k)$	discounted profit at time k.
ρ	discount rate.
$L(k)$	cumulative profit at time k.
K_f	simulation horizon over which cumulative profit is to be maximized.
$s_{h,\max}$	maximum shipping capacity.
$s_{t,\max}$	maximum warehouse capacity.

corresponding equation is as follows:

$$s_t(k+1) = s_t(k) + x_1(k) - s_e(k). \tag{6.4}$$

In order to describe the sales $s_e(k)$ at time k, observe that sales can only occur if the inventory level $s_t(k)$ plus the received material $x_1(k)$ less the safety stock w is greater than the demand $d(k)$. Thus sales can be written as follows:

$$s_e(k) = d(k) + \min\{0, s_t(k) - w + x_1(k) - d(k)\}. \tag{6.5}$$

Thus the quantity of sales matches the demand $d(k)$ if it is less than the effective available inventory level $s_t(k) - w + x_1(k)$, otherwise it is just equal to the latter.

The costs are expressed as follows:

$$c_o(k) = \alpha_o(d(k) - s_e(k)) \text{ (out-of-stock cost)}, \tag{6.6}$$

$$c_{st}(k) = \alpha_{st} s_t(k) \text{ (storage cost)}, \tag{6.7}$$

$$c_h(k) = \alpha_h(x_1(k) + o(k)) \text{ (handling cost)}, \tag{6.8}$$

$$c_{sh}(k) = \alpha_{sh} \sum_{i=2}^{D} x_i(k) \text{ (shipping cost)}, \tag{6.9}$$

$$c_t(k) = c_o(k) + c_{st}(k) + c_h(k) + c_{sh}(k) \text{ (total cost)}. \tag{6.10}$$

Discounted profit, also referred to as EVA, is the revenue from sales less the total cost (all at time k), appropriately discounted:

$$d_p(k) = (ps_e(k) - c_t(k))e^{-\rho(k-D)}. \tag{6.11}$$

The cumulative profit $L(k)$, also called cumulative EVA, accumulates the discounted profit:

$$L(k+1) = L(k) + d_p(k). \tag{6.12}$$

The objective function to be maximized is the cumulative profit at the end of the time horizon and thus, **given the demand** $d(k), k = D, \ldots, K_f - 1$ **over the whole simulation horizon**, the optimization problem to be solved is in fact an optimal control problem, which will be referred to as the **omniscient** optimal control problem (since the demand over the entire simulation horizon is assumed to be known), and can be written as follows:

$$\underset{\{o(k)\}_{k=D}^{K_f-1}}{\text{maximize}} \quad L(K_f). \tag{6.13}$$

In optimal control terminology, this is the Mayer problem [ST00] of choosing an optimal ordering sequence that maximizes the final cumulative profit $L(K_f)$. More realistically, the following constraints are also needed:

$$o(k) \geq 0, \quad k = 0, \ldots, K_f - 1, \tag{6.14}$$

$$s_h(k) \leq s_{h,\max}, \quad k = 0, \ldots, K_f - 1, \tag{6.15}$$

$$s_t(k) \leq s_{t,\max}, \quad k = 0, \ldots, K_f - 1. \tag{6.16}$$

Observe that (6.1) through (6.12) are all linear with the exception of (6.5). Since (6.5) is piecewise linear, it will now be shown how to write the optimal control problem described in (6.13), as a linear program. The function min can be written equivalently as

$$\min\{0, y\} = \frac{1}{2}(y - |y|). \tag{6.17}$$

The variable y can be written as the difference of two nonnegative functions y_+ and y_- so that

$$y = y_+ - y_-, \tag{6.18}$$

$$|y| = y_+ + y_-, \tag{6.19}$$

$$\text{provided that } y_+ y_- = 0. \tag{6.20}$$

Furthermore, it is easy to see graphically that

$$\min\{0, y\} = \frac{1}{2}(y - |y|) = -y_-. \tag{6.21}$$

Denoting the effective available inventory level less the demand as $y(k)$,

$$y(k) = s_t(k) - w + x_1(k) - d(k) \tag{6.22}$$

and using (6.21), (6.5) is rewritten as follows:

$$s_e(k) = d(k) + \min\{0, y(k)\} \tag{6.23}$$

$$= d(k) - y_-(k), \tag{6.24}$$

where $y_-(k)$ is defined from (6.22), i.e.,

$$y_+(k) - y_-(k) = s_t(k) - w + x_1(k) - d(k), \tag{6.25}$$

which is now recognizably a linear equation involving the additional nonnegative variables:

$$y_+(k), y_-(k) \geq 0. \tag{6.26}$$

In order to ensure that (6.20) is satisfied, it is modeled equivalently as the two mutually exclusive logical statements:

$$\text{if } y_+(k) > 0, \text{ then } y_-(k) = 0, \tag{6.27}$$

$$\text{if } y_-(k) > 0, \text{ then } y_+(k) = 0. \tag{6.28}$$

Let M be any upper bound for y_+, y_-. Then, it is easy to check that statements (6.27) and (6.28) are equivalent to the following linear constraints:

$$y_+(k) \leq M\delta_1(k), \tag{6.29}$$

$$y_-(k) \leq M\delta_2(k), \tag{6.30}$$

$$\delta_1(k) + \delta_2(k) = 1, \tag{6.31}$$

where δ_1 and δ_2 are **binary** variables, i.e., $\delta_i(k) \in \{0, 1\}\ \forall i, k$.

The omniscient optimal control problem (6.13) can now be transcribed (cf. [CCP70]), as the following mixed integer linear program (MILP):

$$\begin{array}{lll} \underset{\{o(k)\}_{k=D}^{K_f-1}}{\text{maximize}} & L(K_f) & \\ \text{subject to } (6.1), (6.2), (6.4), (6.12), (6.24), (6.25) & \forall\, k \in [D, K_f - 1] & \\ \text{and } (6.14), (6.15), (6.16), (6.26) & \forall\, k \in [D, K_f - 1] & \\ \text{and } (6.29), (6.30), (6.31) & \forall\, k \in [D, K_f - 1], & \end{array} \tag{6.32}$$

where (6.1), (6.2), (6.4), (6.12), (6.24), and (6.25) are equality constraints that describe the single echelon supply chain (SESC) dynamics. Equations (6.14) and (6.26) are nonnegativity constraints. Equations (6.15) and (6.16) are capacity constraints on shipping and inventory. Last, (6.29), (6.30), and (6.31) are constraints that involve the binary variables.

For future reference, the **state vector** of the SESC at instant k is denoted as $\mathbf{z}(k)$ and defined as

$$\mathbf{z}(k) = [x_1(k), \ldots, x_D(k), s_t(k)]. \tag{6.33}$$

From (6.1), (6.2) it follows that the state vector $\mathbf{z}(k)$ can be written equivalently as

$$\mathbf{z}(k) = [o(k - D), o(k - D + 1), \ldots, o(k - 1), s_t(k)]. \tag{6.34}$$

Remarks: It should be noted that the omniscient optimal control problem has $(D+3)(K_f - D)$ decision variables, i.e., (the $D + 1$ variables in the state vector $\mathbf{z}(k)$ together with $y_+(k)$ and $y_-(k)$) times the length $(K_f - D)$ of the simulation horizon. There are $4(K_f - D)$ inequality constraints due to maximum shipping, warehouse capacities, and upper bounds of $y_+(k), y_-(k)$. There are $3(K_f - D)$ nonnegativity constraints and $(D + 4)(K_f - D)$ equality constraints that describe the SESC dynamics plus the $(K_f - D)$ equality constraints that ensure $\delta_1(k)$ and $\delta_2(k)$ are mutually exclusive.

The omniscient cumulative EVA, even though it is unattainable, serves as a global optimum and as a reference against which the cumulative EVA achieved by causal ordering sequences, obtained by implementable controllers, can be evaluated. The omniscient optimal solution requires knowledge of future peaks and troughs in the demand and uses it, when required, to make anticipative (i.e., noncausal) ordering, ensuring that cumulative profit is maximized. Such noncausal behavior is not possible for any real world controller, which must necessarily be causal or nonanticipative, since it cannot have access to future demands.

6.3 ▪ One step ahead optimal control of inventory

In practice, of course, only past demands are known to the supply chain manager, who has to make ordering decisions based on this information and observation of the current variables, such as inventory level, amount of goods in the shipping pipeline, sales levels, etc. This section formulates the so called **one step ahead optimal control (OSAOC) problem**, that respects practical information constraints, and is shown schematically in Fig. 6.2.

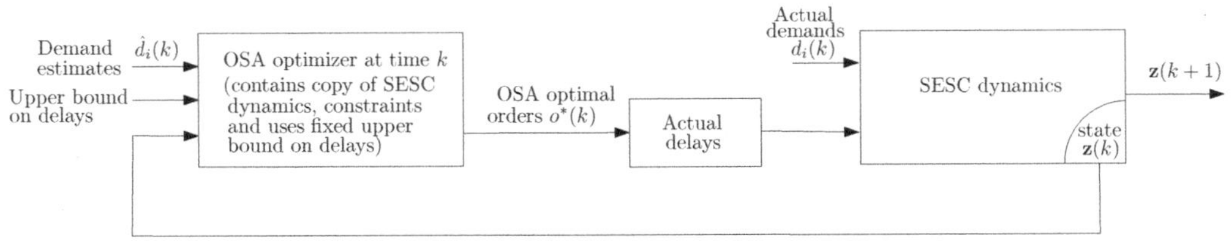

Figure 6.2. *The one step ahead optimal control scheme in the case where the actual delays and demands differ from the values used in the one step ahead optimizer. In sect. 6.7, the actual delays are chosen from a random distribution, while the one step ahead optimizer uses upper bounds. Similarly, the actual demands are used to update the supply chain state $\mathbf{z}(k)$, defined in (6.34), while the one step ahead optimizer uses only past demands and estimates the current demand $\hat{d}(k)$ as $d(k-1)$.*

6.3.1 ▪ Linear programming formulation of one step ahead optimal control

Given the delay D between ordering and receiving, it is clear that, at time instant k, the value of the objective function $L(k+1)$ (the cumulative profit) at the next time instant $k+1$ is dictated by the ordering $o(k-D)$. This means that, since the past demands are known and we can estimate the current demand as $\hat{d}(k) = d(k-1)$, one can then optimize over the backward horizon $\{k-D, k-D+1, \dots, k\}$ to obtain the optimal sequence $\{o^*(i)\}_{i=k-D}^{k}$, assuming the state $\mathbf{z}(k) = [x_1(k), \dots, x_D(k), s_t(k)]$ to be given and initializing $\mathbf{z}_0 = \mathbf{z}(k)$. The OSAOC problem just described is denoted $OSA(\mathbf{z}(k))$ and transcribed as the following MILP problem, the structure of which is inherited from the corresponding omniscient problem (6.32):

$$\begin{array}{ll} \underset{\{o(i)\}_{i=k-D}^{k}}{\text{maximize}} & L(k+1) \\ \text{subject to (6.1), (6.2), (6.4), (6.12), (6.24), (6.25)} \; \forall\, i \in [k-D, k] \\ \text{and (6.14), (6.15), (6.16), (6.26)} \qquad \forall\, i \in [k-D, k] \\ \text{and (6.29), (6.30), (6.31)} \qquad \forall\, i \in [k-D, k] \\ \text{and } \mathbf{z}_0 = \mathbf{z}(k) \text{ (specified initial conditions).} \end{array} \tag{6.35}$$

Now, let the optimal control computed as the solution to (6.35) be denoted as follows:

$$[o^*(k-D), \dots, o^*(k)] := \text{argmax}_{\{o(i)\}_{i=k-D}^{k}} \; L(k+1). \tag{6.36}$$

Although the entire vector $\{o^*(i)\}_{i=k}^{k+D}$ is determined in (6.36), examination of (6.1) through (6.12) and Fig. 6.1(B) shows that only the optimal ordering $o^*(k-D)$ affects the value of the objective function (profit) $L(k+1)$. Thus, the computed values $o^*(k-D+1), \dots, o^*(k)$ are discarded and the variables at these instants maintain their preoptimization values.

As pointed out in (6.34), the state $\mathbf{z}(k)$ can also be expressed as

$$\mathbf{z}(k) = [o(k-D), \dots, o(k-1), s_t(k)].$$

Thus, after the optimization step is carried out, the state is updated to $\mathbf{z}(k+1) = [o(k-D+1), \ldots, o(k-1), o_{osao}(k), s_t(k+1)]$, where $s_t(k+1)$ is obtained by evaluating (6.4). From this new initial condition, a new optimization step can be performed. With this notation in place, the iterative one step ahead control (OSAOC) scheme over the backward horizon can be written as shown (Algorithm 6.1).

ALGORITHM 6.1. One step ahead optimal control of inventory.

Initial state $\mathbf{z}_0 := \mathbf{z}(k_0)$, $k_0 = D$ given
while $D \leq k \leq K_f - 1$ **do**
  $\mathbf{z}(k) := \mathbf{z}_0$
  solve $OSA(\mathbf{z}(k))$ defined in (6.35)
  to get $[o^*(k-D); \ldots; o^*(k)]$
  Discard all computed optimal orderings except $o^*(k-D)$
  $o_{osao}(k) \leftarrow o^*(k-D)$
  Evaluate RHS of (6.4) to obtain $s_t(k+1)$
  $\mathbf{z}_0 \leftarrow [o(k-D+1), \ldots, o(k-1), o_{osao}(k), s_t(k+1)]$
  $k \leftarrow k+1$
end while

Remark. Algorithm 6.1 relies only on past values of the demand and the current demand estimate $\hat{d}(k) = d(k-1)$: at each instant k, it solves a linear program with $(D+3)(D+1)$ decision variables, $(D+4)(D+1)$ equality constraints describing the SESC dynamics, $3(D+1)$ nonnegativity constraints, $4(D+1)$ upper bound constraints, and $(D+1)$ equality constraints that ensure the binary variables are mutually exclusive. This is a linear program that is significantly smaller in terms of the number of decision variables and constraints than the corresponding omniscient optimal control problem (6.32), whenever the simulation horizon K_f is much larger than the lead time D. For example, assuming $D = 7$ there would be a total of 80 decision variables, 88 equality constraints describing the dynamics, 24 nonnegative constraints, 32 upper bound constraints, and 8 equality constraints that ensure the binary variables are mutually exclusive. In contrast, for $K_f = 30$, the omniscient optimal control problem would have 230 decision variables, 253 equality constraints, 69 nonnegative constraints, 92 upper bound constraints, and 23 equality constraints involving the binary variables. Even though it has to be solved at each step, it is a computationally tractable method, which is desirable for real time inventory control. Furthermore, if ordering is made only at the end of the current day, then, of course, current demand $d(k)$ is known and the estimate $\hat{d}(k) = d(k-1)$ does not need to be used.

6.4 ▪ Classical inventory control schemes

This section summarizes the classical control theory based APIOBPCS controller generalized in [Tos+08] and the well known (s, S) control policy [AHM51], chosen as candidates for comparison with the proposed OSAOC controller. These two controllers are chosen because the first is a representative of a family of controllers much discussed and cited in the literature [SNT94], while the second is widely used by practitioners, and commonly discussed in textbooks, e.g., [MS10]. Another reason for the choice is that they are feedback controllers with roughly the same level of simplicity as the proposed controller, although, in contrast to it, the first does require demand forecasting as well as tuning of three controller parameters (T_p, T_i, T_w) and the second requires tuning of the low (s) and high (S) stock level parameters. It is crucial to note, however, that good or optimal parameter tuning for a given demand, will not, in general, be optimal for some other demand. Thus, for fair comparisons, a suitable approach to parameter tuning for the APIOBPCS and (s, S) controllers is required and one is proposed in sect. 6.5.3.

6.4.1 ▪ The APIOBPCS controller

The ordering policy of the APIOBPCS controller [Tos+08, p. 2888, eq. 6] is rewritten as follows:

$$o(k) = \hat{d}(k) + \frac{I_{ref}(k) - s_t(k)}{T_i} + \frac{T_p \hat{d}(k) - s_h(k)}{T_w}, \tag{6.37}$$

where $\hat{d}(k)$ is the estimated demand. $I_{ref}(k)$ is the inventory level reference, the choice of which is based on some heuristic. Parameter T_i is the time constant associated with the adjustment of inventory level, parameter T_p is the lead time or shipping delay, and parameter T_w is the time constant associated with shipping level adjustment.

6.4.2 ▪ The (s, S) inventory controller

The classical (s, S) controller [AHM51] is also chosen for purposes of comparison with the proposed one step ahead optimal control. This is an inventory control policy that is extremely simple to state, and has also proven to be practical and effective, in the seventy years since it was first proposed [BG21]. It involves the choice of two levels of stock, denoted by s and $S > s$ and proposes ordering to bring the inventory level back in the vicinity of S as soon as it drops below s, and not ordering when it exceeds s. This can be expressed as follows:

$$o(k) = \begin{cases} S - s_t(k) & \text{if } s_t(k) \le s, \\ 0 & \text{otherwise}, \end{cases} \tag{6.38}$$

making it clear that it is a threshold based output feedback control policy (i.e., based only on the component s_t of the entire state vector $\mathbf{z}$), switching between 0 and the deficit between S (desired stock level) and the actual current stock level s_t, whenever the latter goes below the threshold value s. It is also obvious that, for a given demand, the performance of an (s, S) controller depends on the choice of the parameters s and S. This implies, in turn, that these parameters can be optimized for a given demand, but, of course, there is no guarantee that these values will remain optimal for a different demand. This is discussed further in sect. 6.5.3, where comparisons between the different controllers are made.

6.5 ▪ Numerical examples of OSAOC versus classical controllers

A demand sequence is generated from a normal distribution, "...the most popular distribution for making inventory management decisions" [Mur06] (also see [SKM15]). In the first numerical example, this normally distributed demand is used to show the solution of the one step ahead optimal control. For the purpose of a fair comparison, both OSAO and APIOBPCS controllers use the same (and very simple) demand forecast $\hat{d}(k) = d(k-1)$.

Next, the parameters of the APIOBPCS and (s, S) controllers are optimized using a data driven methodology. The previous numerical example is repeated using the optimized values obtained for these parameters.

In all cases, the cumulative profit L_{osao} obtained for the OSAOC is compared to the final value L_{omni} attained by the omniscient solution for the same demand sequence. Furthermore, these results are also compared to the cumulative profits $L_{apiobpcs}$ and L_{ss} attained, respectively, by the APIOBPCS controller proposed in [SNT94], derived from classical control theory, and the (s, S) controller proposed in [AHM51].

The ratio between the cumulative profits L_x/L_{omni} is referred to as the *efficiency* η_x, where subscript x specifies the control applied (i.e., x can be one of the subscripts $\{apiobpcs, osao, ss\}$).

The supply chain to be controlled is the single echelon plant described by the dynamics presented in sect. 6.2. Ordering is constrained to be nonnegative, meaning that stock cannot be returned to the supplier. The shipping delay D is taken to be 7 time units and K_f is chosen to be equal to 44 time units. All comparisons are carried out over the interval $[D, K_f - 1 - D]$ to exclude the effect of the final transient due to the turnpike effect [TZ15] that occurs for the omniscient solution, i.e., the comparison interval is $[7, 36]$, which is equivalent to a period of 30 time units.

For all numerical examples, the pipeline was considered initially empty and the other parameters were set as indicated in Table 6.2. The values of parameters T_p, T_i, T_w (of the APIOBPCS controller), s and S (of the (s, S) controller) are specified in each related subsection since their values change for each numerical example.

Table 6.2. *Parameters for the SESC inventory control example problem.*

Symbol	α_{os}	α_{st}	α_h	α_{sh}	p	ρ	$s_{h,\max}$	$s_{t,\max}$	w	$s_h(0)$	$s_t(0)$
Value	20	5	10	5	100	0.05	100	50	1	0	30

6.5.1 ▪ Software implementation details of inventory controllers

The omniscient solution and the OSAO, APIOBPCS, and (s, S) controllers were implemented in the scientific computing language Julia [Bez+17] using JuMP [DHL17], an acronym for Julia mathematical programming, which is an algebraic modeling language for mathematical optimization embedded in Julia with a wrapper for the CLP (coin-OR *linear programming*) and CBC (coin-OR *branch and cut*) MILP solvers. JuMP allows users to express a wide range of optimization problems (linear, mixed integer, quadratic, conic quadratic, semidefinite, and nonlinear) since it supports different types of solvers. It also defines variables, constraints, and the objective using a simple syntax that closely resembles the mathematical formulation shown in Algorithm 6.1.

The optimization of the APIOBPCS and (s, S) tuning parameters discussed in sect. 6.5.3 was obtained by MATLAB implementations of these two controllers that uses the Optimization Toolbox, which is set up to carry out black box optimization of a function, using interior-point, sequential quadratic programming (SQP) and active set methods, amongst others. The black box in question is the system model (6.1)–(6.5) of the SESC dynamics, and the `fmincon` command was used to optimize the tuning parameters, with the algorithm being chosen as interior point.

6.5.2 ▪ Illustrative example of inventory control: Single normally distributed demand

Experiments in this subsection are carried out with a demand d that has a normal distribution with $\mu = 10$ and $\sigma = 3$. This demand is generated by Julia command `d = rand(Normal(10,3),Kf)` using the Distributions package. Note that for this distribution there is a 99.7% probability of $1 \leq d(k) \leq 19$ for $k = 0, \ldots, K_f$. If, however, a demand with negative values is generated, it is discarded and replaced with a new one until a nonnegative demand sequence is generated. The OSAO controller uses the approach detailed by Algorithm 6.1. Both OSAO and APIOBPCS controllers use $\hat{d}(k) = d(k-1)$ as an estimate of the unknown current demand. For the APIOBPCS, the gains were set as $T_i = T_w = T_p = D = 7$, which is based on the setting used by [Tos+08].

Last, the setpoint I_{ref} was chosen to be equal to 10, which is the average demand over the interval $[7, 36]$. For the (s, S) controller, the stock levels were set as $s = \mu - \sigma + w = 8$ and $S = \mu + \sigma + w = 14$, which are the first deviations from the mean plus the safety stock, noting that this presupposes knowledge of the demand distribution used in the numerical experiment. Such prior knowledge is not required for the proposed OSAO controller.

The attained cumulative profits (6.12) and the respective efficiencies with regard to the global optimum (omniscient solution) for each controller are presented in Table 6.3. Figures 6.3 to 6.10 show plots of the important variables for each of the three controllers, in order to make a comparison. Further observations are made in subsection 6.5.2.

Table 6.3. *Cumulative profits and efficiencies.*

Controller	Profit (L)	Efficiency (η_x)
APIOBPCS	7306.21	62.80%
OSAO	9968.63	85.69%
(s, S)	6728.56	57.84%
Omniscient solution	11633.35	100%

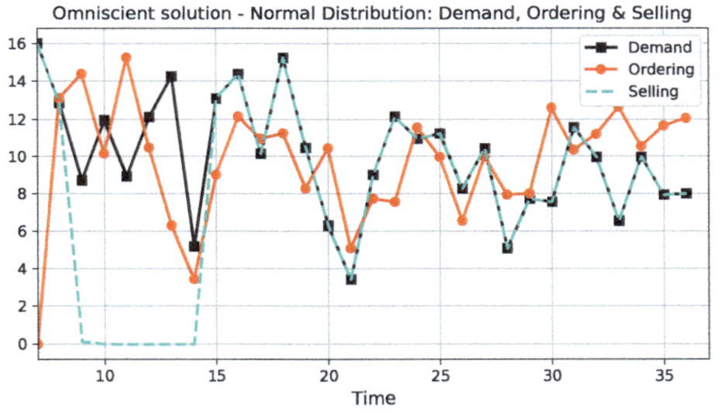

Figure 6.3. *Ordering and selling for the omniscient solution with $D = 7$, assuming that demands from $k = 0$ to $k = 6$ are used as the initial past demands, to $k = (K_f - 1 - D) = 36$, in order to remove the turnpike effect, for a normally distributed demand. Thus, the simulated horizon is equivalent to a period of 30 time units.*

Discussion of numerical Example 1

Figure 6.3 depicts the ordering and selling for the omniscient solution. Since it assumes knowledge of the demand over the entire simulation horizon, it can anticipate the ordering of stock by D instants and overcome the potentially adverse effects of shipping delay. Note that the demand is not matched at instants $k = 9$ to $k = 14$ due to the initially empty pipeline, but, if the warehouse inventory level is sufficiently large, lost sales (Fig. 6.9) can be avoided.

Figures 6.4 to 6.6 show the ordering and selling responses for the APIOBPCS, OSAO, and (s, S) policies, respectively. As expected, all controllers exhibit the same pattern of lost sales due to initialization as the omniscient solution. The OSAO and (s, S) controllers also have lost sales after instant $k = 14$. The APIOBPCS was the only causal (nonanticipative) controller to avoid lost sales after instant $k = 14$, but this was achieved at the cost of a higher usage of the storage space and violation of both maximum warehouse ($s_{t,\max} = 50$) and shipping ($s_{h,\max} = 100$) capacities as can be seen in Figs. 6.7 and 6.8. Unlike the anticipative noncausal omniscient solution, the causal controllers are not able to keep the inventory level at the minimum, which is the specified safety stock of $w = 1$, after the initial pipeline transient.

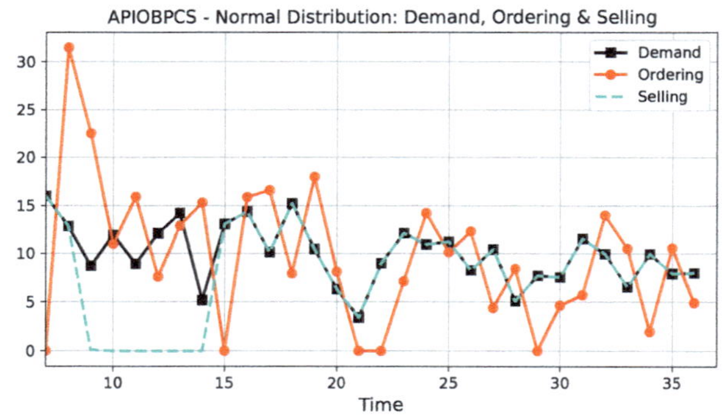

Figure 6.4. *Ordering and selling for the APIOBPCS controller with $\hat{d} = d(k-1)$ and $D = 7$, assuming that demands from $k = 0$ to $k = 6$ are used as the initial past demands, to $k = (K_f - 1 - D) = 36$ for a normally distributed demand. Note that selling tracks demand exactly after the initial transient, i.e., for $k \geq 15$.*

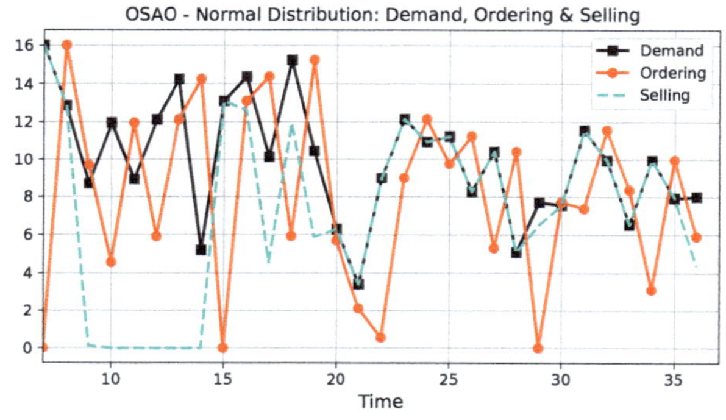

Figure 6.5. *Ordering and selling for the OSAO controller with $D = 7$, assuming that demands from $k = 0$ to $k = 6$ are used as the initial past demands, to $k = (K_f - 1 - D) = 36$ for a normally distributed demand.*

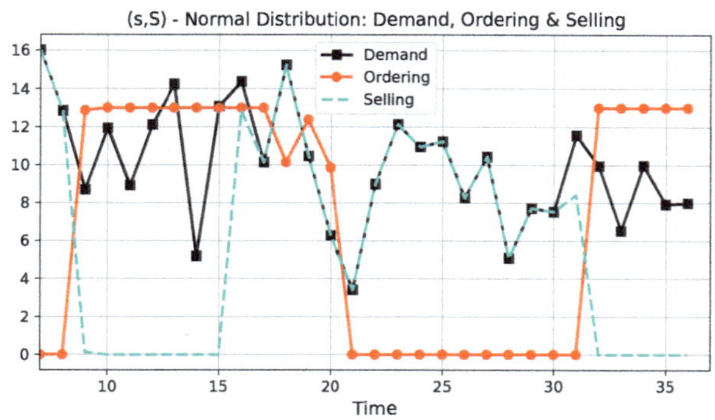

Figure 6.6. *Ordering and selling for the (s, S) controller with $D = 7$, assuming that demands from $k = 0$ to $k = 6$ are used as the initial past demands, to $k = (K_f - 1 - D) = 36$ for a normally distributed demand.*

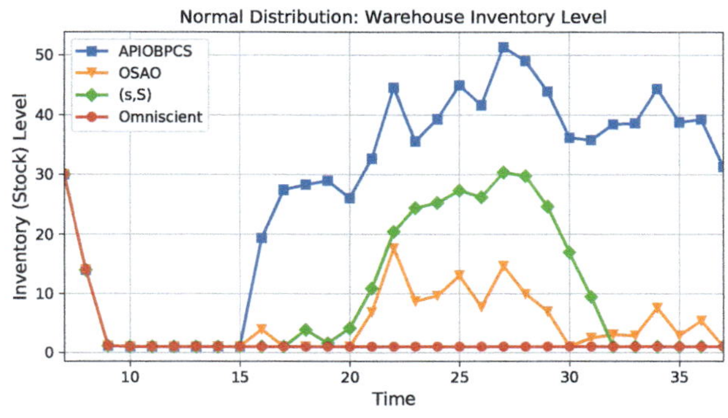

Figure 6.7. *Inventory level for all controllers with* $D = 7$*, assuming that demands from* $k = 0$ *to* $k = 6$ *are used as the initial past demands, to* $k = (K_f - D) = 37$ *for a normally distributed demand. Note that the APIOBPCS controller violates the maximum warehouse capacity* ($s_{t,\max} = 50$) *at instant* $k = 27$.

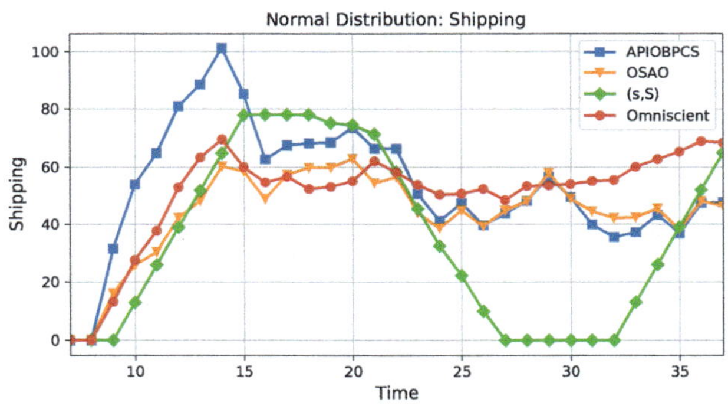

Figure 6.8. *Shipping for all controllers with* $D = 7$*, assuming that demands from* $k = 0$ *to* $k = 6$ *are used as the initial past demands, to* $k = (K_f - D) = 37$ *for a normally distributed demand. Note that the APIOBPCS controller violates the maximum shipping capacity* ($s_{h,\max} = 100$) *at instant* $k = 14$.

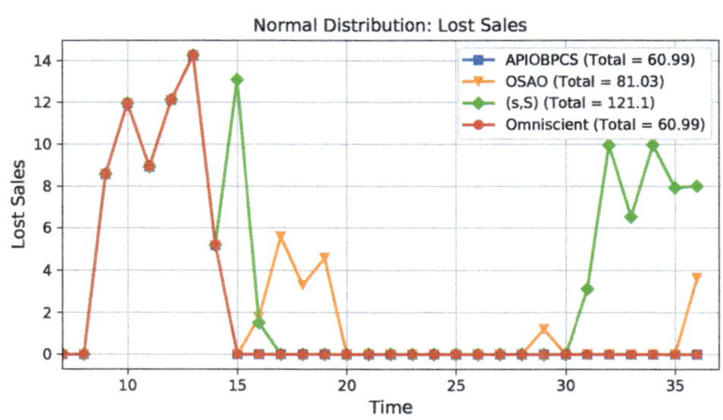

Figure 6.9. *Lost sales for all controllers over the simulated horizon, for a normally distributed demand. All controllers lead to lost sales in the initial segment, up to* $k = 14$*, because the pipeline is initially empty. Both the noncausal omniscient solution and the APIOBPCS controller manage to avoid lost sales after* $k = 14$.

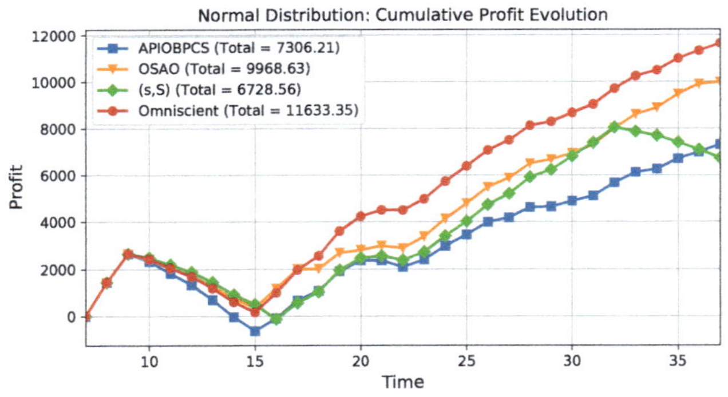

Figure 6.10. *Cumulative profit for all controllers over the simulated horizon, for a normally distributed demand. The efficiencies of the causal controllers, at the end of the simulation horizon, with respect to the global optimum (noncausal omniscient solution) are* $\eta_{apiobpcs} = 62.80\%$, $\eta_{osao} = 85.69\%$, *and* $\eta_{ss} = 57.84\%$.

Figure 6.10 depicts the evolution of the cumulative profits. The efficiencies of the causal controllers, at the end of the simulation horizon, with respect to the global optimum (noncausal omniscient solution) are $\eta^L_{apiobpcs} = 62.80\%$, $\eta^L_{osao} = 85.69\%$, and $\eta^L_{ss} = 57.84\%$.

6.5.3 ▪ Data driven methodology to optimize the APIOBPCS and (s, S) controllers

The tuning parameters of the APIOBPCS controller and the stock levels of the (s, S) controller chosen heuristically in section 6.5.2 yielded results that were considerably inferior to the OSAO controller, raising the question of tuning or optimizing these parameters to improve their performance. Note that, in order to compare the controllers with regard to a specific normally distributed demand d_{spec}, it would not be fair to optimize the APIOBPCS and (s, S) controllers with respect to d_{spec}, because this amounts to giving these two controllers omniscient information (i.e., the demand over the whole period is assumed to be known and is used for the parameter optimization), while the proposed OSAO controller does not use this omniscient information. A reasonable alternative is to optimize the parameters of the APIOBPCS and (s, S) controllers using a set of normally distributed demands similar to the demand d_{spec}. The specific demand d_{spec}, however, cannot be included in this set. The following methodology is used. First, a training set, consisting of N randomly generated and normally distributed nonnegative demands with a given mean μ and standard deviation σ is generated. Evidently, if a dataset of real demands is known it should be used and the optimization is then data driven, with real data, as opposed to synthetic data. With the training set in hand, the parameters of the APIOBPCS and (s, S) controllers are optimized for the demands in the training set using the Matlab Optimization Toolbox and the solver `fmincon`, set to the default interior-point algorithm.

The problem of optimizing the parameter triple (T_p, T_i, T_w) of the APIOBPCS-based controller and the stock levels of the (s, S) controller is now formulated as a black box optimization problem. The black box, which contains the dynamics and constraints, receives either the triple (T_p, T_i, T_w) (when optimizing the APIOBPCS-based controller) or the pair (s, S) (when optimizing the (s, S) controller), in addition to a given demand sequence, and returns the cumulative profit L for this demand. The goal of the optimization is to find the solution (triple (T_p, T_i, T_w) or pair (s, S)) that maximizes the average cumulative profit L of the given demand. For the APIOBPCS controller, the optimization problem to be solved is unconstrained with respect to its parameters. However, given the definition of the (s, S) controller, which requires $S > s$, it is necessary to impose the inequality constraint

$$s - S < 0. \tag{6.39}$$

The capacity constraints on shipping and the warehouse are treated using a penalty function, P, that adds a cost to the cumulative functions L and C whenever $s_t(k) > s_{t,\max}$ or $s_h(k) > s_{h,\max}$ and is defined as follows,

$$P(k) = \omega_1 P_1(k) + \omega_2 P_2(k), \tag{6.40}$$

where

$$P_1(k) = s_t(k) - s_{t,\max} \qquad \text{(store penalty)}, \tag{6.41}$$

$$P_2(k) = s_h(k) - s_{h,\max} \qquad \text{(shipping penalty)}. \tag{6.42}$$

Even though it is possible to select the weights ω_1 and ω_2 to be large enough in order to find an optimal solution that generates feasible ordering sequences for all training demands, there are no guarantees that this will remain true for any demand with the same distribution, but outside the training set. Also note that this methodology not only requires the type of distribution to be known in advance, but also its parameters, i.e., the mean (μ) and standard deviation (σ) in the case of a normal distribution, and such information may not always be available in practice. It is important to emphasize that, in contrast, no information about the demand distribution is required for the OSAO controller. Furthermore, if the value of the demand distribution parameters expected in the training set differ from the ones in the test set, then the solution found by this method does not guarantee good results for the APIOBPCS and (s, S) controllers, which, unlike the proposed parameter-free OSAO controller, depend on good tuning of their parameters (see section 6.6).

The previous example in section 6.5.2 considered a normally distributed demand of $\mu = 10$ and $\sigma = 3$. By randomly generating a training set of $N = 10$ demands with the same $\mu = 10$ and $\sigma = 3$, the fixed gains of the APIOBPCS-based controller that maximized the average profit L of the demands in the training set were found to be $T_p = 5.03$, $T_i = 16.71$, and $T_w = 15.63$. Analogously, the optimal stock levels for the (s, S) controller were found to be $s = 9.27$ and $S = 10.06$. The weights were set as $\omega_1 = \omega_2 = 20$. All other parameters remained the same as indicated in Table 6.2.

Figures 6.11–6.16 show the results of replacing the parameters used for the APIOBPCS and (s, S) controllers in the example of section 6.5.2 with the optimal values obtained in this section. Table 6.4 summarizes the results and demonstrates the significant improvement in performance of the APIOBPCS and (s, S) controllers tuned by the proposed method. The result for the OSAO control, which is parameter free, is, of course, the same as in Table 6.3 and is repeated in Table 6.4 only for the purposes of convenient comparison. Further comments and observations are made in subsection 6.5.3 below.

Table 6.4. *Cumulative profits and efficiencies (normal demand of sect. 6.5.2) after optimizing APIOBPCS and (s, S) controllers. Compare with the results of Table 6.3.*

Controller	Profit (L)	Efficiency (η_x)
APIOBPCS	9706.35	83.44%
OSAO	9968.63	85.69%
(s, S)	7684.53	66.06%
Omniscient solution	11633.35	100%

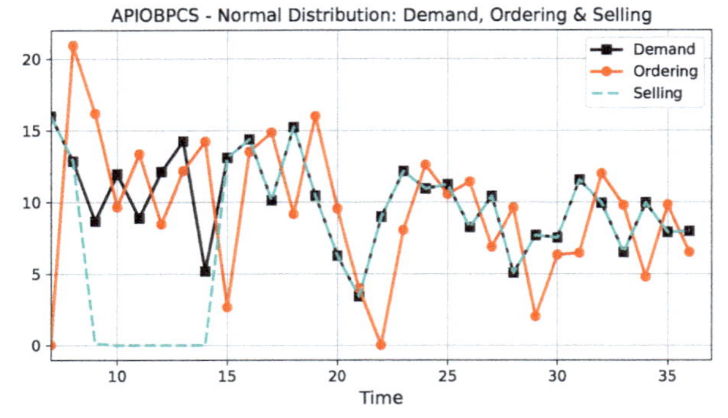

Figure 6.11. *Ordering and selling for the APIOBPCS controller with $D = 7$, assuming that demands from $k = 0$ to $k = 6$ are used as the initial past demands, to $k = (K_f - 1 - D) = 36$ for a normally distributed demand. Compare with the results obtained with the unoptimized control in Fig. 6.4.*

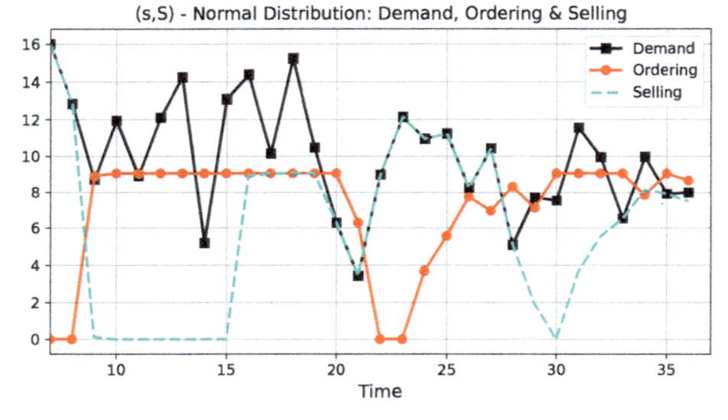

Figure 6.12. *Ordering and selling for the (s, S) controller with $D = 7$, assuming that demands from $k = 0$ to $k = 6$ are used as the initial past demands, to $k = (K_f - 1 - D) = 36$ for a normally distributed demand. Compare with the results obtained with the unoptimized control in Fig. 6.6.*

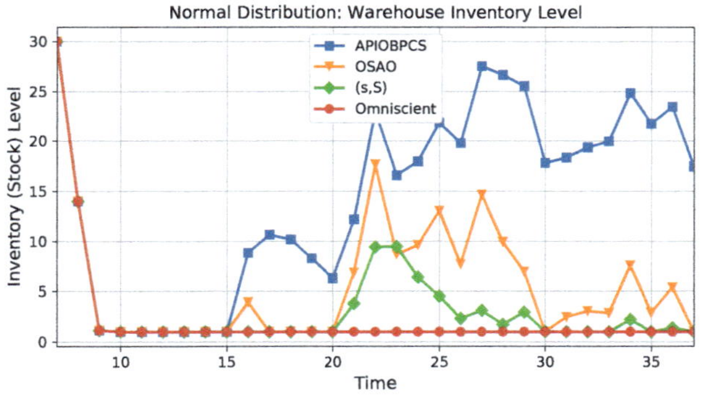

Figure 6.13. *Inventory level for all controllers with $D = 7$, assuming that demands from $k = 0$ to $k = 6$ are used as the initial past demands, to $k = (K_f - D) = 37$ for a normally distributed demand. Compare with the results obtained with the unoptimized control in Fig. 6.7.*

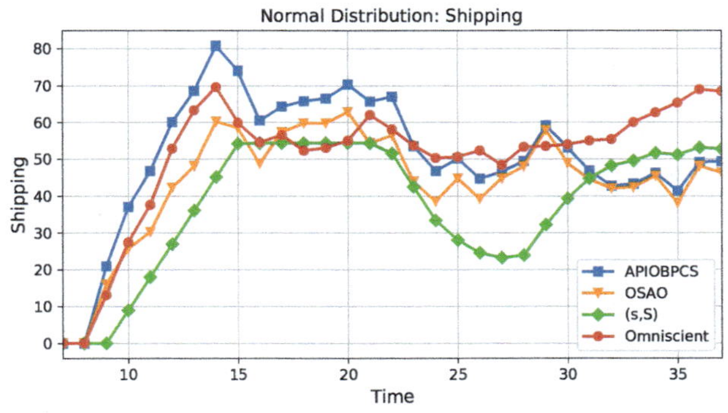

Figure 6.14. *Shipping for all controllers with $D = 7$, assuming that demands from $k = 0$ to $k = 6$ are used as the initial past demands, to $k = (K_f - D) = 37$ for a normally distributed demand. Compare with the results obtained with the unoptimized control in Fig.* 6.8.

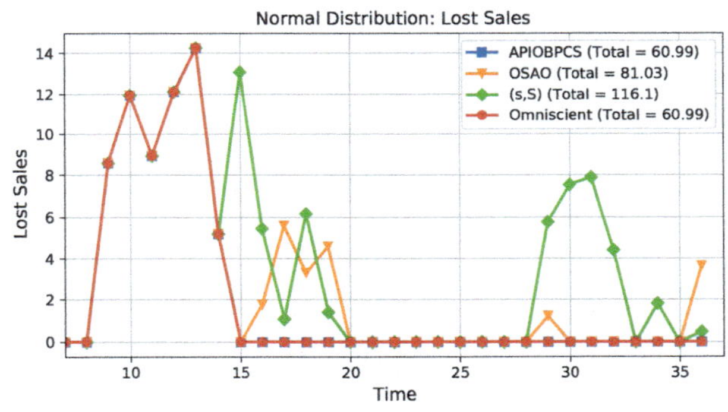

Figure 6.15. *Lost sales for all controllers over the simulated horizon, with a normally distributed demand. Compare with the results obtained with the unoptimized control in Fig.* 6.9.

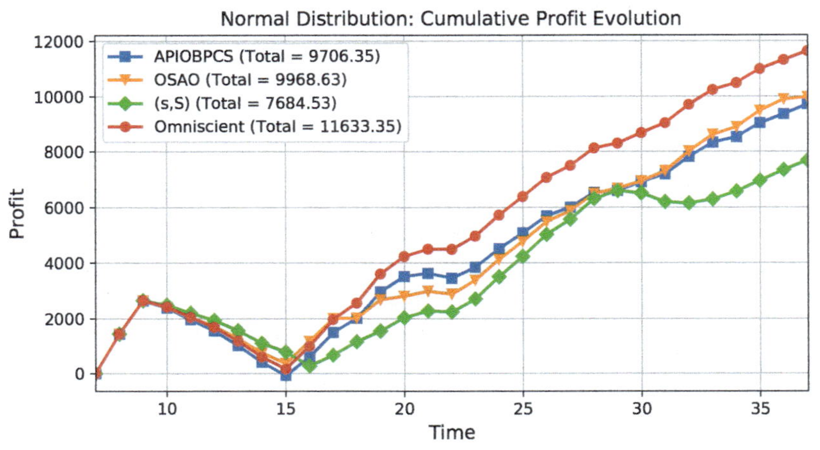

Figure 6.16. *Cumulative profit for all controllers over the simulated horizon, with a normally distributed demand. The efficiencies of the causal controllers, at the end of the simulation horizon, with respect to the global optimum (noncausal omniscient solution) are $\eta_{apiobpcs} = 83.44\%$, $\eta_{osao} = 85.69\%$, and $\eta_{ss} = 66.06\%$. Compare with the results obtained with the unoptimized control in Fig.* 6.10.

Comparison of inventory controllers: Discussion of numerical examples

Figures 6.11 and 6.12 show the ordering and selling for the optimized APIOBPCS and (s, S) controllers, respectively. There is a significantly lower bullwhip effect in the inventory (stock) level produced by the optimized APIOBPCS controller (compare Figs. 6.7 and 6.13). Furthermore, Figs. 6.13 and 6.14 show that the APIOBPCS controller reaches lower peaks in the warehouse inventory and shipping levels and no longer violates the upper bounds in maximum warehouse ($s_{t,\max} = 50$) and shipping ($s_{h,\max} = 100$) capacities, in contrast to Figs. 6.7 and 6.8, respectively. As for the optimized (s, S) controller, a reduction in the warehouse inventory level is noticeable in Fig. 6.13, compared to Fig. 6.7. Unlike the anticipative omniscient solution, the implementable controllers are not able to keep the inventory level at the minimum, which is the specified safety stock of $w = 1$, after the initial transient. Figure 6.15 shows a slight decrease in the lost sales of the optimized (s, S) controller. Last, Fig. 6.16 shows that the efficiencies increased from the previous $\eta_{apiobpcs} = 62.80\%$ to 83.44% for the optimized APIOBPCS and from $\eta_{ss} = 57.84\%$ to 66.06% for the optimized (s, S) controller, showing the effectiveness of the proposed optimization (tuning) method.

6.5.4 ▪ Comparison of average performances for test sets of normally distributed demand

A common problem associated with many inventory control policies is the bullwhip effect of demand uncertainty resulting in larger amplitudes of system variables, such as inventory level. To examine this behavior, two measures are proposed in this chapter: the normalized average used capacity A_{st} and the normalized peak stock level M_{st}. The normalized average used capacity A_{st} measures the average level of stock in the warehouse and is defined as the ratio of the mean of the warehouse inventory level s_t over the simulation horizon to the maximum storage capacity $s_{t,\max}$:

$$A_{st} = \frac{\text{average use of warehouse capacity}}{\text{maximum warehouse capacity}}. \tag{6.43}$$

The normalized peak warehouse level M_{st} measures the peak level of stock in the warehouse and is defined as the ratio of the peak value of the warehouse inventory level s_t over the simulation horizon to the maximum storage capacity $s_{t,\max}$:

$$M_{st} = \frac{\text{peak stock value}}{\text{maximum warehouse capacity}}. \tag{6.44}$$

Both these coefficients are calculated over the interval $[2D + 1, K_f - D]$, so as to exclude the initial transient due to pipeline initialization as well as the turnpike effect, and are used to quantify the effect of the variation of demand on the inventory level. Low A_{st} and M_{st} indicate a maximum storage capacity that is larger than required by the current demand level. Low A_{st} and high M_{st} indicate a bullwhip effect in the inventory. Last, high A_{st} and M_{st} indicate the inventory is being used close to its full capacity. These inferences are collected in Table 6.5.

Remark. The bullwhip effect is commonly defined in inventory control literature as the ratio of the coefficients of variation of the ordering and the demand. Measures greater than unity are an indication of the bullwhip effect due to the amplification of demand variability. However, in our experiments, we found some of these measures to be occasionally misleading, in particular, for the omniscient solution, whose optimal ordering anticipates the demand by D time units

Table 6.5. *Inferences from combinations of the average used capacity A_{st} and peak warehouse level M_{st} values for a given set of demands and simulation horizon.*

A_{st}	M_{st}	Inference
Low	Low	Max. storage capacity larger than required for the current demand level.
Low	High	Bullwhip effect in the warehouse inventory.
High	High	Inventory being used close to full capacity and danger of bullwhip induced overflow.

(as discussed in section 6.5.2). For this reason, we decided to characterize the bullwhip effect using indexes (6.43) and (6.44), as explained in Table 6.5.

Training and test set methodology to evaluate inventory control approaches

This section utilizes the approach illustrated in the previous section, for a single test demand, to a set of test demands, in order to compare average performances. Ten samples of normally distributed demands with $\mu = 10$ and $\sigma = 3$ were generated and grouped in a separate set, referred to as the test set. The training set, discussed in the previous section (and henceforth denoted as S_1), and the test set (henceforth denoted as S_2) are two distinct sets and it is ensured that $S_1 \cap S_2 = \emptyset$. The parameters for the APIOBPCS controller were optimized using the methodology described in section 6.5.3 and the solutions found were $T_p = 5.03$, $T_i = 16.71$, $T_w = 15.63$. Analogously, the optimal stock levels for the (s, S) controller were found to be $s = 9.27$ and $S = 10.06$. The average efficiencies (resp., standard deviation) considering the cumulative profit with respect to the globally optimum (noncausal omniscient solution) are presented in Table 6.6, along with the average used capacities and peak warehouse values for these 10 normally distributed demands. These results indicate that all controllers are operating well below the lower bound specified on the right-hand side of (6.16) and are not being subjected to stressful operating conditions.

Table 6.6. *Average profit efficiencies, average used capacities, peak warehouse levels, and respective standard deviations for* 10 *normal demands* ($\mu = 10$, $\sigma = 3$).

Controller	Efficiency (η_x)	Used capacity (A_{st})	Peak level (M_{st})
APIOBPCS	81.71 ($\pm$ 5.33)%	27.69 ($\pm$ 11.00)%	59.76 ($\pm$ 13.84)%
OSAO	83.56 ($\pm$ 5.03)%	10.72 ($\pm$ 3.70)%	31.99 ($\pm$ 8.65)%
(s, S) policy	67.95 ($\pm$ 5.92)%	4.77 ($\pm$ 0.93)%	17.08 ($\pm$ 5.88)%

Thus, in order to test the controllers under more extreme circumstances, a test set, S_2, comprised of 10 samples of normally distributed demands with $\mu = 20$ and $\sigma = 3$ was generated, thus increasing the mean demand by one hundred percent. Once again, the tuning parameters of the APIOBPCS controller and the stock levels of the (s, S) controller were adjusted using the methodology described in section 6.5.3.Using the same parameters in Table 6.2 and defining the setpoint $I_{ref} = 20$, i.e., the mean of the normal distribution, led to the stock levels $s = 16.57$ and $S = 17.67$ of the (s, S) controller, and the fixed gains $T_p = 2.86$, $T_i = 174.42$, $T_w = 10.63$ of the APIOBPCS controller. Table 6.7 summarizes the average results ($\pm$ standard deviation) obtained for a test set of 10 normally distributed demands with $\mu = 20$ and $\sigma = 3$. The proposed OSAO controller maintains a higher efficiency than the others (after they have been tuned).

Table 6.7. *Average profit efficiencies, average used capacities, peak warehouse levels, and respective standard deviations for* 10 *normal demands* ($\mu = 20$, $\sigma = 3$).

Controller	Efficiency (η_x)	Used capacity (A_{st})	Peak level (M_{st})
APIOBPCS	87.52 ($\pm$ 4.09)%	7.79 ($\pm$ 4.17)%	31.38 ($\pm$ 16.10)%
OSAO	93.87 ($\pm$ 2.26)%	4.52 ($\pm$ 1.93)%	17.98 ($\pm$ 10.82)%
(s, S) policy	90.41 ($\pm$ 1.87)%	2.42 ($\pm$ 0.34)%	7.43 ($\pm$ 3.70)%

6.6 ▪ Robustness of inventory control schemes to demand uncertainty

This section reports on an experimental investigation of the robustness of the APIOBPCS, OSAO, and (s, S) controllers with respect to normally distributed demands of uncertain mean and standard deviation. The experiment is designed as follows. The means (resp., standard deviations) of the normally distributed demands are allowed to vary in the intervals $[10, 20]$ (resp., $[1, 3]$), in steps of size 1 (resp., 0.25). At each point on this grid in the (μ, σ)-space, a test set of 10 normally distributed demands is generated. The parameters of the APIOBPCS and (s, S) controllers are optimized, using a training set of 10 normally distributed demands, at the central point $(15, 2)$ of the (μ, σ)-grid and held fixed for the entire experiment. As before, the test and training sets are disjoint. The average efficiency over the test set of each of the four controllers is computed at each grid point and gives rise to the average efficiency surfaces plotted in Fig. 6.17.

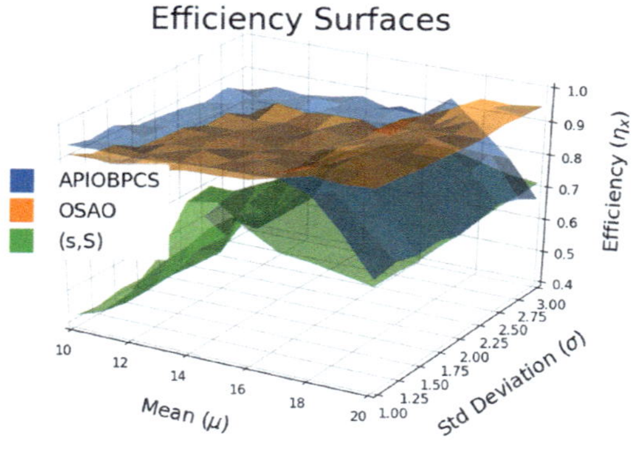

Figure 6.17. *Efficiency surfaces for each controller x with respect to the objective function L. Each point on a surface represents the average efficiency ηx^L for* 10 *normally distributed demands from the test set. Observe that the efficiency of the OSAO controller stays at or above levels of* 80% *of the (unattainable) omniscient global optimum profit for all combinations of* $10 \leq \mu \leq 20$ *and* $1 \leq \sigma \leq 3$, *while the efficiencies of the* (s, S) *and APIOBPCS controllers fall off considerably in certain areas of the* (μ, σ)*-space.*

At the central point $\mu = 15, \sigma = 2$ of the (μ, σ) grid, the optimized stock levels of the (s, S) controller were found to be $s = 14.44$ and $S = 15.21$ while, the optimized parameters of the APIOBPCS-based controller were found to be $T_p = 2.52$, $T_i = 172.29$, and $T_w = 80.98$, and these optimized parameters were kept fixed throughout the experiment. The setpoint was defined as $I_{ref} = 15$, the central value of μ, and all other parameters used in this numerical experiment were the same as indicated in Table 6.2. As can be seen in Fig. 6.17, the (s, S) controller proved to be less robust as the value of the mean decreased ($\mu < 15$). On the other hand, the APIOBPCS-based controller proved to be less robust as the value of the mean increased ($\mu > 15$). Since the

OSAO controller does not require the setting of control parameters (such as stock levels, fixed gains, or setpoint), it is seen to be robust over the entire space defined by the intervals of μ and σ, attaining an average profit of at least 80% of the (unattainable) omniscient global maximum profit, and this is one of the significant advantages of the scheme proposed in this book.

6.7 ▪ Robustness of inventory control schemes to lead time (delay) uncertainty

So far, all experiments in this chapter have assumed a constant lead time D. However, the time elapsed from the placement of an order up to the instant the good is received at the warehouse can vary in real-life inventory control problems. Unlike the case with demand uncertainty, the introduction of lead time (delay) uncertainty requires a few adjustments to be made in the single echelon supply chain dynamics discussed in section 6.2.

First, a sequence of lead times, denoted D_{var}, is defined as follows,

$$D_{var} = \{D_1, D_2, \ldots, D_{K_f}\}, \tag{6.45}$$

where the kth element of D_{var}, denoted D_k, corresponds to the actual lead time for an order placed at time instant k for $k = 1, \ldots, K_f$. As with the demand sequence, D_{var} is assumed to be **known in advance only while computing the omniscient solution** and not known by the implemented controllers OSAO, APIOBPCS, and (s, S).

The length of the conveyor, described by (6.1) and (6.2), needs to be increased taking into account the maximum lead time, denoted D_{max} and defined as

$$D_{\max} = \max\{D_1, D_2, \ldots, D_{K_f}\}, \tag{6.46}$$

which can be greater than the expected constant lead time D used previously.

As noted in [Ste21, p. 507], knowledge of lead times and lead time variation is needed for management to be effective. Therefore, the assumption of $D_{\max}$ being known beforehand is reasonable. Furthermore, (6.46) provides the minimum required length of the conveyor (i.e., the number of conveyor states) in order for the SESC dynamics to be able to account for all lead times in D_{var}. For real-life applications where lead time variation may not be known, $D_{\max}$ only needs to be greater than the maximum expected lead time, i.e., $D_{\max} > E\left[\max\left(D_{var}\right)\right]$. The simple choice of $D_{\max} = \max(D_{var})$ is made below.

Last, the position of the conveyor in which the ordering $o(k)$ is inserted, denoted by the subscript $p(k)$ of x, is no longer fixed and equal to D. Instead, $p(k)$ is equal to the current lead time value $D_k \in [1, D_{max}]$ at each time instant k for $k = 1, \ldots, K_f$. The conveyor state dynamics described in (6.1) and (6.2) can, then, be generalized as follows:

$$x_i(k+1) = x_{i+1}(k),\ i \in \{1, \ldots, D_{\max}\} - \{p(k)\}, \tag{6.47}$$

$$x_{p(k)}(k+1) = x_{p(k)+1}(k) + o(k), \tag{6.48}$$

where $x_{p(k)+1}(k) = 0$ when $p(k) = D_{\max}$.

Figure 6.18 illustrates how the ordering $o(k)$, placed at time instant k, is inserted at the position $p(k)$ of the conveyor for varying values of D_k.

The number of goods being shipped at a time can be rewritten as

$$s_h(k) = \sum_{i=2}^{D_{max}} x_i(k). \tag{6.49}$$

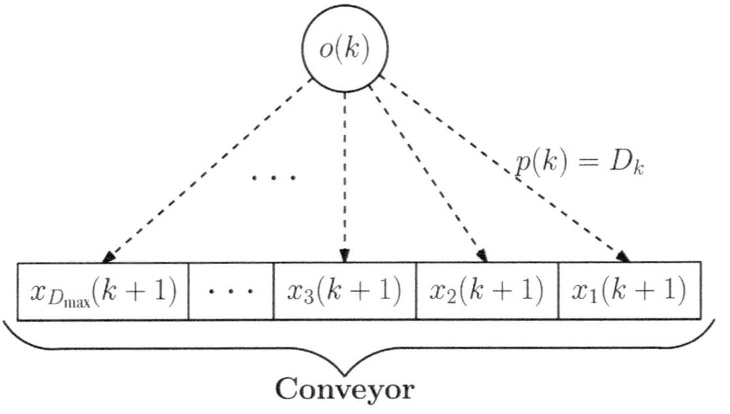

Figure 6.18. *Functioning of the conveyor. The ordering $o(k)$, placed at time instant k, is inserted at the position $p(k) = D_k \in [1, D_{\max}]$ of the conveyor, yielding (6.48). The contents of the first position of the conveyor, $x_1(k)$ represent the quantity of goods that arrive at the warehouse at instant k, while the contents of the other positions, x_2 through $x_{D_{\max}}$, represent the quantity of goods currently in transit (being shipped) in each conveyor position.*

Hence, the omniscient solution can be obtained by solving the following MILP:

$$\begin{array}{lll} \underset{\{o(k)\}_{k=D}^{K_f-1}}{\text{maximize}} & L(K_f) & \\ \text{subject to (6.47), (6.48), (6.4), (6.12), (6.24), (6.25)} & \forall\, k \in [D, K_f - 1] & \\ \text{and (6.14), (6.15), (6.16), (6.26)} & \forall\, k \in [D, K_f - 1] & \\ \text{and (6.29), (6.30), (6.31)} & \forall\, k \in [D, K_f - 1]. & \end{array} \tag{6.50}$$

The **state vector** of the supply chain under lead time uncertainty at instant k is denoted as $\mathbf{z}(k)$ and defined as:

$$\mathbf{z}(k) = [x_1(k), \ldots, x_{D_{max}}(k), s_t(k)]. \tag{6.51}$$

The OSA optimizer (see Fig. 6.2), however, does not have any knowledge of the lead time sequence D_{var} in advance other than the highest possible lead time value $D_{\max}$, which sets the length of the new state vector. Instead, it assumes a constant lead time of $D \leq D_{\max}$ time units. Thus, the conveyor state dynamics for the OSA optimizer block of the OSAO controller can be rewritten as

$$x_i(k+1) = x_{i+1}(k),\ i \in \{1, \ldots, D_{\max}\} - \{D\}, \tag{6.52}$$

$$x_D(k+1) = x_{D+1}(k) + o(k). \tag{6.53}$$

For the particular case where $D = D_{\max}$, (6.52) and (6.53) become identical to (6.1) and (6.2), respectively, since the position $x_{D+1}(k)$ lies outside of the conveyor's boundary and, therefore, is equal to zero.

The OSAOC problem for variable delays, denoted as $OSA(\mathbf{z}(k), D)$, can be transcribed in the following MILP problem:

$$\begin{array}{ll} \underset{\{o(i)\}_{i=k-D}^{k}}{\text{maximize}} & L(k+1) \\ \text{subject to (6.52), (6.53), (6.4), (6.12), (6.24), (6.25)} & \forall\, i \in [k - D, k] \\ \text{and (6.14), (6.15), (6.16), (6.26)} & \forall\, i \in [k - D, k] \\ \text{and (6.29), (6.30), (6.31)} & \forall\, i \in [k - D, k] \\ \text{and } \mathbf{z}_0 = \mathbf{z}(k) \text{ (specified initial conditions).} & \end{array} \tag{6.54}$$

The optimal ordering sequence for the OSAO controller can be obtained by following similar steps as the ones described in section 6.3. By solving (6.54) at a given instant k, we find the optimal ordering $o_{osao}(k)$. This procedure corresponds to the OSA optimizer block in Fig. 6.2 and assumes no knowledge of D_{var}, using the conveyor state dynamics described by (6.52) and (6.53). After the optimal ordering $o_{osao}(k)$ has been placed, and its value can no longer be changed, the actual conveyor is updated according to (6.47) and (6.48), using the information (now known) about the lead time $D_k \in [1, D_{\max}]$ that actually occurred at time instant k. Last, the SESC dynamics are evaluated using the now known actual demand and the state vector $\mathbf{z}(k+1)$ is updated. From this new initial condition, a new optimization step can be performed. Algorithm 6.2 summarizes the necessary changes made to the OSAO controller in order to account for lead time uncertainty.

ALGORITHM 6.2. Inventory control with delay (lead time) uncertainty.

Initial state $\mathbf{z}_0 := \mathbf{z}(k_0)$, $k_0 = D_{\max}$ given
while $D \leq k \leq K_f - 1$ **do**
  $\mathbf{z}(k) := \mathbf{z}_0$
  solve $OSA(\mathbf{z}(k), D)$ defined in (6.54)
  to get $[o^*(k-D); \ldots; o^*(k)]$
  Discard all computed optimal orderings except $o^*(k-D)$
  $o_{osao}(k) \leftarrow o^*(k-D)$
  Evaluate RHS of (6.4) to obtain $s_t(k+1)$
  Update the conveyor state (6.47, 6.48) according to D_k
  $\mathbf{z}_0 \leftarrow [x_1(k+1), \ldots, x_{D_{\max}}(k+1), s_t(k+1)]$
  $k \leftarrow k+1$
end while

This section reports on an experimental investigation of the robustness of the APIOBPCS, OSAO, and (s, S) controllers with respect to 10 randomly generated and uniformly distributed delay sequences, with values in the interval $[5, 9]$, i.e., $D_k \in [5, 9]$ for $k = 1, \ldots, K_f$. In this experiment, each controller has its cumulative profit L and efficiency η_x evaluated for all 10 different delay sequences. The overall performance of each controller is, then, calculated by taking the average (and standard deviation) of the 10 cumulative profits obtained for each delay sequence.

Throughout the experiment, the system parameters are set to the values indicated in Table 6.2 and the same demand profile, used in the first three numerical examples of section 6.5, is adopted for all performance evaluations. The tuning parameters of the APIOBPCS and (s, S) controllers are set to the optimized values obtained in section 6.5.3 for $D = 7$ time units, which are $T_p = 5.03$, $T_i = 16.71$, $T_w = 15.63$ for the APIOBPCS controller and $s = 9.27$ and $S = 10.06$ for the (s, S) controller.

Table 6.8 shows the performance (average efficiency and standard deviation) evaluated for each controller with respect to 10 uniformly distributed delay sequences. As can be seen, the

Table 6.8. *Efficiency ($\pm$ standard deviation) of the APIOBPCS, OSAO, and (s, S) controllers with respect to constant ($D = 7$) and variable ($D_k \in [5, 9]$) delay sequences.*

Controller	Variable delay efficiency	Constant delay efficiency
APIOBPCS	63.65 ($\pm$ 8.38)%	83.44%
OSAO	70.32 ($\pm$ 3.68)%	85.69%
(s, S)	48.44 ($\pm$ 8.96)%	66.06%

OSAO controller achieved both the highest average efficiency (above 70%) and lowest standard deviation (below 5%), meaning that its performance suffered less from different delay sequences. For the purpose of convenient comparison, Table 6.8 also shows the efficiency of the controllers with respect to the constant lead time $D = 7$ (first presented in Table 6.4).

6.8 ▪ Chapter summary

This chapter proposed a novel one step ahead optimal control scheme for a single echelon supply chain model, that does not require prediction. The proposed control scheme requires the solution of a low-dimensional (in terms of the number of decision variables) optimization problem at each time step, thus being perfectly adequate for real time supply chain operation. The one step ahead control is shown to be efficient, robustly attaining an average profit of at least 80% of the (unattainable) omniscient global optimum. The use of a controller with a fixed structure such as the popular class of proportional-integral-derivative controllers requires the tuning of parameters (setpoints and gains) associated with this structure. It is difficult to find fixed choices of parameters that work well over a range of demands. In other words, if a set of these parameters is chosen to be adequate or even optimal for a given nominal demand d_{nom}, it will, in general, be worse for some other demand d, even if d is close, in some appropriate metric, to the demand d_{nom}. The degradation of performance will increase as the demand d moves further away from d_{nom} in the given metric. This is to be contrasted with the proposed OSAO controller, which is always locally optimal and does not need any tuning, as changes occur in the demand, for example, in its distribution or its mean and standard deviation. This is one of the main advantages of the proposed approach. It was also shown how to rewrite the OSAOC problem as a linear programming problem with a relatively small number of decision variables. From a computational viewpoint, this implies that the simple examples in this chapter can easily be scaled to much larger dimension. It should also be noted that a large number of supply chain problems, including the multiechelon case, are in fact described by linear or piecewise linear dynamics. Thus, the proposed scheme is scalable and can (i) be generalized to large multiechelon supply chains and (ii) be used in a planning mode, to choose inventory size, shipping capacity requirements and prices that ensure profit margins, since these choices can be recast as feasibility problems. It should also be pointed out that, although this chapter used the example of a simple warehouse supply chain, with dynamics such that the resulting OSAO problems were linear programs, the OSAO approach is not limited to dynamics and objective functions that necessarily lead to linear programming problems. The generalization of the single good warehouse model presented in this chapter to a multiple goods warehouse model is straightforward, if it is assumed that some upper bounds on the stock of each good are given, together with some lower bounds on their safety stocks. The upper bounds would be constrained by the physical capacity of the warehouse. Similarly, if several goods are shipped together, the model could put a common upper bound on the shipping of these goods, and so on. The fact that the proposed OSAOC approach does not require demand prediction makes it a strong contender for a cheap and universal control scheme that could be adopted by practitioners who might not be comfortable with the considerably greater sophistication of schemes that require prediction, such as the class of model predictive control schemes.

Notes and references

An early example of feedback control in supply chains occurred in the pioneering paper of Arrow, Harris, and Marschak [AHM51] which introduced the two stock level (s, S) policy and proved its optimality under certain conditions. Study of the (s, S) policy has continued to the present day (see, for example, [BG21] and references therein).

Forrester [For61; For68] pioneered the use of systems thinking and feedback control theory in the study of the dynamics of industrial systems and, in particular, of supply chains, which were, at the time, more commonly referred to as production-distribution systems. These ideas were followed up by the systems dynamics school [MH04; Mor07; Ste00] as well as some practitioners of control theory (see the survey [OL04]). Rivera and Pew [RP05] and Tosetti et al. [Tos+08] are among the many who propose a PID setpoint or regulatory control approach to inventory management in a simple supply chain problem. Jansen, de Kok, and Fransoo [JKF11] and Ignaciuk [Ign12] are examples of papers that apply lead time compensation to linear supply chain models in order to mitigate effects of delay, such as bullwhip. A preliminary version of this chapter, making comparisons of the one step ahead optimal controller with the APIOBPCS controller [Tos+08] appeared in [BKR20].

Another approach that has been proposed more recently is based on MPC, or, if a performance index based on economic objective is specified, the terminology becomes economic MPC. A model of the plant is used, together with available demand data, to predict future demand and use the predictions to find an ordering sequence that optimizes the specified performance index. Finally, one or more of the computed optimal controls is applied, before a new predict-optimize-control sequence is embarked upon. The reader is referred to [PLYG03; SRM14; WRK07] and the references therein, for examples of MPC and economic MPC.

Zu and Chen [ZC17] assert that, in the supply chain management context, most managers prefer myopic decisions.

Chapter 7

Market share dynamics under advertising in monopolies

This chapter changes gear and examines business models that originate in the field of marketing science. Models of sales response to advertising, also referred to as market share dynamics under advertising have been the concern first of economists and later of researchers in marketing, starting from the late 1950s. Vidale and Wolfe, in 1957, proposed their now eponymous model based on sales data, and, in 1962, Nerlove and Arrow proposed a related model to which they applied optimal control methods, in order to derive optimal advertising policies. Since then, most of the work in the field has centered around the application of optimal control methods, leading to open-loop control of the Vidale–Wolfe and Nerlove–Arrow models and variants, in order to achieve a given market share, while minimizing advertising expenditures. This chapter revisits the Vidale–Wolfe model and a recent variant, in the context of achieving a target market share using one step ahead optimal control, which constitutes a closed-loop control. The one step ahead optimal control applied in this chapter differs from the ones in Chapters 3, 4, and 5 in two respects: the presence of a target in the objective function and the fact that the market share dynamics are nonlinear, as opposed to the dynamics in all the previous chapters, which were either linear or piecewise linear.

7.1 ▪ Market share dynamics in monopolies

Vidale and Wolfe [VW57] proposed the following, now classical, model for sales response to advertising of a particular brand,

$$\dot{S} = rA(t)(1 - S/M) - \lambda S, \tag{7.1}$$

where S represents the rate of sales at time t, $A(t)$ is the advertising expenditure (to be designed), r is referred to as the response constant, M the market saturation level, and λ the exponential sales decay rate. The interpretation is that the increase in the rate of sales, $\dot{S}$, is proportional to the intensity of the advertising effort (or control) $A(t)$ reaching the fraction of potential customers $(1 - S/M)$, less the number of defecting customers (λS). In what follows, the parameter λ will be referred to as the defection rate, rather than sales decay rate, since, in the more general case of market share models involving competition between firms, sales decay will be attributed to defection of the customer from the firm. In order to rewrite model (7.1) in normalized form, i.e., in terms of the fraction of customers S/M, which can also be denominated as the market share, denoted as x, a change of variables ($x = S/M$) is made, to yield

$$\dot{x} = \frac{rA(k)}{M}(1 - x) - \lambda x. \tag{7.2}$$

In **discrete time**, the **Vidale–Wolfe market share dynamics** can be written as follows:

$$x(k+1) = x(k) + \frac{rA(k)}{M}(1 - x(k)) - \lambda x(k). \tag{7.3}$$

Thus, under the assumption of a constant advertising expenditure $A(k) = A$, the market share converges globally (i.e., for all initial conditions) and exponentially to the equilibrium value $B/(B + \lambda)$, where $B = rA/M$, which is always less than one. Thus, this model assumes that positive defection rate ($\lambda > 0$) impedes the brand from reaching the full market share of unity, but does not go into any detail as to where the "missing" market share (or deficit, from the point of view of the firm) might have gone. This will be discussed further in section 7.3.

Despite the simplicity of this model, it has been the subject of intense research, notably by Sethi [Set77; ST00] who derived optimal advertising efforts (controls) for this class of models, under different assumptions on the cost functions. The bulk of the literature on the Vidale–Wolfe model does not, however, propose significant or structural modifications to the original Vidale–Wolfe model dating from 1957.

7.2 ▪ The discrete-time Vidale–Wolfe model under omniscient optimal control

The Vidale–Wolfe dynamics can be written compactly as follows,

$$x(k+1) = x(k) + u(k)(1 - x(k)) - \lambda x(k), \tag{7.4}$$

where $u(k) \geq 0$ and $\lambda \geq 0$ for $k = 1, \ldots, K_f$.

Suppose that a linear performance index J_ℓ is defined as

$$J_\ell = \sum_{k=1}^{K_f} (x(k+1) - \alpha u(k)), \tag{7.5}$$

where α is a nonnegative weighting parameter that controls the trade-off between market share and advertising expenditure.

Similarly, suppose that a quadratic performance index J_q is defined as

$$J_q = \sum_{k=1}^{K_f} (x(k+1)^2 - \alpha u(k)^2), \tag{7.6}$$

where α is a nonnegative weighting parameter that controls the trade-off between market share and advertising expenditure.

The **omniscient optimal control of market share** is formulated as follows:

$$\begin{aligned}
&\text{maximize } J_i(K_f), i = \ell \text{ or } q \\
&\text{subject to the dynamics (7.4),} \\
&\text{the control constraint } 0 \leq u(k) \leq 1, \\
&\text{and the nonnegativity constraint } x(k) \geq 0.
\end{aligned} \tag{7.7}$$

7.2.1 ▪ The discrete-time Vidale–Wolfe model under OSAOC with a linear performance function: Analytic solution

In order to lighten notation, at any given time k, let $x(k)$ be denoted as x, $x(k+1)$ as x_+, and $u(k)$ as u. Then the discrete-time Vidale–Wolfe model can be written as

$$x_+ = x + h(u(1-x) - \lambda x) = (1-h\lambda)x + h(1-x)u.$$

Let the OSA index be defined as

$$J_{\ell,1} := x_+ - \alpha u.$$

Substituting the dynamics into the performance function yields

$$J_{\ell,1} = x + hu(1-x) - h\lambda x - \alpha u = (1-h\lambda)x + [h(1-x) - \alpha]u,$$

which is, in terms of the decision variable u, the equation of a straight line with an intercept $(1-h\lambda)x$ and slope $[h(1-x)-\alpha]$. If this slope is positive (resp., negative), the maximum of J_1 occurs at the right (resp., left) endpoint of the interval to which u belongs, i.e., for its maximum (resp., minimum) value.

From this analysis it follows that

$$u^*_{\text{osa}} = \begin{cases} 0 & \text{if } h(1-x) - \alpha < 0, \\ 1 & \text{if } h(1-x) - \alpha > 0. \end{cases} \tag{7.8}$$

Remark. Observe that (7.8) defines an on-off or bang-bang type control, where the control is of the all or nothing type, based on whether the current state vector x is above or below the threshold value $1 - \frac{\alpha}{h}$.

7.2.2 ▪ The discrete-time Vidale–Wolfe model under OSAOC with a quadratic performance function: Analytic solution

At any given time k, let $x(k)$ be denoted as x, $x(k+1)$ as x_+, and $u(k)$ as u. Then the discrete-time Vidale–Wolfe model can be written as

$$x_+ = x + h(u(1-x) - \lambda x) = (1-h\lambda)x + h(1-x)u.$$

Let the OSA index be defined as

$$J_{q,1} := x_+^2 - \alpha u^2.$$

Observe that, in J, the market share to be maximized x_+ results from the application of u and the weight α allows a trade-off between how fast the market share is reached and how much advertising effort is used to do this. Writing J in terms of u (the control or decision variable) and the other variables and parameters yields

$$J_{q,1} = [(1-h\lambda)x + h(1-x)u]^2 - \alpha u^2.$$

By setting $\frac{dJ}{du}$ to zero, an extremizing value of u is

$$u_{\text{ext}} = -\frac{(1-h\lambda)x}{h^2(1-x)^2 - \alpha}$$

provided that $u_{\text{ext}} \geq 0$, since the advertising effort is required to be nonnegative.

A necessary condition for a maximum (unconstrained) is that the second derivative be negative. Since

$$\frac{d^2 J_{q,1}}{du} = 2[h^2(1-x)^2 - \alpha],$$

this means that $h^2(1-x)^2 - \alpha < 0$. Notice that if this condition is satisfied, then it implies that u_{ext} is positive and it follows that a maximum is indeed attained at $u_{\text{ext}} = u_{\text{osa}}$.

The other possibility is that $\frac{d^2 J}{du} > 0$ which, in turn, implies that $u_{\text{ext}} < 0$, in which case, the parabola J is convex and it follows that $u_{\text{osa}} = 1$ (its upper bound).

From this analysis it follows that

$$u^*_{\text{osa}} = \begin{cases} -\frac{(1-h\lambda)x}{h^2(1-x)^2-\alpha} & \text{if } h^2(1-x)^2 - \alpha < 0, \\ 1 & \text{otherwise.} \end{cases} \tag{7.9}$$

Remark. It should be noted that it is only possible to use analytic methods of solution in cases where the dynamics are very simple, as is the case for the discrete-time Vidale–Wolfe model with scalar and relatively simple nonlinear dynamics. In cases where the dynamics are more complex (e.g., nonlinear, vector), numerical optimization software has to be used in order to compute the one step ahead optimal control.

7.2.3 ▪ Numerical examples comparing evolution of market share

This section shows the evolution of market share of the discrete-time Vidale–Wolfe model subject to OSAOC and omniscient control, using the linear and quadratic performance indices.

Comparison of one step ahead and omniscient control of market share dynamics

Figure 7.1 compares the evolution of the market share with the dynamics (7.4), subject to OSAOC and omniscient control, using the linear performance index.

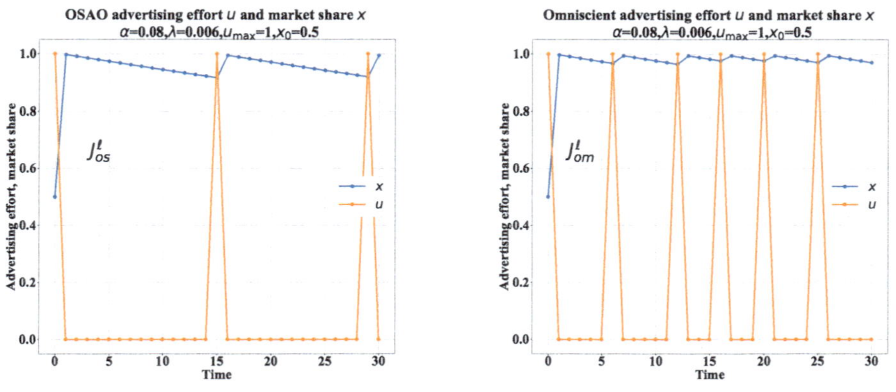

(a) Market share under one step ahead optimal control.

(b) Market share: omniscient solution.

Figure 7.1. (a) *Evolution of market share governed by* (7.4) *under OSAOC, showing the periodic bang-bang nature of the control, as calculated in* (7.8). *This periodic bang-bang nature of the control is maintained under omniscient control* (b), *although with a higher frequency.*

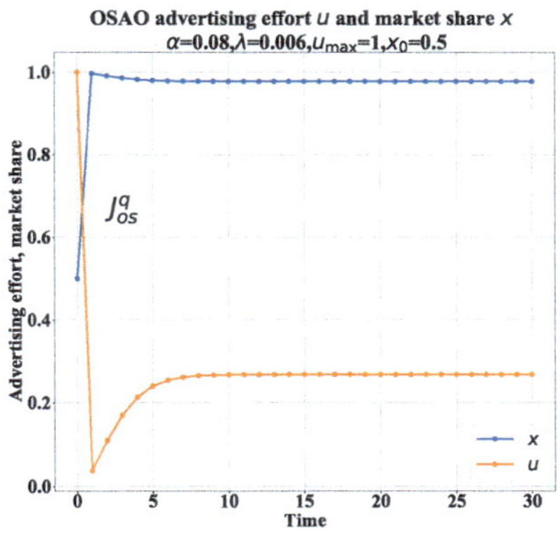

(a) Market share under one step ahead optimal control.

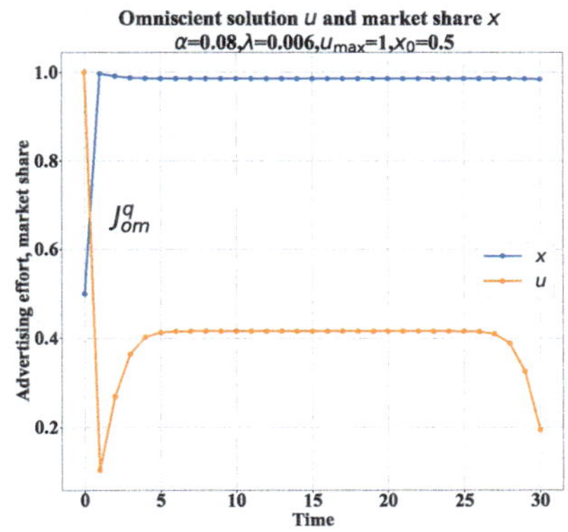

(b) Market share: omniscient solution.

Figure 7.2. (a) *Evolution of market share governed by* (7.4) *under OSAOC, showing that, for the quadratic performance index, in contrast to the case of the linear performance index, depicted in Fig.* 7.1, *the control is smooth, except for the initial transient, and then settles to the equilibrium value, calculated in* (7.9). *Under omniscient control (right panel), the qualitative nature of the control is similar, although its equilibrium value is higher. As expected, the turnpike effect towards the end of the planning horizon, is also noticeable in the omniscient case.*

Figure 7.2 compares the evolution of the market share with the dynamics (7.4), subject to OSAOC and omniscient control, using the quadratic performance index.

7.2.4 ▪ Analysis of the origin of periodic oscillations in the discrete-time Vidale–Wolfe model under one step ahead control

A Lamerey diagram [Arn92], also called a cobweb plot, is a graphical tool to investigate the qualitative behavior of one-dimensional dynamical systems. Using a Lamerey diagram, it is possible to infer the long-term behavior of the dynamical system under repeated application of a map. In the context of this section, it may be defined as follows:

For a given dynamical system $x(k+1) = f(x(k))$, the plot, in the x-y plane, starts with a line of slope one ($y = x$) and a curve representing $y = f(x)$. The **procedure to construct the Lamerey diagram of the map** f (i.e., the behavior of the initial condition $x(0)$ under repeated applications of the map f) is as follows:

1. Find the point $(x(0), f(x(0)))$.
2. Join this point to the diagonal line with a horizontal line segment to arrive at the point $(f(x(0)), f(x(0)))$.
3. Plot vertically from the point $(f(x(0)), f(x(0)))$ on the diagonal to the function curve, obtaining the point with coordinates $(f(x(0)), f(f(x(0))))$.
4. Repeat steps 2 and 3 for as many iterations of the map as required.

On the Lamerey diagram, a stable equilibrium corresponds to an inward spiral of the graph constructed using the above procedure, while an unstable equilibrium is an outward one. It follows from the definition of an equilibrium that these spirals will be centered at a point where the diagonal line $y = x$ crosses the function graph. A period 2 orbit is represented by a rectangle, while cycles of larger periods produce further, more complex closed loops. Loosely speaking, an orbit is said to be stable if all trajectories originating "inside" it converge to it (spiraling "outwards"), and all trajectories originating "outside" it also converge to it (spiraling "inwards"). For more details on Lamerey or cobweb diagrams, as well as formal methods of analysis, instead of the graphical analysis referred to here, see [Dev92].

From a geometric analysis of possible Lamerey diagrams for the discrete Vidale–Wolfe model, the picture which emerges is as follows.

The **discrete-time Vidale–Wolfe dynamics**, under **OSAOC with linear performance index**, has the following **possible behaviors**:
• If $\alpha < 0.5$ and $\lambda < \frac{\alpha}{1-\alpha}$, then period 4 oscillations occur.
• If $\alpha < 0.5$ and $\lambda = \frac{\alpha}{1-\alpha}$, period 2 oscillations occur.
• If $\alpha < 0.5$ and $\lambda > \frac{\alpha}{1-\alpha}$, then damped oscillations occur converging to an equilibrium at $x_{\text{eq}} = \frac{1}{1+\lambda}$.
• If $0.5 < \alpha \leq 1$, then period X oscillations occur (e.g., for $\lambda = 0.1, \alpha = 0.6, X = 10$).
• If $\alpha > 1$, then exponential decay to the equilibrium $x_{\text{eq}} = 0$ occurs, for all $\lambda \in [0, 1]$.

Numerical examples: Lamerey diagrams and periodic orbits

This section shows examples of Lamerey diagrams and corresponding periodic orbits for two choices of the parameters α and λ, in Figs. 7.3 and 7.4.

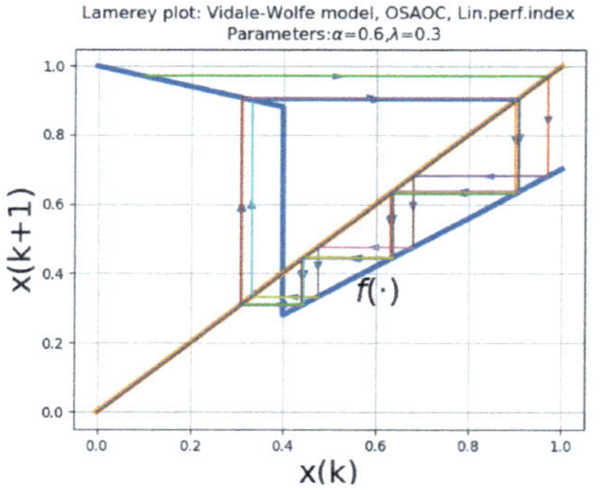

(a) Lamerey plot for parameters in the figure title.

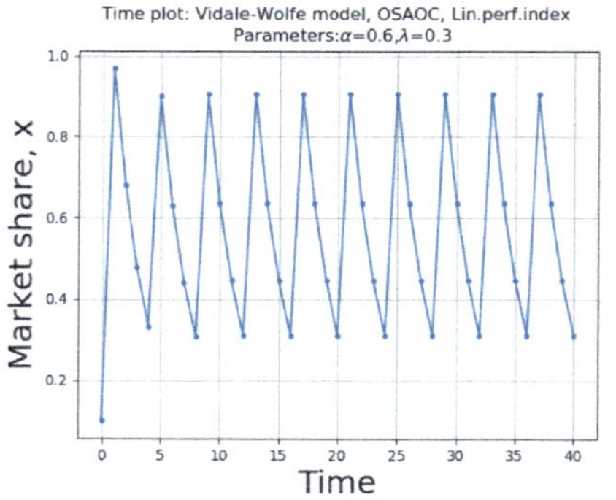

(b) Time plot for parameters in the figure title.

Figure 7.3. (a) *The heavy blue line is the graph of the function f, defined by the Vidale–Wolfe dynamics under one step ahead optimal control, used with the line $x(k+1) = x(k)$, in order to plot the Lamerey diagram in accordance with the procedure given in section* 7.2.4. (b) *Time plot of the market share x showing its periodic behavior.*

7.3 ▪ A three population model of monopolistic market share dynamics

One possibility of explaining the deficit or missing market share, alluded to in section 7.1, is to assume that it has gone to a competing brand and model the second brand as well, i.e., a duopoly instead of a monopoly. This was, to some extent, the route taken by Deal [Dea79] who proposed the following.

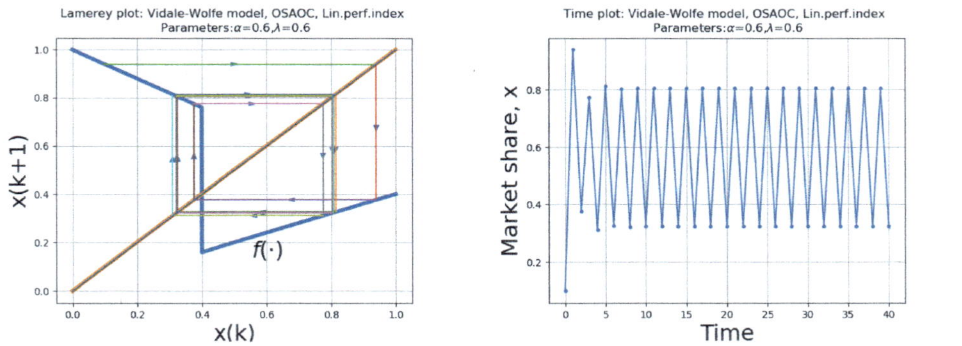

(a) Lamerey plot for parameters in the figure title. (b) Time plot for parameters in the figure title.

Figure 7.4. (a) *The heavy blue line is the graph of the function f, defined by the Vidale–Wolfe dynamics under one step ahead optimal control, used with the line $x(k+1) = x(k)$, in order to plot the Lamerey diagram in accordance with the procedure given in section* 7.2.4. (b) *Time plot of the market share x showing its periodic behavior.*

The duopolistic generalization of the Vidale–Wolfe model, written here in discrete-time:

$$x_1(k+1) = x_1(k) + u_1(1 - x_1(k) - x_2(k)) - \lambda_1 x_1(k), \tag{7.10}$$
$$x_2(k+1) = x_2(k) + u_2(1 - x_1(k) - x_2(k)) - \lambda_2 x_2(k), \tag{7.11}$$

where, for $i = 1, 2$, x_i (resp., u_i) denotes the market share (resp., advertising policy) of firm i and λ_i are the respective defection rates.

Note, however, that even in Deal's generalization of the Vidale–Wolfe model, the two defection rates do not solve the mystery of the "missing" market share, since it is easy to show that, under constant advertising effort, the equilibrium market shares of the two brands do not add up to one.

Also in the context of a duopoly, Kimball [Kim57] cited the Lanchester model as being a successful model to describe the effect of advertising, when the market is assumed to be "saturated" (i.e., the market shares of the two brands sum to unity).

The **Lanchester model in discrete time**, for the **saturated market**, is written as follows:

$$x_1(k+1) = x_1(k) - \rho_2 u_2 x_1(k) + \rho_1 u_1 x_2(k), \tag{7.12}$$
$$x_2(k+1) = x_2(k) + \rho_2 u_2 x_1(k) - \rho_1 u_1 x_2(k). \tag{7.13}$$

Observe that the Lanchester model is really a unidimensional model, since the market share of one brand is always the complement of the share of the other brand. In fact, Little [Lit79], seeking to unify the Vidale–Wolfe and Lanchester models [Lan16], observed that, for the continuous-time models, the substitutions $x_2 = 1 - x_1$, $\rho_2 u_2 = \lambda$, and $\rho_1 = 1$, in the Lanchester model make it identical to the Vidale–Wolfe model. He concluded that the Lanchester model is a generalization of the Vidale–Wolfe model that considers competition. Another interpretation is that the decay term $(-\lambda x)$ in the Vidale–Wolfe model, which is only justified in the original paper [VW57] as a sales decay term, is actually a way of identifying the deficit or missing market share as explicitly belonging to the competing brand.

The most popular models are still those proposed by Vidale and Wolfe for monopolies [VW57], and Lanchester [Lan16] for duopolies. However, each model has limitations: the Vidale–Wolfe model does not consider competition explicitly, whereas the Lanchester model does not consider behavior of the firms before the so-called market saturation is reached.

Moving forward 60 years in time, El Ouardighi et al. write the following in the context of Word-of-Mouth (WOM) and contagion models; we quote from [El +16]:

> As a marketing instrument dedicated to attracting new customers and, ultimately, brand image building, advertising-dependent WOM may interact with channels of social influence that are not under the firm's direct control. Such channels, termed autonomous WOM, have recently gained much attention in the marketing literature, notably because of the development of online product ratings. While advertising-dependent WOM involves satisfied current customers only, autonomous WOM includes both negative WOM of dissatisfied current customers and positive WOM of satisfied current customers. Both influences can significantly influence the effectiveness of advertising-dependent WOM and thus the attraction of new customers.

It is in this context of considerable current interest that a new model for market share dynamics of a single brand under advertising was proposed in [KB18], with the objective of unifying the Vidale–Wolfe and Lanchester models, but also including WOM effects. The primary objective of the proposed model is to understand the dynamics of the market share of a particular brand which advertises and is subject to WOM effects, from defectors, who oppose the brand, but have not necessarily become consumers of a competing brand. To contextualize, in today's world of social networks, it is common to have dissatisfied consumers of a particular brand making negative publicity with regard to it (thus referred to as *defectors* henceforth), but who do not necessarily endorse a competitor. Similarly, it is also common to have uncommitted or undecided potential customers of the brand who might interact with either brand customers or defectors and be influenced by them, without seeking to influence them.

Section 7.3.1 gives the mathematical formulation of a discrete-time version of the model in [KB18].

7.3.1 ▪ Discrete-time dynamics of the three population model for a monopoly

This section details a mathematical model of market share dynamics under advertising. The model is inspired by Lotka–Volterra type models of three interacting populations of customers: one that is satisfied with the brand that the model seeks to describe, its market share at time k (fraction of the total customer population) being denoted $x_b(k)$, the fraction that of defectors from the brand, denoted $x_d(k)$, and the fraction of undecided customers being denoted $x_i(k)$. For brevity, the three populations are referred to as brand, defector, and undecided.

The **three population model for monopoly market share dynamics** is as follows:

$$x_b(k+1) = x_b(k) + k_b u + k_{bi} x_b(k) x_i(k) - k_{bd} x_b(k) x_d(k), \tag{7.14}$$
$$x_d(k+1) = x_d(k) - k_d u + k_{di} x_d(k) x_i(k) + k_{bd} x_b(k) x_d(k), \tag{7.15}$$
$$x_i(k+1) = x_i(k) + (-k_b + k_d) u - k_{di} x_d(k) x_i(k) - k_{bi} x_b(k) x_i(k) \tag{7.16}$$

with u denoting **positive advertising effort by the brand.**

The five model parameters ($k_b, k_d, k_{bd}, k_{bi}, k_{di}$) and u are discussed and interpreted in section 7.3.1 below. Observe that (7.14)–(7.16) are set up such that

$$x_b(k+1) + x_d(k+1) + x_i(k+1) = x_b(k) + x_d(k) + x_i(k)\ \forall\, k. \tag{7.17}$$

Thus, if initial conditions are chosen such that $x_b(0) + x_d(0) + x_i(0) = 1$, then the market share fractions must sum to unity at all times, i.e., this model assumes that the advertising (or control) effort u made by the brand causes an increase in its fraction (market share) with corresponding decreases in the undecided and possibly also in the defector fractions. Furthermore, it is assumed that the undecided population is analogous to a prey and subject to predation by both the brand and defector (predator) populations . In analogy with Lotka–Volterra type models, it is assumed that all predation terms are proportional to the interactions between the populations. Such an assumption is also similar to the one made in WOM or electronic WOM (eWOM) models [El +16], and also in competitive dynamics of web sites [MH03]. Once again, increases or decreases in a given population must be matched by corresponding changes (decreases or increases) in the others, in order that (7.17) hold true for all time. Observe that (7.17) implies that the trajectory of any one of the populations x_b, x_d, x_i can be inferred from the trajectories of the other two. In particular, in what follows, attention will be focused on the brand and defector dynamics (7.14), (7.15).

The interaction graph between the three populations is shown in Fig. 7.5.

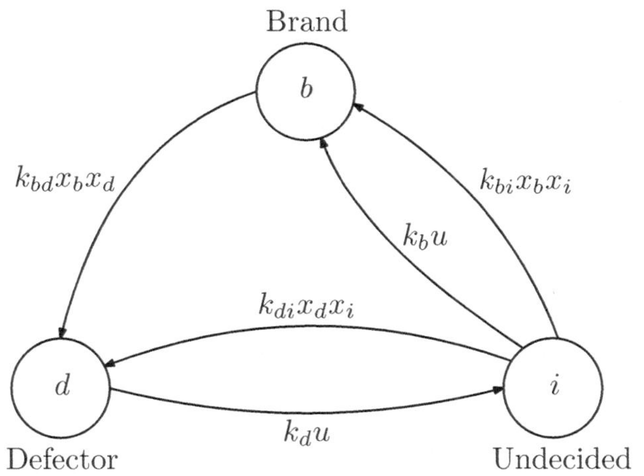

Figure 7.5. *The graph showing interaction between the brand, defector, and undecided populations (nodes). Arrows are labeled with a term that indicates the rate at which the population at the tail of the arrow is being depleted and, correspondingly, the population at the head of the arrow is growing. This is in accordance with the sign of each term in* (7.14)–(7.16).

Interpretation of model parameters

We describe the model by discussing its five parameters in words and explain our choices of sign for each one.

- k_b is the parameter describing the effect of brand advertising on its market share, and advertising effort u is positive. It is reasonable to assume that k_b is positive, and that its magnitude expresses the extent to which brand advertising is successful in increasing the brand market share x_b. In the terminology of [El +16], the term k_bu is the advertising-dependent WOM term.

- k_{bi} is assumed to be a nonnegative parameter, reflecting the assumption that, when a WOM interaction between brand and undecided customers occurs, the outcome is a conversion of undecided to brand. The rate of conversion is determined by the magnitude of the parameter k_{bi}. Note that the undecided customer is assumed to be passive, i.e., can be influenced by brand customers, but does not influence them. This is in line with the basic assumption that the goal of advertising is to persuade the undecided customers to buy the advertised brand product. The term k_{bi} is an autonomous WOM term, in the language of [El +16].

- k_{bd} is the parameter associated with the autonomous WOM term $k_{bd}x_bx_d$. Its sign is positive, assuming that defectors may cause brand consumers to defect when mutual encounters occur but that the converse is not true (which accounts for the absence of an arrow from node b to node d in Fig. 7.5).

- k_d is a nonnegative parameter that appears in the advertising-dependent WOM term $-k_du$. This term models the effect that brand advertising might have on defectors. For example, if k_d is zero, brand advertising has no effect on defectors in terms of convincing them to become undecided. A small value of k_d models a situation in which a sufficiently large brand advertising effort u could cause defectors to become undecided, thus becoming susceptible to a subsequent transition to either the brand population or a return transition to the defector population.

- k_{di} is a nonnegative parameter that appears in the autonomous WOM term $k_{di}x_dx_i$, modeling the interaction between the defector and undecided populations, in a manner entirely analogous to the term k_{bi}.

This model of market share dynamics under advertising and WOM interactions accounts explicitly for the so-called decay term, modeling it as the effect of WOM predation by defecting customers. Advertising is deemed to affect not only brand customers, but also to attract undecided ones as well as to possibly make defectors undecided, when it exceeds a certain level.

One important requirement of market share models is that all n market shares x_i, $i = 1, \ldots, n$, must add up to unity and remain nonnegative ($x_i \geq 0$ for all i), which defines a region in $\mathbb{R}^n$, denoted T. Indeed, the region T should remain invariant under any proposed market share dynamics. For the Vidale–Wolfe dynamics (7.4), it is easy to show that, for all $u, \lambda \in [0, 1]$, the market share $x(k) \in [0, 1]$ (which is invariance of T in this one-dimensional case).

In the continuous-time case of a three population model of market share dynamics [KB18], invariance of T is explicitly ensured by the use of projected dynamics. This is also necessary for the discrete-time version (7.14), (7.15), (7.16), however, there are some important differences between the projection operator used in the continuous-time case and the one appropriate for the discrete-time case. This is the subject of the next section.

7.4 ▪ Projected dynamical systems in discrete time

Observe that, in any market share dynamics model, the market share fractions x_i must be nonnegative and sum to at most one. In this section, the notation, x_1, x_2 is used, instead of x_b, x_d, with a view to using the definitions in this section in Chapter 8 as well. Let T denote the closed convex set (triangle in the positive quadrant x_1-x_2) defined as follows:

$$T := \{(x_1, x_2) : x_1 \geq 0, x_2 \geq 0, x_1 + x_2 \leq 1\}. \tag{7.18}$$

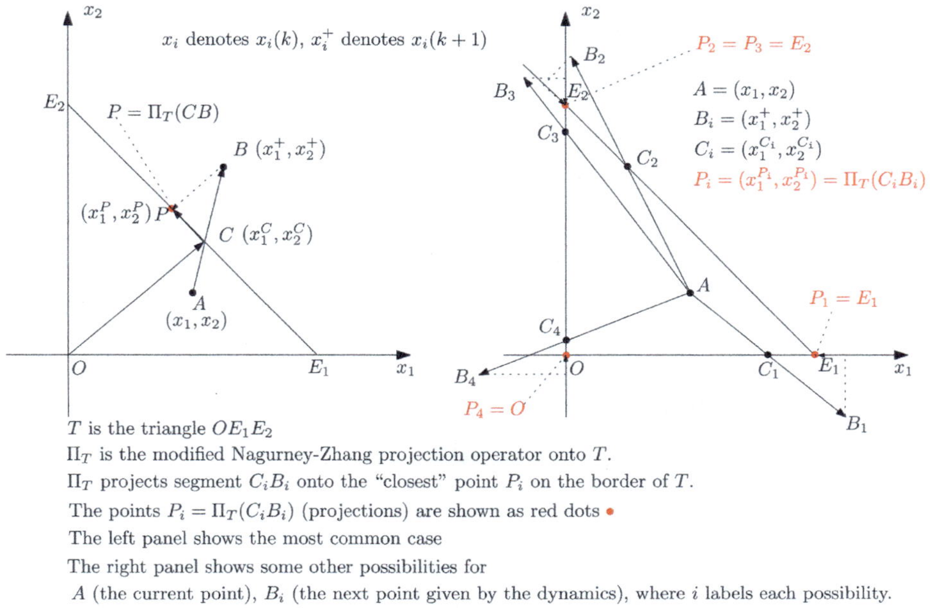

Figure 7.6. *Detailing the modification of the Nagurney–Zhang projection for the discrete-time three population market share dynamics model.*

In other words, for the market share models considered in this chapter (and the next), the complete set of possible states $X_1 \times X_2$ is actually T.

Let $\mathbf{x}$ denote (x_1, x_2), $\mathbf{u}$ denote (u_1, u_2), and $\mathbf{f}(\mathbf{x}, \mathbf{u})$ denote $(x_(k+1), x_2(k+1))$, i.e., the vector of right-hand sides of (7.14), (7.15). In order to ensure the invariance of the triangle T, it is necessary to consider the projected version of (7.14), (7.15), using the notion of projected dynamical systems, which were defined for continuous-time systems in [NZ96].

In the discrete-time case, a modification of the projection mechanism is needed and is defined in Fig. 7.6. The essential difference with respect to the continuous-time case is that there will not be, in general, an exact instant at which a trajectory, which is in the interior of the triangle T, crosses the border of T, creating the need to project onto the border of T. In the discrete-time case, the situation depicted in Fig. 7.6 (left panel) may arise, namely, that the point $A = (x_1(k), x_2(k))$ is in the interior of T and the next point determined by the dynamics $B = (x_1^+(k), x_2^+(k)) := (x_1(k+1), x_2(k+1))$ is outside T. In analogy with the continuous-time case [NZ96], it is necessary to define the projected point in such a way that it lies within T (actually, on the frontier of T). In order to do this, referring once again to the left panel of Fig. 7.6, project the segment CB, where C is the intersection of AB with the line E_1E_2, orthogonally onto the line E_1E_2, since this is the line "crossed" by the trajectory when it leaves the triangle T. The right panel shows some other cases that might arise and the resulting projections. Let $\Pi_T(\mathbf{x}, \mathbf{f}(\mathbf{x}, \mathbf{u}))$ denote the projection with respect to T just defined, noting that Π_T takes as arguments two points: the current point, $\mathbf{x}$ and the next point, $\mathbf{f}(\mathbf{x}, \mathbf{u})$. The projected dynamical system corresponding to (7.14), (7.15) can be written as

$$\mathbf{x}(k+1) = \Pi_T\left(\mathbf{x}(k), \mathbf{f}(\mathbf{x}(k), \mathbf{u}(k))\right). \tag{7.19}$$

Given the definition of the projection operator Π_T, the discrete-time dynamical system (7.14), (7.15) should more precisely be thought of as a projected dynamical system defined as follows.

The **projected dynamical system** for market share dynamics is

$$\mathbf{x}(k+1) = \Pi_T\left(\mathbf{x}(k), \mathbf{f}(\mathbf{x}(k), u(k))\right), \tag{7.20}$$

where $\mathbf{x}(k) := (x_b(k), x_d(k))$ and

$$\mathbf{f}(\mathbf{x}(k), u(k)) := \begin{bmatrix} x_b(k) + k_b u + k_{bi} x_b(k) x_i(k) - k_{bd} x_b(k) x_d(k) \\ x_d(k) - k_d u + k_{di} x_d(k) x_i(k) + k_{bd} x_b(k) x_d(k) \end{bmatrix},$$

i.e., $\mathbf{f}$ is the vector of the right-hand sides of (7.14), (7.15).

7.5 ▪ One step ahead control aiming at a target market share applied to the three population model

This section compares a one step ahead optimal control approach with a switching control for the model of market share dynamics (7.20), discussed in section 7.3.1. Let the target market share for the brand be x_b^* with $x_b^* \leq 1$. Given an advertising effort (control) $u(k)$ at time k and the state $x_b(k+1)$ arising from the application of this advertising effort, as well as positive weights α, β, the index $J_{os}^r(u(k))$ is defined as

$$J_{os}^r(u(k)) := \alpha u(k) + \beta(x_b(k+1) - x_b^*)^2. \tag{7.21}$$

It is also assumed that the control effort is constrained, i.e., $u(k) \in \mathcal{U} := [0, u_{\max}]$, for all k.

The **one step ahead optimal control of market share** is formulated as follows:

$$\begin{aligned} &\text{maximize } J_{os}^r(u(k)), \text{ by choice of } u(k) \\ &\text{subject to the dynamics (7.20)} \\ &\text{and the control constraint } 0 \leq u(k) \leq u_{\max}. \end{aligned} \tag{7.22}$$

7.5.1 ▪ Numerical example of market share dynamics for the three population model

This section shows a numerical example of market share dynamics for the three population model, with parameters specified in Table 7.1, under one step ahead optimal control that aims at achieving a target market share.

Table 7.1. *Parameters for the numerical example of a three population model of market dynamics.*

k_b	k_d	k_{bi}	k_{bd}	k_{di}
2	1	0.03	0.04	0.05

The initial conditions are $x_b(1) = 0.2$, $x_d(1) = 0.4$, $x_i(1) = 0.4$ for the brand, defector, and undecided populations, respectively. The target equilibria are 0.7 (70%) of the market share for the brand, and 0 for the undecided population, so that the defector population is expected to be kept at 0.3 (30%). The maximum advertising effort is normalized to 4 units. The weights in (7.21) are chosen as $\alpha = 5$, $\beta = 50$.

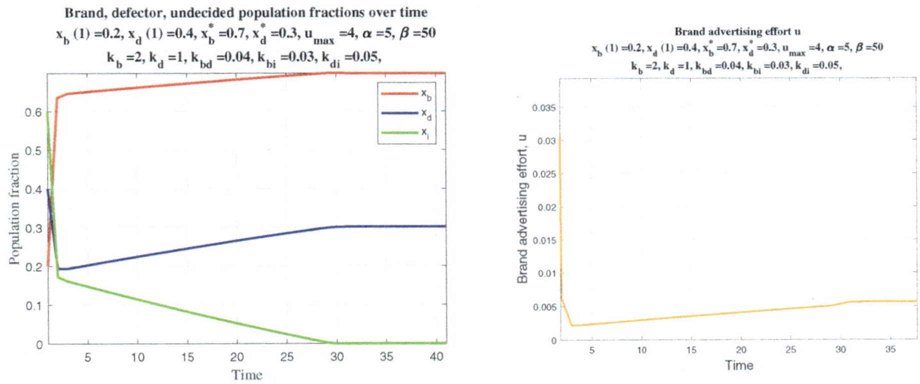

(a) Time plots of brand, defector, undecided population fractions.

(b) Advertising effort over time.

Figure 7.7. (a) *Observe that the growth in the brand population fraction is initially fast, corresponding to a large initial advertising effort shown in* (b)*. The one step ahead optimal advertising effort drops to a low value quickly, causing a slow increase of the brand population fraction to the target value of* 0.7*. A zoom has been applied to the plot in* (b)*, to show more detail in the advertising effort evolution.*

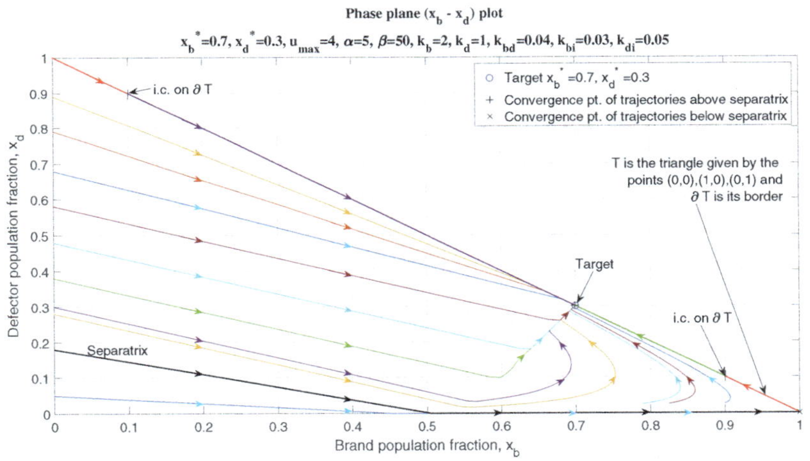

Figure 7.8. *Phase plane plot of brand, defector population fractions. The black trajectory is a separatrix in the sense that for initial defector population fractions above it, the one step ahead optimal control, obtained by solving* (7.22)*, is able to achieve the target market share* x_b^* $(= 0.7)$ *for this example. For initial defector population fractions below it, trajectories converge to the point* $(1, 0)$*, i.e., the one step ahead optimal control achieves full market share* $(= 1)$ *and the defector population goes to zero.*

Figure 7.7(a) shows the evolution of the brand, defector and undecided populations over time. Figure 7.7(b) shows the advertising effort, starting with the maximum value, but then stabilizing at a small value as the brand population approaches its target. Finally, Fig. 7.8 is a phase plane plot illustrating the fact that the equilibrium $(0.7, 0.3)$ (brand, defector) is attained from all initial conditions above the separatrix in the nonnegative quadrant. Observe also that the point $(1, 0)$ is a saddle point for the projected dynamics under one step ahead optimal control, with the horizontal axis as the stable manifold and the segment of the border of the triangle T between the point $(1, 0)$ and the target $(0.7, 0.3)$ being the unstable manifold.

7.6 ▪ Vidale–Wolfe model with delayed forgetting of advertising

We quote the following from Aravindakshan and Nair [AN11]:

> Extant models posit that awareness declines immediately and gradually after the cessation of advertising, whereas anecdotal evidence from managers suggests awareness stays constant for a while and then decays rapidly. This pattern arises because consumers remember advertisements for a finite time before they forget. Hence, we extend advertising models by incorporating the memory for ads. We conceptualize the role of memory as "delayed forgetting of ads."

The continuous-time model introduced by Aravindakshan and Nair [AN11] is as follows:

$$\dot{x} = ru(t)\,(1 - x(t)) - \lambda x(t - \tau). \tag{7.23}$$

Using the forward Euler method, the **discrete-time equivalent of the Vidale–Wolfe model with delayed forgetting of advertising** is

$$x(k+1) = x(k) + h\,(ru(k)\,(1 - x(k)) - \lambda x(k - \tau))\,. \tag{7.24}$$

The linear performance index to be maximized for one step ahead optimal control is chosen as follows,

$$J^{\ell}_{osa}(k) = x(k+1) - \alpha u(k), \tag{7.25}$$

where α is a nonnegative weighting coefficient that permits the manager to trade off market share against advertising expenditure. Reducing advertising expenditure is given priority by choosing a larger value of α.

Correspondingly, the quadratic performance index to be maximized for one step ahead is chosen as follows,

$$J^{q}_{osa}(k) = x(k+1)^2 - \alpha u(k)^2, \tag{7.26}$$

where, again, α is a nonnegative weighting coefficient that permits the manager to trade off market share against advertising expenditure. Maximizing market share is given priority by choosing a smaller value of α.

The **one step ahead optimal control problem for the Vidale–Wolfe model with delayed forgetting** can be written as

$$\begin{array}{l} \max_{0 \le u \le u_{\max}} J^{i}_{osa},\ i = \ell, q \\ \text{subject to the dynamics (7.24).} \end{array} \tag{7.27}$$

Remark. For the linear performance index, $i = \ell$, OSAOCP (7.27) reduces to a linear program, whereas, for $i = q$, to a quadratic program. Both are easily solved using optimization software.

7.6.1 ▪ Vidale–Wolfe model with delayed forgetting under one step ahead optimal control: Numerical examples

This section gives numerical examples of the Vidale–Wolfe model (7.24) under one step ahead optimal control. The results, of solving the OSAOCP (7.27) for the linear and quadratic

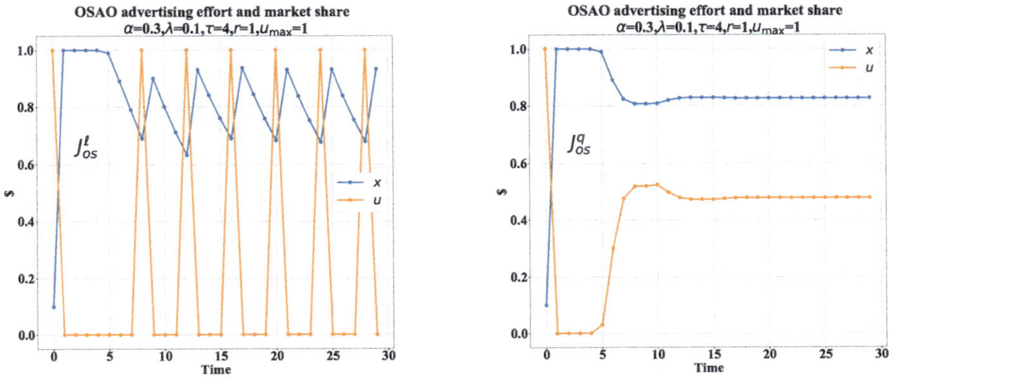

(a) Market share x and advertising effort u for OSAOC with linear performance index.

(b) Market share x and advertising effort u for OSAOC with quadratic performance index.

Figure 7.9. (a) *For the linear performance index, after the initial transient, the one step ahead optimal advertising effort is of the on-off type.* (b) *For a quadratic performance index, the one step ahead optimal advertising effort is initially large, then drops to zero and gradually rises to and remains at a steady state value.*

performance indices defined above, are shown in Fig. 7.9. The parameters are as follows: initial time $k = 1$, final time $K_f = 30$, initial market share $x(0) = 0.1$, advertising cost coefficient $\alpha = 0.3$, sales decay coefficient $\lambda = 0.1$, the delay in forgetting $\tau = 4$, the response coefficient $r = 1$, and the maximum value of the advertising budget $u_{\max} = 1$.

Figure 7.9(a) shows the evolution of market share x and advertising effort u for the Vidale–Wolfe model with delayed forgetting of advertising, using one step ahead optimal control with the linear objective function. The effect of delayed forgetting can be seen every time the advertising effort drops to zero. For example, between instants $k = 10$ and $k = 13$, the market share decays due to the sales decay coefficient λ, but does not drop to zero immediately, even though no control is being applied. Overall, the on-off nature of the control and the market share evolution are similar to the ones that occur in the case without delayed forgetting.

Figure 7.9(b) shows the evolution of market share x and advertising effort u for the Vidale–Wolfe model with delayed forgetting of advertising, using one step ahead optimal control with the quadratic objective function. In contrast with Fig. 7.9(a), note the smoothing effect of the quadratic performance index: the control is now smooth, not on-off, as in the corresponding undelayed case.

7.7 ▪ Chapter summary

This chapter has shown that one step ahead optimal control can be applied to design and implement an advertising effort to obtain a target market share for Vidale–Wolfe and related models of market share dynamics. These models are nonlinear, but the one step ahead approach is still easily applicable. The origin of the oscillatory behavior of the market share dynamics in the Vidale–Wolfe model under one step ahead optimal control with a linear performance index is explained using Lamerey diagrams. Finally, the discrete-time Vidale–Wolfe model with delayed forgetting of advertising, recently proposed in the continuous-time case in the literature, is also subjected to one step ahead control and, except for the transient due to the delay, the results are similar to the ones obtained for the classical Vidale–Wolfe model.

Notes and references

Optimal control of the Vidale–Wolfe model with a time-varying market was studied in [Edi97], building on earlier work of Sethi [Set73].

The theme of modeling or measuring the interaction between sets of individuals in networks has been explored using various techniques: Markov processes [Paa+17], random graphs [KC16], and text analysis [SE14], to cite just a few. In [KB18] the interaction between any pair of populations is modeled by a multiplicative term, familiar from the Lotka–Volterra predator-prey models. These multiplicative interaction terms account for the so-called autonomous WOM effects. The effect of advertising, also referred to as advertising-dependent WOM [El +16] is modeled by a positive term, similar to the approach in the Nerlove–Arrow model [NA62]. However, unlike the classical Vidale–Wolfe model, a constant advertising effort may lead to three different outcomes: an equilibrium between satisfied and dissatisfied customers, or conquest of the full market share by either the satisfied customers or defectors. The main theorem in the continuous-time case [KB18] can be summarized by saying that, if predatory WOM interactions predominate, then the equilibrium in which the brand market share goes to zero, can be avoided by applying a suitably large advertising effort, which causes all trajectories to converge to the (brand favorable) equilibrium $(1, 0)$. The one step ahead optimal control, which alternates between no advertising effort and maximum advertising effort, can result in a desired equilibrium in which neither brand nor defector market shares become one or zero. The progression of behavior from a simple winner-take-all (WTA) model (in which the defectors take all) to one in which the brand market share is less than one, and finally to one in which the brand takes all is achieved by the reasonable method of increasing advertising effort. This kind of WTA behavior, with flips between winners and losers, was also observed in [MH03] in the context of varying the strength of the interaction coefficient, rather than the advertising effort.

The definition of a discrete-time projected dynamical system is made for the first time, in this context, in this book, to the best of the authors' knowledge.

Chapter 8

Competitive duopolies: Market share dynamics under advertising

This chapter studies the extension of the Vidale–Wolfe model to duopolies: the first such extension was made by Deal [Dea79], in the continuous-time case, and this model is thus referred to as the Vidale–Wolfe–Deal model. In this model, two firms compete for market share, the dynamics of which is described by a pair of differential equations, under the assumption that each firm's advertising effort acts only on the undecided customers (i.e., those who are not already customers of either of the competing firms).

Interpreting firms as players competing for market share, the two player decision making problem of allocating advertising expenditure or effort, is referred to as a game. The game is called dynamic if the order in which the decisions are made is important, and is noncooperative if each player involved pursues its own interests which are partly conflicting with interests of the others [BO99]. Furthermore, since a difference (resp., differential) equation in discrete time (resp., in continuous time) describes the evolution of the underlying decision process, the adjective differential is used to qualify the game. Strictly speaking, in the discrete-time case, one should refer to a difference game, but since this terminology is not common in the literature, the term *dynamic game* will be used in this book, and some basic definitions pertaining to dynamic games will be recalled in section 8.2.

We quote the following from Deal [Dea79] (at length, since it describes the objectives of this chapter very clearly)

> The natural form of a differential game explicitly considers the two critical aspects of an economic model ... – competition and dynamics. In management applications of differential games, each competitor attempts to optimize his criterion of performance by manipulating a set of inputs to a common dynamic economic system. There is direct recognition of the necessity of operating in an environment in which some of the determinants of an entity's behavior are controlled by opponents. The dynamic reaction of the market system to changes in the values of the variables controllable by the firms and those that describe the state of the environment must be defined and modeled by each of the competitors. Consequently, rather than ignoring these competitive and dynamic components of economic problems, differential games thrust the analysis of these elements on the investigator. It is intended that the construction and manipulation of ... models provide marketing academics and managers with a tool through which a more complete and satisfactory understanding of competitive dynamic marketing systems is possible.

In the literature, the Vidale–Wolfe–Deal model has mainly been studied in the continuous-time case, from a theoretical viewpoint, using the techniques of differential games. It is often difficult to obtain analytical or even computational results using the differential game approach, owing to the complexity of solving Hamilton–Jacobi–Bellman equations. The main objective in this chapter is to show that the one step ahead optimal control is applicable, and easily computable, in the discrete-time context, provided that the competition is assumed to occur according to a given procedure: for example, with firms alternating in the computation of their optimal actions. This chapter studies the Vidale–Wolfe–Deal model, as well as three more general models, in which advertising effort can affect both customers who are undecided as well as those who patronize the competing brand, using the one step ahead optimal control approach.

The sections that follow describe the main ingredients of a discrete-time dynamic game. First, the models used to describe market share dynamics are introduced and discussed briefly, together with the definition of possible performance indices that are relevant. This is followed by a quick recapitulation of some basic definitions of dynamic games, as well as the introduction of two basic procedures of game playing that define alternating and simultaneous modes of play. The concluding section gives numerical examples of some sample cases. Since there are many different choices of models, performance indices, game playing procedures, and parameters, it is clear that, combinatorially speaking, there is potentially a large number of cases to be investigated. However, the scope of this chapter is not to make an exhaustive study, but rather to showcase some of the most illustrative or representative cases.

8.1 ▪ Models of market share dynamics for duopolies

This section introduces discrete-time versions of four models of market share dynamics, referred to by the initials of the authors who first proposed the models. In all four models, x_i denotes the market share of firm i and u_i the corresponding advertising effort, while λ_i denotes the market share decay rate of firm i. Other parameters, specific to each model are defined when it becomes necessary. Performance indices applicable to all three models are also defined.

The Vidale–Wolfe–Deal (VWD) model

Discrete-time Vidale–Wolfe–Deal dynamics for two firms, whose market shares are represented by the variables x_1 and x_2, are as follows,

$$x_1(k+1) = x_1(k) + b_1(1 - x_1(k) - x_2(k))u_1(k) - \lambda_1 x_1(k), \tag{8.1}$$
$$x_2(k+1) = x_2(k) + b_2(1 - x_1(k) - x_2(k))u_2(k) - \lambda_2 x_2(k), \tag{8.2}$$

where $u_i(k) \geq 0$ for $k = 1, \ldots, K_f$ and $\lambda_i \geq 0, i = 1, 2$. The nonnegative b_i is referred to as the market share response parameter.

The Aliaga–Bhaya–Kaszkurewicz (ABK) model

An alternative proposal for dynamics of market shares in a duopoly was made in [ABK20] and the **discrete-time ABK dynamics** is as follows,

$$x_1(k+1) = x_1(k) + b_1(1 - x_1(k))u_1(k) - k_1 x_1(k) u_2(k) - \lambda_1 x_1(k), \tag{8.3}$$
$$x_2(k+1) = x_1(k) + b_2(1 - x_2(k))u_2(k) - k_2 x_2(k) u_1(k) - \lambda_2 x_2(k), \tag{8.4}$$

where $u_i(k) \geq 0$ for $k = 1, \ldots, K_f$ and $\lambda_i \geq 0, i = 1, 2$. The nonnegative b_i is referred to as the market share response parameter and the nonnegative k_i as the predation parameter, $i = 1, 2$.

The Deal–Sethi–Thompson (DST) model

Discrete-time Deal–Sethi–Thompson dynamics for two firms, whose market shares are represented by the variables x_1 and x_2 are as follows,

$$\begin{aligned} x_1(k+1) &= x_1(k) + b_1(1 - x_1(k) - x_2(k))u_1(k) \\ &\quad + e_1(x_1(k) + x_2(k))(u_1(k) - u_2(k)) - \lambda_1 x_1(k), \end{aligned} \tag{8.5}$$

$$\begin{aligned} x_2(k+1) &= x_2(k) + b_2(1 - x_1(k) - x_2(k))u_2(k) \\ &\quad + e_2(x_1(k) + x_2(k))(u_2(k) - u_1(k)) - \lambda_2 x_2(k), \end{aligned} \tag{8.6}$$

where $u_i(k) \geq 0$ for $k = 1, \ldots, K_f$ and $\lambda_i \geq 0, i = 1, 2$. The nonnegative b_i is referred to as the market share response parameter, and the nonnegative e_i as the excess advertising effect parameter.

8.1.1 ▪ Brief comparative discussion of duopoly market share models

As pointed out by Deal [Dea79], the time-varying aspects that must be treated in a market share model must include the market share response to advertising expenditures, as well as the possibility of diminishing returns to cumulative advertising expenditures. The four models considered above deal with these issues in different ways. There are several surveys [Eri95; FHS94; HLL12; Jør82] and even book length expositions [Eri03; JZ04] which propose different classifications of these models to which the reader is referred for greater detail. The discussion below is limited to a brief description of the main features of each model.

The VWD model (8.1)–(8.2) is the simplest model since it does not have a competitive term and the competitor's advertising effort has no direct effect on a firm's market share. However, the presence of the term $b_i(1 - x_1(k) - x_2(k))u_i(k)$ implies that if the market share of the competitor increases, the size of the unconquered market $(1 - x_1(k) - x_2(k))$ decreases, which, in turn, diminishes the effectiveness of advertising effort for the firm, thus modeling the effect of competition and diminishing returns. This is sometimes referred to as a (market) saturation effect.

The ABK model (8.3)–(8.4), introduced in continuous time in [ABK20] and inspired by population biology models, is a variant of the VWD model, which considers three populations: two composed of customers of firms 1 and 2 and a third composed of undecided customers. The new feature of the ABK model is to consider the effects of advertising on the undecided population $x_3(k)$ defined as $1 - x_1(k) - x_2(k)$. Thus, for firm 1, the saturation effect term $b_1(1 - x_1(k) - x_2(k))u_1(k)$ of the VWD model is replaced by the term $b_i(1 - x_1(k))u_1(k)$. The term which has been removed, namely, $-b_1 x_2(k)u_1(k)$ is replaced by the term $-k_1 x_1(k)u_2(k)$. The first change implies that the advertising effort of firm 1 applies to both the competitor population as well as the undecided one. The second change implies that the advertising effort of firm 2 has a direct (predatory) effect on the firm 1 population, proportional to the latter's size.

The salient feature of the DST model (8.5)–(8.6), which is another variant of the VWD model, is that it contains reaction terms of the form $e_1(u_1 - u_2)(x_1 + x_2)$ and $e_2(u_2 - u_1)(x_1 + x_2)$. To explain these terms, Deal, Sethi, and Thompson [DST79] assume that $u_1 > u_2$, so that the term $e_1(u_1 - u_2)x_2$ represents the fraction of the x_2 population that switched from firm 2 to firm

1 because of the excess advertising of firm 1. Next, the term $e_1(u_1 - u_2)x_1$ is referred to as an approximation of $e_1(u_1 - u_2)x_1x_2$. The latter term is typical of Lotka–Volterra type dynamics, representing the rate of encounters or interaction between individuals belonging to the x_1 and x_2 populations and represents the fraction of the x_2 population switching from firm 2 to firm 1 as a result of the excess advertising of firm 1. This term has, more recently, also been described as modeling WOM interaction between populations. Summing the two terms leads to the term $e_1(u_1 - u_2)(x_1 + x_2)$. Similar arguments lead to the corresponding term $e_2(u_2 - u_1)(x_1 + x_2)$ in the x_2-dynamics.

8.1.2 ▪ Performance indices for dynamic games

Performance indices of two types will be defined: the first type captures the desire to maximize market share while minimizing advertising effort, while the second establishes target market shares for each party, so that the deviation of the actual market share from the target is sought to be minimized, while simultaneously keeping the advertising effort as small as possible. From these descriptions, it is clear that these indices apply to all models of competitive duopolies. A further subdivision of the performance indices without targets is made according to whether it is linear or quadratic. In the case that targets are specified, only quadratic performance indices are considered, for simplicity.

Linear performance index without target market shares, $J_i^\ell(k)$

The **linear one step ahead performance index for firm i (with market share x_i at instant k)**, denoted $J_i^\ell(k)$, is defined as follows,

$$J_i^\ell(k) = x_i(k+1) - \alpha_i u_i(k), \tag{8.7}$$

where α_i is a nonnegative weight and the index $J_i^\ell(k)$ is to be maximized at each instant k for each i.

Quadratic performance index without target market shares, $J_i^q(k)$

The **quadratic one step ahead performance index for firm i (with market share x_i) at instant** k, denoted $J_i^q(k)$, is defined as follows,

$$J_i^q(k) = x_i(k+1)^2 - \alpha_i u_i(k)^2, \tag{8.8}$$

where α_i is a nonnegative weight and the index $J_i^q(k)$ is to be maximized at each instant k, for each i.

Quadratic performance index with target market shares specified, $J_i^r(k)$

Given target values $x_{i,ref}, i = 1, 2$, a **quadratic one step ahead performance index at instant k, denoted $J_i^r(k)$, for firm i (with market share x_i)** is defined as follows,

$$J_i^r(k) = \beta_i(x_i(k+1) - x_{i,ref})^2 + \alpha_i u_i(k)^2, \tag{8.9}$$

where α_i, β_i are positive weights and the index $J_i(k)$ is to be minimized at each instant k for each i.

8.2 ▪ Brief review of some concepts from dynamic game theory

In this section, some basic concepts from dynamic game theory are reviewed, relying mainly on [Baş87]. The main reason for doing this is to frame the discussions in this chapter in this terminology, rather than to derive rigorous results within the full formalism of game theory. Most papers, in the literature on continuous-time differential game theory, in the competitive setting, focus on defining Nash equilibria and deriving conditions for the stability of such equilibria, but this will not be the main focus of this chapter, which focuses more on showing the applicability and computational simplicity of one step ahead optimal control in the dynamic game setting.

The general formulation of a dynamic game in [Baş87] will be given below, in order to highlight some important differences which arise in the discrete-time case. The discussion will be limited, for simplicity, to two-person deterministic games, but there is no difficulty in generalizing to N-person games.

Informally, an equilibrium solution of a two-person game, either a zero or nonzero sum, is said to be stable if, after any deviation from it, unilateral optimal actions by both players cause a return to this solution. Note that this definition assumes that each player only needs to know its own performance index (cost function) as well as the most recently utilized and publicly broadcasted action of its adversary, but not its adversary's cost function.

It is pointed out in [Baş87] that not all equilibrium (saddle-point or Nash) solutions are stable. In fact, as examples given in section 8.3 show, in the discrete-time case, it may happen that a competitive two-person dynamic game results in a (stable) limit cycle, rather than a stable equilibrium, and this is, to the best of the authors' knowledge, a novel observation in the context of discrete-time two-person dynamic games.

A **two-person non-zero-sum dynamic game** in normal form (see [BO99] for a formal definition) is completely characterized by the input (also called action or strategy) spaces U_1, U_2, for players 1 and 2, who have the corresponding cost functions (also called performance indices) J_1, J_2 to be maximized. Let $u_i \in U_i, i = 1, 2$, denote the action of player i. Then $u_i^* \in U_i$ is a **noncooperative Nash equilibrium** if

$$J_1(u_1^*, u_2^*) = \max_{u_1 \in U_1} J_1(u_1, u_2^*), \tag{8.10}$$

$$J_2(u_1^*, u_2^*) = \max_{u_2 \in U_2} J_1(u_1^*, u_2). \tag{8.11}$$

In the special case in which $J_1 = -J_2$, the corresponding game is called *zero-sum* and its equilibrium is also referred to as a *saddle-point solution*.

Let L_i be the **optimal action function**, also called the optimal response function, defined as follows:

$$L_i(u_j) := \text{argmax}_{u_i \in U_i} J_i(u_i, u_j), j \neq i. \tag{8.12}$$

Note that, in the definition of L_i, u_j is assumed fixed and the optimization variable is u_i.

Using this notation, two iterative procedures can be described. The first corresponds to alternate play by each of the players and, following [Baş87], will be referred to as the *Gauss–Seidel procedure*, since it is reminiscent of the numerical iterative method with the same name. The second corresponds to simultaneous play by both players and is referred to as the Jacobi procedure, once again in analogy with the numerical iterative method.

Formally, the **Gauss–Seidel procedure** is written as

$$u_1(k+1) = L_1(u_2(k)) = \text{argmax}_{u_1 \in U_1} J_1(u_1, u_2(k)), \quad u_2(1) \in U_2 \text{ given}, \tag{8.13}$$
$$u_2(k+1) = L_2(u_1(k+1)) = \text{argmax}_{u_2 \in U_2} J_2(u_1(k+1), u_2), \quad k = 1, \ldots. \tag{8.14}$$

Note, furthermore, that the iteration (8.13)–(8.14) can be written equivalently as

$$u_2(k+1) = (L_2 \circ L_1)(u_2(k)) = L_{GS}(u_2(k)), \quad u_2(1) \in U_2 \text{ given}, \tag{8.15}$$

where $L_{GS} := L_2 \circ L_1$ is the composition of the optimal action functions.

An equilibrium solution (u_1^*, u_2^*) of the game (J_1, J_2, U_1, U_2) is *stable* if and only if it is the limit point of the sequence $\{u_1(k), u_2(k)\}_{k=1}^{\infty}$ generated by (8.13)–(8.14), or, equivalently, by (8.15), for all initial actions $u_2(1) \in U_2$. Note that this means that an equilibrium can also be thought of as a fixed point of the composite map L_{GS}. Observe also that, if $L_{GS} = L_1 \circ L_2$, this just means that the Gauss–Seidel procedure begins with firm 2 instead of firm 1, so that the initial action $u_1(1)$ must be specified, but the resulting equilibrium solution is the same as the one found using the inverted order $L_2 \circ L_1$.

The **Jacobi procedure**, in which the players compute their optimal actions simultaneously (i.e., in parallel), rather than sequentially, is written formally as follows:

$$u_1(k+1) = L_1(u_2(k)) \quad u_2(1) \text{ given}, k = 1, 2, \ldots, \tag{8.16}$$
$$u_2(k+1) = L_2(u_1(k)) \quad u_1(1) \text{ given}, k = 1, 2, \ldots. \tag{8.17}$$

Once again, defining, the map

$$L_J : U_1 \times U_2 \to U_1 \times U_2 : (u_1, u_2) \mapsto (L_1(u_2), L_2(u_1)), \tag{8.18}$$

an equilibrium solution of the Jacobi procedure is just a fixed point of the map L_J.

Finally, using the notation L_μ, where the subscript μ can be either GS or J, it may be the case that L_μ does not have a fixed point, but that L_μ^N does, for some positive integer N, where the superscript denotes N successive applications of the map L_μ. This means that the dynamic game (J_1, J_2, U_1, U_2) possesses a stable limit cycle of period N. In view of the fact that the game playing procedure (so far, Gauss–Seidel or Jacobi), determines the outcome of a game, a complete description of a two player dynamic game should include the procedure as well. In other words, thus far, a two player dynamic game is characterized by $(J_1, J_2, U_1, U_2, \mathcal{P})$, where $\mathcal{P}$ refers to the game playing procedure.

We will now introduce a slight extension of these concepts, needed for the application to dynamic games of the type that we are interested in studying in this chapter. The setting is the same as above, except that the performance indices J_i now depend on state variables $x_i \in X_i$, as well as the inputs or actions $u_i \in U_i$, where X_i is the set of all possible states for the i-dynamics, and U_i is the set of all possible inputs for the player i. The state variables, in turn, evolve according to discrete-time dynamics, involving both state and input variables. Specifically, the discrete-time dynamics are given as follows:

$$x_1(k+1) = f_1(x_1(k), x_2(k), u_1(k), u_2(k)), \quad k = 1, 2, \ldots, \tag{8.19}$$
$$x_2(k+1) = f_2(x_1(k), x_2(k), u_1(k), u_2(k)), \quad k = 1, 2, \ldots. \tag{8.20}$$

Note that the general form of the dynamics (8.19)–(8.20) is chosen so as to encompass all the market share models discussed in section 8.1. For the VWD model, the function f_i does not depend on u_j, but this is not true of the other three models. On the other hand, for the ABK model, f_i does not depend on x_j, but this is not true of the other two models. These details are important in determining the information required for the game playing procedures discussed below.

It is assumed that, at time instant k, player i wishes to choose its action $u_i(k)$ so as to maximize the performance index evaluated at the state resulting from the action $u_i(k)$, i.e., one step ahead optimization. Observe that this is a case in which one step ahead optimal control arises naturally. Given the general form of the dynamics (8.19), (8.20), and the performance indices defined in section 8.1.2, it is clear that, in order to optimize these indices, it is also necessary, for player i, to have information on the current state $x_j(k)$ of its adversary, player j, as well as its current input or action $u_j(k)$. Of course, as discussed in the previous paragraph, for specific instances of the general model, less information may be required. For example, for dynamic games based on the ABK model, knowledge of the adversary's state is not required, but knowledge of its action is necessary. The VWD model is the only one for which dynamic games based on it do not require knowledge of the adversary's action. There is a hierarchy of mutual information requirements for dynamic games based on these models, with the VWD model requiring the least amount and the DST model requiring the most information (adversary's current state and action). Dynamic games based on the ABK model require the same amount of information (adversary's current action, but not its state). Finally, for the sake of formality, it should be pointed out that, in this setting, a two player dynamic game is characterized by $(J_1, J_2, X_1, X_2, U_1, U_2, \mathcal{P})$, where J_is are the performance indices, X_is are the state spaces, U_is are the action or input spaces, and $\mathcal{P}$ refers to the game playing procedure (Gauss–Seidel or Jacobi). With this notation in place, it is now possible to define Gauss–Seidel and Jacobi procedures for the case in which performance indices depend on the state as well as the inputs, and the states in turn are governed by the dynamics (8.19), (8.20).

Consider the map $L_1 : X_1 \times X_2 \times U_2 \to U_1$ defined by the following equality constrained optimization problem:

$$
\begin{aligned}
&L_1(x_1(k), x_2(k), u_2(k)) \\
&\quad = \begin{cases} \operatorname{argmax}_{u_1 \in U_1} J_1(x_1(k+1), x_2(k), u_1, u_2(k)) \\ \text{s.t. } x_1(k+1) = f_1(x_1(k), x_2(k), u_1, u_2(k)), \;\; x_i(k), u_2(k) \text{ given.} \end{cases}
\end{aligned} \tag{8.21}
$$

Observe that the argument u_1 that maximizes J_1 in (8.21) is denoted $u_1^*(k)$ and is the one step ahead optimal control for player 1 at instant k. Formally,

$$
u_1^*(k) = L_1(x_1(k), x_2(k), u_2(k)).
$$

The map $L_2 : X_1 \times X_2 \times U_1 \to U_2$ can be defined similarly and the Gauss–Seidel procedure can then be defined in terms of L_1 and L_2. Observe that, by using the dynamics to substitute $x_1(k+1)$ by the right-hand side of (8.19), the nonlinearly constrained problem (8.21) can be written in terms of the following unconstrained nonlinear optimization problem:

$$
\begin{aligned}
&L_1(x_1(k), x_2(k), u_2(k)) \\
&= \operatorname{argmax}_{u_1 \in U_1} J_1(f_1(x_1(k), x_2(k), u_1, u_2(k)), x_2(k), u_1, u_2(k)).
\end{aligned} \tag{8.22}
$$

Instead of pursuing this general formulation further, the next important ingredient of projections is now introduced and subsequently, in section 8.2.2, the two procedures are made explicit in the case of the VWD discrete-time model of market share dynamics. Finally, note that the J_i in this discussion can be either J_i^ℓ or J_i^q; if, however, it is desired to use J_i^r, then the argmax in (8.21) and (8.22) should both be changed to argmin.

A final remark, that applies to this chapter as a whole, is that the omniscient paradigm of the previous chapters, is inappropriate in the dynamic game context of this chapter, because computing optimal actions for each player requires perfect knowledge of the adversary's actions and variables over the entire planning horizon.

8.2.1 ▪ Complete description of a dynamic game with projections

In light of the discussion above, it is clear that the previous descriptions of the Gauss–Seidel and Jacobi procedures must be augmented with a projection step (described in section 7.4), in order to guarantee that the triangle T is maintained invariant during the dynamic game. The complete descriptions of the procedures are as follows.

The Gauss–Seidel procedure for a dynamic advertising game

This iterative procedure or algorithm can be written as follows.

ALGORITHM 8.1. Gauss–Seidel procedure for advertising game.

$k = 0$; $x_1(0), x_2(0), u_2(0)$, and horizon K_f given.
while $k \leq K_f - 1$ **do**
    $u_1^*(k) = L_1(x_1(k), x_2(k), u_2(k))$.
    $x_1^t(k+1) := f_1(x_1(k), x_2(k), u_1^*(k), u_2(k))$.
    $u_2^*(k) = L_2(x_1^t(k+1), x_2(k), u_1^*(k))$.
    $x_2^t(k+1) := f_2(x_1^t(k+1), x_2(k), u_1^*(k), u_2^*(k))$.
    $(x_1(k+1), x_2(k+1)) = \Pi_T\left((x_1(k), x_2(k)), (x_1^t(k+1), x_2^t(k+1))\right)$.
    $k \leftarrow k+1$
end while

The Jacobi procedure for a dynamic advertising game

This iterative procedure or algorithm can be written as follows.

ALGORITHM 8.2. Jacobi procedure for advertising game.

$k = 0$; $x_1(0), x_2(0), u_1(0), u_2(0)$, and horizon K_f given.
while $k \leq K_f - 1$ **do**
    $u_1^*(k) = L_1(x_1(k), x_2(k), u_2(k))$.
    $u_2^*(k) = L_2(x_1(k), x_2(k), u_1(k))$.
    $x_1^t(k+1) := f_1(x_1(k), x_2(k), u_1^*(k), u_2(k))$.
    $x_2^t(k+1) := f_2(x_1(k), x_2(k), u_1(k), u_2^*(k))$.
    $(x_1(k+1), x_2(k+1)) = \Pi_T\left((x_1(k), x_2(k)), (x_1^t(k+1), x_2^t(k+1))\right)$.
    $k \leftarrow k+1$
end while

Note the appearance of the superscript t in both procedures, to indicate that the calculation of the superscripted "next" states is temporary, because the point $(x_1^t(k+1), x_2^t(k+1))$ may not belong to the triangle T. This is only ensured in line 7 of both procedures by application of the projection Π_T. Observe also that the one step ahead optimal control is computed in the steps in which the L_i appears on the right-hand sides.

8.2.2 ▪ Dynamic game based on the VWD dynamics

This section writes out the Gauss–Seidel and Jacobi dynamic games based on the VWD model explicitly, and then shows how the one step ahead optimal controls can be found analytically.

Gauss–Seidel procedure for VWD duopoly game

The **Gauss–Seidel procedure** described in general terms in section 8.2 can be written formally **for the VWD dynamics** as follows:

$$
\begin{aligned}
&u_1^*(k) = \text{argmax}_{u_1} J_1(x_1(k), x_2(k), u_1) \text{ [given } x_1(k), x_2(k)],\\
&x_1^t(k+1) = x_1(k) + u_1^*(k)(1 - x_1(k) - x_2(k)) - \lambda_1 x_1(k),\\
&u_2^*(k) = \text{argmax}_{u_2} J_2(x_1(k+1), x_2(k), u_2) \text{ [given } x_1^t(k+1), x_2(k)],\\
&x_2^t(k+1) = x_2(k) + u_2^*(k)(1 - x_1^t(k+1) - x_2(k)) - \lambda_2 x_2(k),\\
&(x_1(k+1), x_2(k+1)) = \Pi_T\left((x_1(k), x_2(k)), (x_1^t(k+1), x_2^t(k+1))\right).
\end{aligned}
\tag{8.23}
$$

The notation $x_i^t(k+1)$ refers to a temporary or preprojection value of the state $x_i(k+1)$. The actual values $x_i(k+1)$ are computed in the last step, which is the projection.

Jacobi procedure for VWD duopoly game

The **Jacobi procedure** described in general terms in section 8.2 can be written formally **for the VWD dynamics** as follows:

$$
\begin{aligned}
&u_1^*(k) = \text{argmax}_{u_1} J_1(x_1(k), x_2(k), u_1) \quad \text{[given } x_1(k), x_2(k)],\\
&u_2^*(k) = \text{argmax}_{u_2} J_2(x_1(k), x_2(k), u_2) \quad \text{[given } x_1(k), x_2(k)],\\
&x_1^t(k+1) = x_1(k) + u_1^*(k)(1 - x_1(k) - x_2(k)) - \lambda_1 x_1(k),\\
&x_2^t(k+1) = x_2(k) + u_2^*(k)(1 - x_1(k) - x_2(k)) - \lambda_2 x_2(k),\\
&(x_1(k+1), x_2(k+1)) = \Pi_T\left((x_1(k), x_2(k)), (x_1^t(k+1), x_2^t(k+1))\right).
\end{aligned}
\tag{8.24}
$$

8.2.3 ▪ Analytic solution of the OSAOCP for VWD duopoly game using a linear performance index

For the simple choice of linear index, the one step ahead optimal control problem can be solved analytically. The linear index J_i can be written as

$$
J_i(x_1(k), x_2(k), u_i(k)) = \underbrace{(1 - \lambda_i)x_i(k)}_{A_i(k)} + \underbrace{(1 - x_1(k) - x_2(k) - \alpha_i)}_{B_i(k)} u_i(k). \tag{8.25}
$$

In order to maximize J_i by choice of u_i, the sign of $B_i(k)$ is crucial, since $A_i(k)$ is positive.

Observe that, with $A > 0$,

$$\operatorname{argmax}_u (A + Bu) = \begin{cases} u_{\max} & \text{if } B > 0, \\ 0 & \text{otherwise.} \end{cases} \tag{8.26}$$

Thus the solution $u_i^*(k)$ to maximizing J_i can be written explicitly as

$$u_i^*(k) = \begin{cases} u_{\max} & \text{if } \alpha_i < 1 - x_1(k) - x_2(k), \\ 0 & \text{otherwise.} \end{cases} \tag{8.27}$$

Observe that the one step ahead optimal control is of the bang-bang (all or nothing) type.

Explicit version of the Gauss–Seidel and Jacobi procedures for VWD duopoly game using a linear performance index

Using the results of the previous section, the Gauss–Seidel procedure can be written explicitly as

$$\begin{aligned} &u_1^*(k) = \begin{cases} u_{1,\max} & \text{if } \alpha_1 < 1 - x_1(k) - x_2(k), \\ 0 & \text{otherwise,} \end{cases} \\ &x_1^t(k+1) = x_1(k) + u_1^*(k)(1 - x_1(k) - x_2(k)) - \lambda_1 x_1(k), \\ &u_2^*(k) = \begin{cases} u_{2,\max} & \text{if } \alpha_2 < 1 - x_1(k+1) - x_2(k), \\ 0 & \text{otherwise,} \end{cases} \\ &x_2^t(k+1) = x_2(k) + u_2^*(k)(1 - x_1(k+1) - x_2(k)) - \lambda_2 x_2(k), \\ &(x_1(k+1), x_2(k+1)) = \Pi_T\left((x_1(k), x_2(k)), (x_1^t(k+1), x_2^t(k+1))\right). \end{aligned} \tag{8.28}$$

The Jacobi procedure, in turn, can be written explicitly as

$$\begin{aligned} &u_1^*(k) = \begin{cases} u_{1,\max} & \text{if } \alpha_1 < 1 - x_1(k) - x_2(k), \\ 0 & \text{otherwise,} \end{cases} \\ &x_1^t(k+1) = x_1(k) + u_1^*(k)(1 - x_1(k) - x_2(k)) - \lambda_1 x_1(k) \\ &u_2^*(k) = \begin{cases} u_{2,\max} & \text{if } \alpha_2 < 1 - x_1(k) - x_2(k), \\ 0 & \text{otherwise,} \end{cases} \\ &x_2^t(k+1) = x_2(k) + u_2^*(k)(1 - x_1(k) - x_2(k)) - \lambda_2 x_2(k), \\ &(x_1(k+1), x_2(k+1)) = \Pi_T\left((x_1(k), x_2(k)), (x_1^t(k+1), x_2^t(k+1))\right). \end{aligned} \tag{8.29}$$

8.2.4 ▪ Analytic solution of the OSAOCP for VWD duopoly game using a quadratic performance index

Consider the quadratic one step ahead performance indices at instant k, denoted $J_i^q(k)$, for firms 1 (associated with x_1) and firm 2 (associated with x_2):

$$J_i^q(k) = x_i(k+1)^2 - \alpha_i u_i(k)^2, \tag{8.30}$$

where the α_is are nonnegative weights and the indices $J_i(k)$ are to be maximized at each instant k. Observe first that

$$x_i(k+1)^2 = (\underbrace{(1-\lambda_i)x_i(k)}_{A_i(k)} + [\underbrace{(1 - x_1(k) - x_2(k))}_{B(k)}\, u_i(k)]^2) \tag{8.31}$$

$$= A_i(k)^2 + 2A_i(k)B(k)u_i(k) + B(k)^2 u_i(k)^2. \tag{8.32}$$

We can now rewrite (8.30), displaying its functional dependence explicitly:

$$J_i^q(x_1(k), x_2(k), u_i(k)) = A_i(k)^2 + 2A_i(k)B(k)u_i(k) + (B(k)^2 - \alpha_i)u_i(k)^2 \tag{8.33}$$

which is the equation of a convex (resp., concave) parabola, if $\alpha_i < B(k)^2$ (resp., $\alpha_i > B(k)^2$). The extremizing argument of either parabola is

$$u_i^{ext}(k) = -\frac{A_i(k)B(k)}{B(k)^2 - \alpha_i}. \tag{8.34}$$

From the geometry of the parabolas, and the fact that the optimal control $u_i^*(k)$ is constrained to be nonnegative, defining

$$C := \left|\frac{A_i(k)B(k)}{B(k)^2 - \alpha_i}\right| \tag{8.35}$$

it follows that

$$u_i^*(k) = \begin{cases} 0 \text{ if } \alpha_i < B(k)^2, \\ C \text{ if } \alpha_i > B(k)^2, \text{ and } C < 1, \\ 1 \text{ if } \alpha_i > B(k)^2, \text{ and } C > 1. \end{cases} \tag{8.36}$$

Using (8.36), it is possible to write explicit versions of the Gauss–Seidel and Jacobi procedures just as was done in section 8.2.3, but this will be omitted here. In fact, similar exercises can be carried out for the performance indices J_i^r with targets, as well as for all the other models discussed in section 8.1, but, in keeping with the general spirit of the book, for all models, numerical optimization software will be used to solve the one step ahead optimal control problems that are part of the dynamic game procedures, and samples of this are given in the next section.

8.3 ▪ Numerical examples of VWD duopoly games for linear performance indices

In order to describe the numerical examples, the terms λ-gap and α-gap are introduced. The *λ-gap* refers to the difference between λ_1 and λ_2 and is said to be in favor of firm i if $\lambda_i < \lambda_j$, $i \neq j$. This is because, in the case of constant control (u_i), a smaller decay factor should lead to a larger equilibrium value of market share. The *α-gap* refers to the difference between α_1 and α_2 and is said to be in favor of firm i if $\alpha_i < \alpha_j, j \neq i$, because a smaller positive weight implies that a larger control effort can be applied if necessary, leading, in principle, to a larger market share. This terminology is useful in describing different combinations of parameter choices compactly and describing the qualitatively different types of behavior associated with these choices.

8.3.1 ▪ Zero α- and λ-gaps

With zero gaps, it is to be expected that the VWD duopoly game will lead to a situation in which both firms end up having roughly equal market shares. The simulations below show that this is indeed the case, although, for the parameter values chosen, the end result is a limit cycle rather than a (Nash) equilibrium. Phase plane and limit cycle plots (resp., time plots of the states and advertising efforts) are shown in Fig. 8.1 (resp., 8.2) (Gauss–Seidel procedure) and Fig. 8.3 (resp., 8.4) (Jacobi procedure).

The Gauss–Seidel procedure for linear performance indices J_i^ℓ

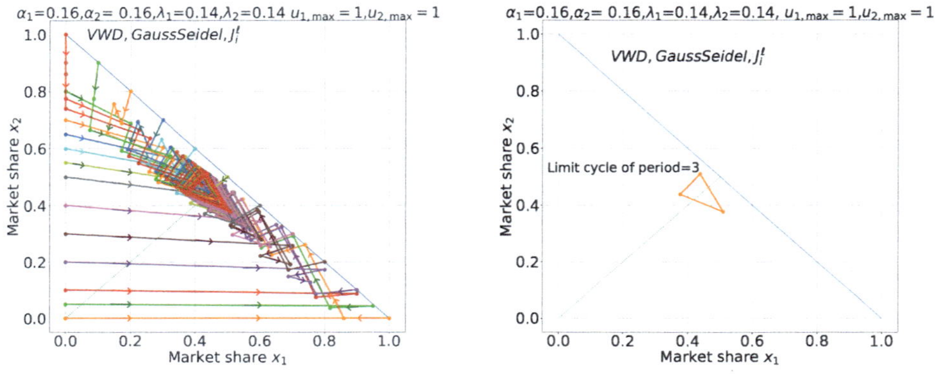

(a) Phase plane plot, showing convergence to the limit cycle, from all initial conditions.

(b) Period 3 limit cycle, symmetrically located around the green dotted equal market share line.

Figure 8.1. *Phase plane* (a) *and limit cycle* (b) *plots for the VWD duopoly game, with linear performance index* J_i^ℓ*, following the Gauss–Seidel procedure, and with zero* α*- and* λ*-gaps.*

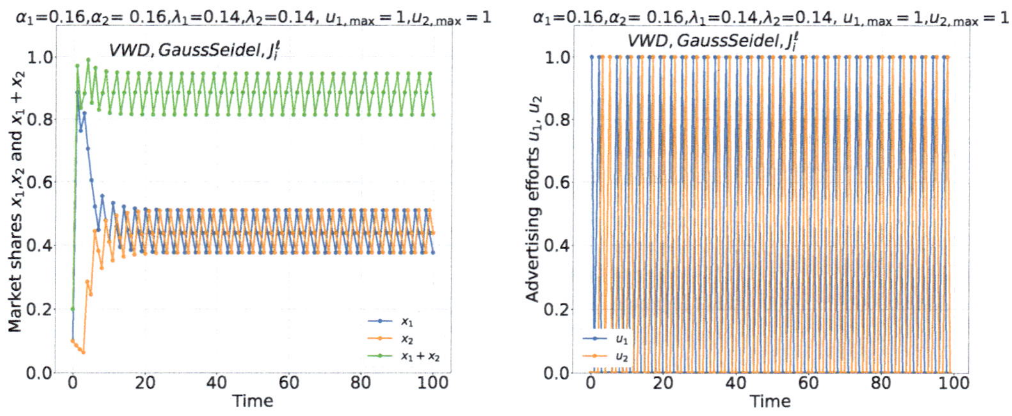

(a) Initial conditions: $x_1(1) = 0.1, x_2(1) = 0.1$

(b) Initial conditions: $x_1(1) = 0.1, x_2(1) = 0.1$

Figure 8.2. (a) *Typical time plots of market share for the VWD duopoly game, with linear performance index* J_i^ℓ*, following the Gauss–Seidel procedure, and with zero* α*- and* λ*-gaps, showing convergence to period 3 oscillations for different initial conditions. The oscillations are out of phase, but have the same amplitude.* (b) *Corresponding advertising efforts of each firm, the alternating and bang-bang nature being clearly visible.*

The Jacobi procedure for linear performance indices J_i^ℓ

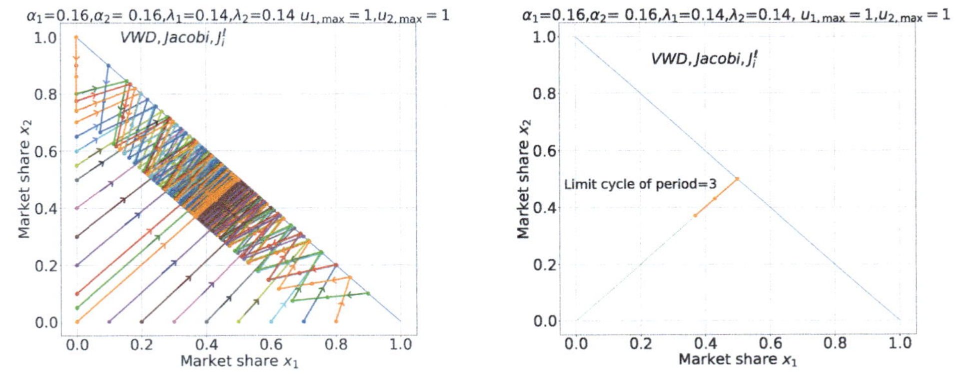

(a) Showing convergence to the limit cycle, from all initial conditions.

(b) Period 3 limit cycle, located on the equal market share line.

Figure 8.3. *Showing* (a) *phase plane, and* (b) *limit cycle plots for the VWD duopoly game, with linear index J_i^ℓ, following the Jacobi procedure, and with zero α- and λ-gaps.*

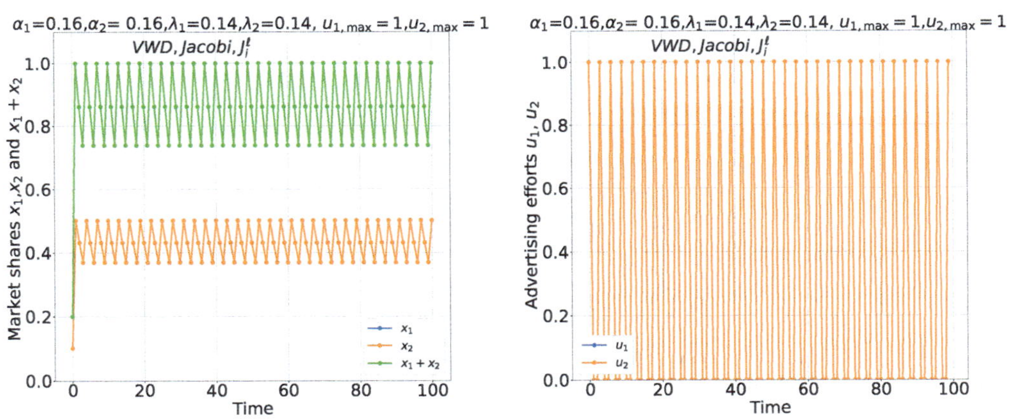

(a) Initial conditions: $x_1(1) = 0.1, x_2(1) = 0.9$

(b) Initial conditions: $x_1(1) = 0.1, x_2(1) = 0.9$

Figure 8.4. (a) *Time plots for the VWD duopoly game, with a linear index, following the Jacobi procedure, and with zero α- and λ-gaps, showing convergence to the same period 3 oscillations, in phase and of equal amplitude.* (b) *Corresponding advertising efforts of each firm, the in-phase, bang-bang nature being clearly visible.*

8.3.2 ▪ α- and λ-gaps both in favor of firm 1

With both gaps in favor of firm 1, it is to be expected that the VWD duopoly game will lead to a situation in which firm 1 ends up having a larger market share. The simulations below show that this is indeed the case, although, for the parameter values chosen in Figs. 8.5 and 8.7, the end result is a limit cycle rather than a (Nash) equilibrium. Phase plane and limit cycle plots (resp., time plots of the states and advertising efforts) are shown in Fig. 8.5 (resp., 8.6) (Gauss–Seidel procedure) and Fig. 8.7 (resp., 8.8) (Jacobi procedure).

The Gauss–Seidel procedure for linear performance indices J_i^ℓ

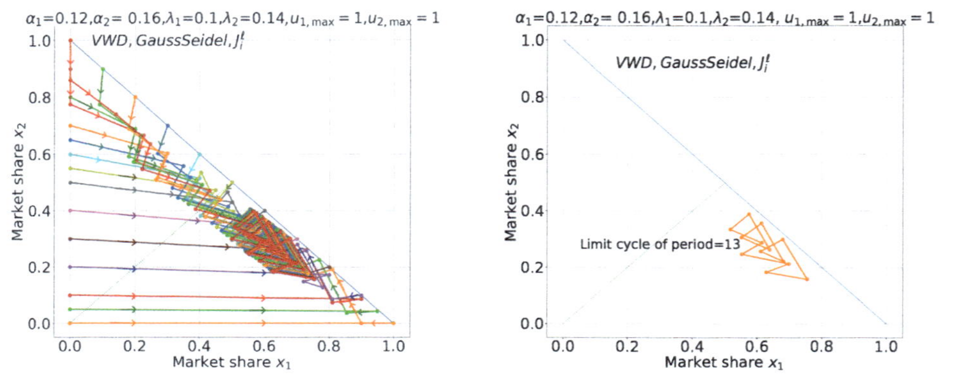

(a) Phase plane plot, showing convergence to the limit cycle, from all initial conditions.

(b) Period 13 limit cycle, located below the green dotted equal market share line.

Figure 8.5. *Showing phase plane* (a) *and limit cycle* (b) *plots for the VWD duopoly game, with linear index* J_i^ℓ*, following the Gauss–Seidel procedure, and with* α*- and* λ*-gaps in favor of firm* 1.

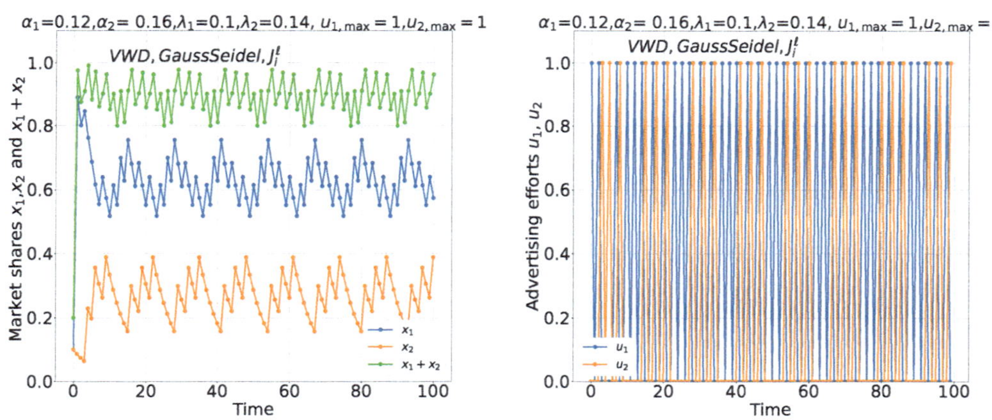

(a) Initial conditions: $x_1(1) = 0.1, x_2(1) = 0.1$

(b) Initial conditions: $x_1(1) = 0.1, x_2(1) = 0.1$

Figure 8.6. (a) *Time plots for the VWD duopoly game, with linear index* J_i^ℓ*, following the Gauss–Seidel procedure, and with* α*- and* λ*-gaps in favor of firm* 1*, showing convergence to period* 13 *oscillations. The oscillations are out of phase and the mean value of market share is higher for firm* 1*, which is favored by both the* α*- and* λ*-gaps.* (b) *Corresponding advertising efforts of each firm.*

The Jacobi procedure for linear performance indices J_i^ℓ

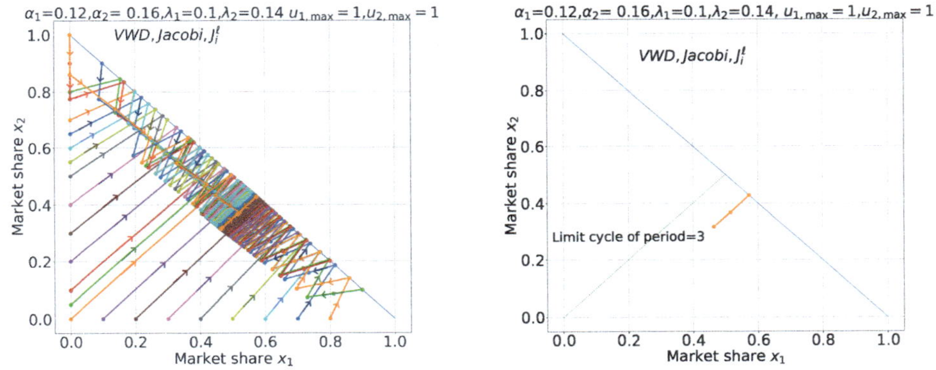

(a) Phase plane plot, showing convergence to the limit cycle, from all initial conditions.

(b) Period 3 limit cycle, located below the green dotted equal market share line.

Figure 8.7. *Showing phase plane* (a) *and limit cycle* (b) *plots for the VWD duopoly game, with linear index J_i^ℓ, following the Jacobi procedure, and with α- and λ-gaps in favor of firm* 1.

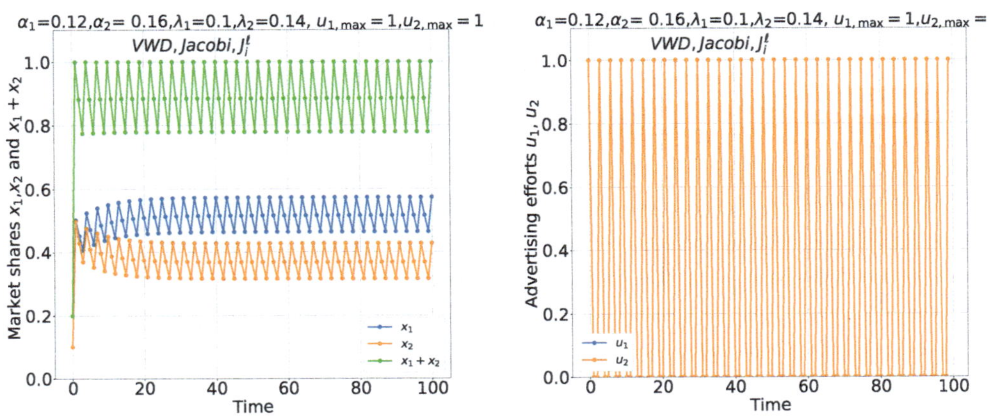

(a) Initial conditions: $x_1(1) = 0.1, x_2(1) = 0.1$

(b) Initial conditions: $x_1(1) = 0.1, x_2(1) = 0.9$

Figure 8.8. (a) *Time plots for the VWD duopoly game, with linear index J_i^ℓ, following the Jacobi procedure, and with α- and λ-gaps in favor of firm* 1, *showing convergence to period* 2 *oscillations for different initial conditions. The oscillations are in phase, and of similar amplitude, but the average market share of firm* 1, *favored by both gaps, is larger.* (b) *Corresponding advertising efforts of each firm.*

8.3.3 ▪ α-gap in favor of firm 1 and λ-gap in favor of firm 2

With the α-gap in favor of firm 1, and the λ-gap in favor of firm 2, the relative sizes of the gaps could be traded off, resulting in a situation in which both firms have roughly equal market shares. Such a choice of parameters, resulting in a slight advantage for firm 2, are shown in the figures below. Phase plane and limit cycle plots (resp., time plots of the states and advertising efforts) are shown in Fig. 8.9 (resp., 8.10) for the Gauss–Seidel procedure.

The Gauss–Seidel procedure for linear performance indices J_i^ℓ

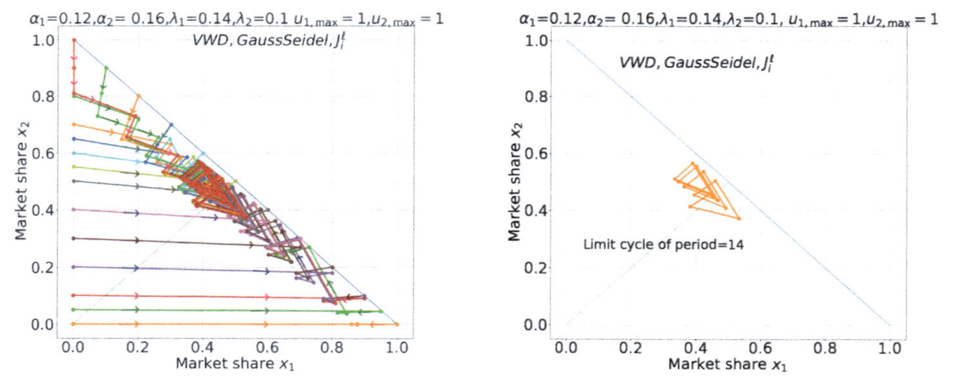

(a) Phase plane plot, showing convergence to the limit cycle, from all initial conditions.

(b) Period 14 limit cycle, located around the green dotted equal market share line, mostly above it.

Figure 8.9. *Showing phase plane* (a) *and limit cycle* (b) *plots for the VWD duopoly game, with linear index* J_i^ℓ*, following the Gauss–Seidel procedure, and with* α*-gap in favor of firm* 1 *and* λ*-gap in favor of firm* 2.

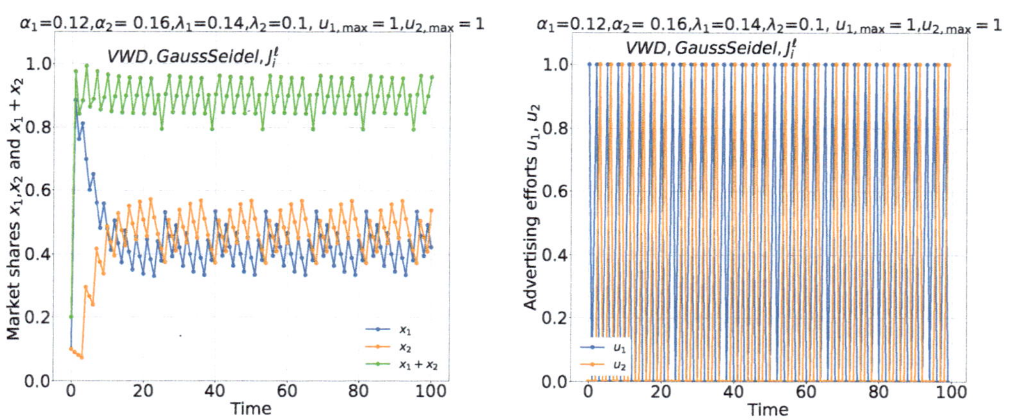

(a) Initial conditions: $x_1(1) = 0.1, x_2(1) = 0.1$

(b) Initial conditions: $x_1(1) = 0.1, x_2(1) = 0.9$

Figure 8.10. (a) *Typical time plots for the VWD duopoly game, with linear index* J_i^ℓ*, following the Gauss–Seidel procedure, and with* α*-gap in favor of firm* 1 *and* λ*-gap in favor of firm* 2*, showing convergence to period* 14 *oscillations. The oscillations are out of phase and of roughly equal amplitude, but with a slightly higher mean value for firm* 2*, showing a slight advantage in market share.* (b) *Corresponding advertising efforts of each firm.*

The Jacobi procedure for linear performance indices J_i^ℓ

For this particular choice of parameters, the Jacobi procedure can lead to one of two limit cycles, depending on the location of the initial condition. This can be seen clearly in the phase plane plots in Fig. 8.11. The plot on the left shows initial conditions originating above the equal market share line E ($x_1 = x_2$), and it can be seen that trajectories emanating from initial conditions above E appear to converge to a limit cycle above it, while the plot on the right shows that those emanating from initial conditions below E converge to a limit cycle below it. This is confirmed in the plots shown in Fig. 8.12. Time plots of the market share for initial conditions above and below the equal market share line are shown in Fig. 8.13.

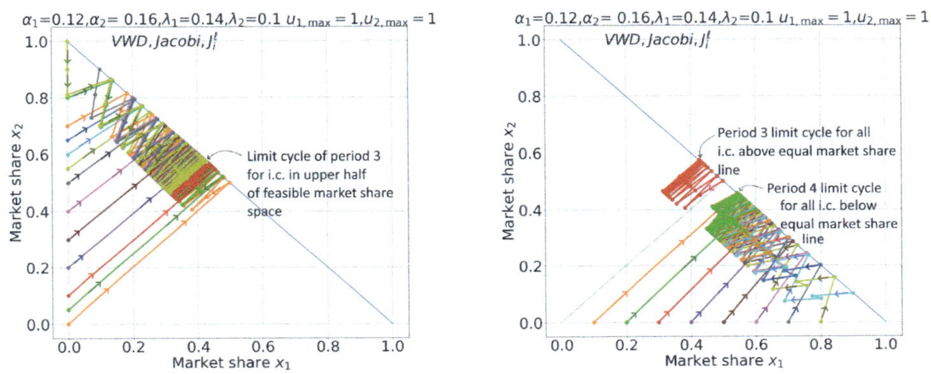

(a) Phase plane plot for initial conditions above the green dotted equal market share line.

(b) Phase plane plot for initial conditions below the green dotted equal market share line.

Figure 8.11. (a) *Phase plane plot for initial conditions above E (the green dotted equal market share line), for the VWD duopoly game, with linear index J_i^ℓ, following the Jacobi procedure, and with α-gap in favor of firm* 1 *and λ-gap in favor of firm* 2. (b) *Phase plane plot for initial conditions below E. The equal market share line E is a separatrix, in the sense that trajectories with initial conditions above (resp., below) it, remain above (resp., below) it and never cross E.*

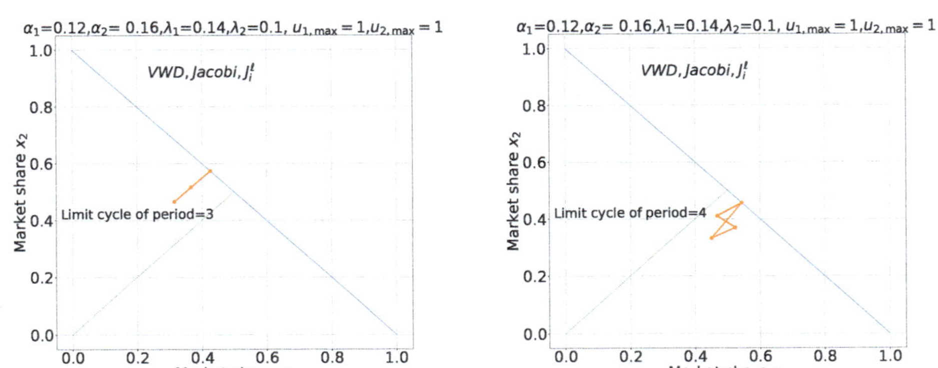

(a) Period 3 limit cycle, located above the equal market share line E.

(b) Period 4 limit cycle, located below the equal market share line E.

Figure 8.12. *Convergence to different limit cycles:* (a) *to a period* 3 *limit cycle for initial conditions above the equal share market line,* (b) *to a period* 4 *limit cycle for initial conditions below the equal share market line, for the VWD duopoly game, with linear index J_i^ℓ, following the Jacobi procedure, and with α-gap in favor of firm* 1 *and λ-gap in favor of firm* 2.

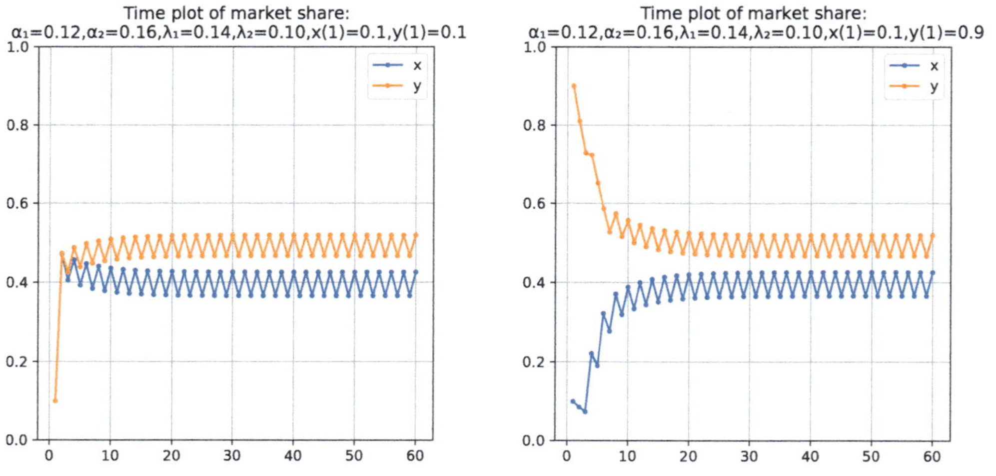

(a) Initial conditions: $x_1(1) = 0.1, x_2(1) = 0.1$ (b) Initial conditions: $x_1(1) = 0.1, x_2(1) = 0.9$

Figure 8.13. *Time plots for the VWD duopoly game, with a linear index, following the Jacobi procedure, and with α-gap in favor of firm 1 and λ-gap in favor of firm 2, showing convergence to period 2 oscillations for different initial conditions, shown in* (a) *and* (b). *The oscillations are in phase, and of similar amplitude, but the average market share of firm 2 is larger.*

8.4 ▪ Numerical examples of VWD duopoly games for quadratic performance indices

This section presents some results for VWD duopoly games using a quadratic index. Figure 8.14 is a phase plane plot showing the emergence of multiple equilibria for the Gauss–Seidel procedure, while Fig. 8.15 shows corresponding market share plots. Figure 8.16 is a phase plane plot showing a similar phenomenon of multiple equilibria for the Jacobi procedure. Finally, Fig. 8.17 is a phase plane plot showing that multiple equilibria, as well as limit cycles, can arise for certain parameter values when the Jacobi procedure is used.

8.4.1 ▪ Zero α- and λ-gaps

The Gauss–Seidel procedure with quadratic performance indices

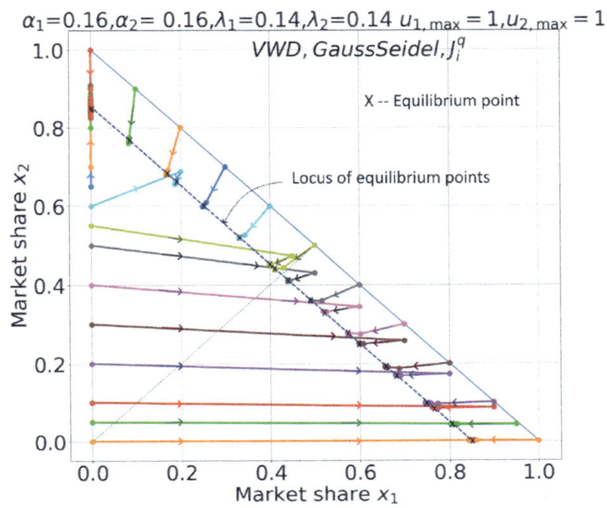

Figure 8.14. *Phase plane plot for the quadratic index J_i^q. The new feature, with respect to the case of the linear index, is the appearance of multiple equilibria. The initial market shares determine the outcome of the game, which is always an equilibrium. All these equilibrium points lie on a straight line (shown as dashed dark blue line in the figure), which is parallel to the saturated market line $x_1 + x_2 = 1$.*

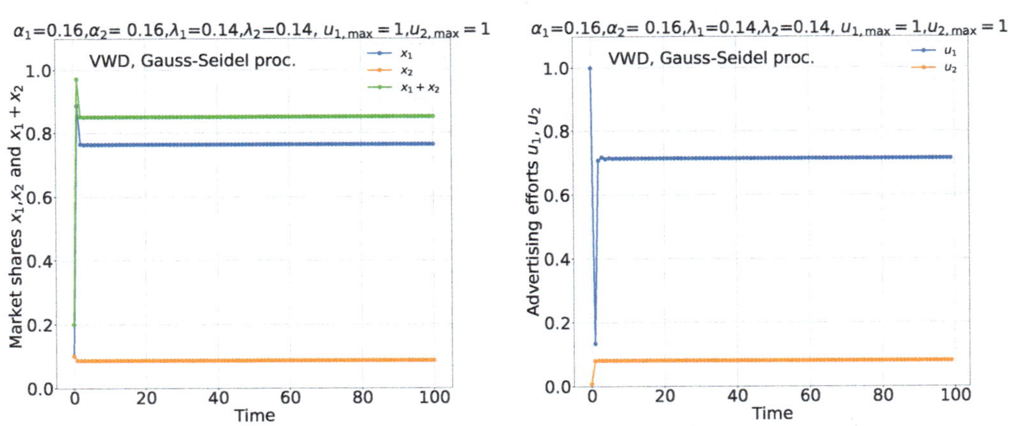

(a) Initial conditions: $x_1(1) = 0.1, x_2(1) = 0.1$

(b) Initial conditions: $x_1(1) = 0.1, x_2(1) = 0.1$

Figure 8.15. (a) *Typical time plots for the VWD duopoly game, with quadratic index J_i^q, following the Gauss–Seidel procedure, and with both the α-gap and λ-gaps in favor of firm* 1, *showing quick convergence to the equilibrium point corresponding to the specified initial condition.* (b) *Corresponding OSAO advertising efforts of each firm, showing quick convergence to constant values corresponding to the equilibrium market shares.*

The Jacobi procedure with quadratic performance indices

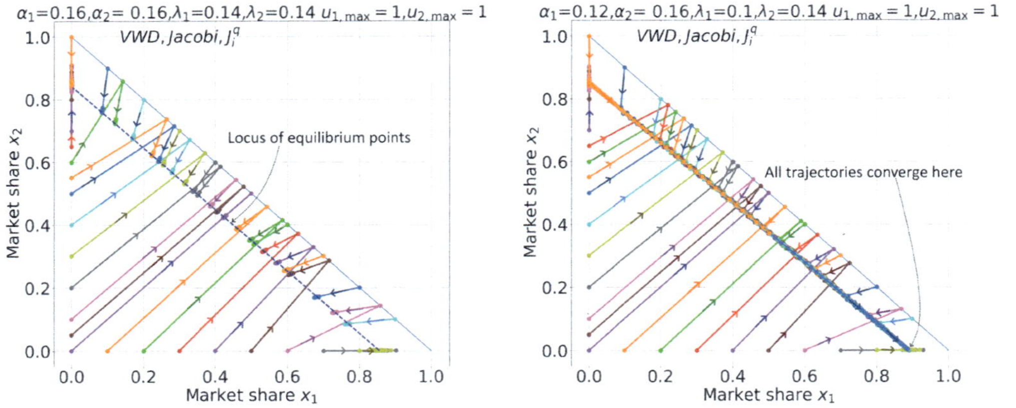

(a) Phase plane plot (b) Phase plane plot

Figure 8.16. *Phase plane plot for the quadratic index J_i^q. The new feature, with respect to the case of the linear index, is the appearance of multiple equilibria. The initial market shares determine the outcome of the game, which is always an equilibrium. All these equilibrium points lie on a straight line (shown as dashed dark blue line in the figure), which is parallel to the saturated market line $x_1 + x_2 = 1$.*

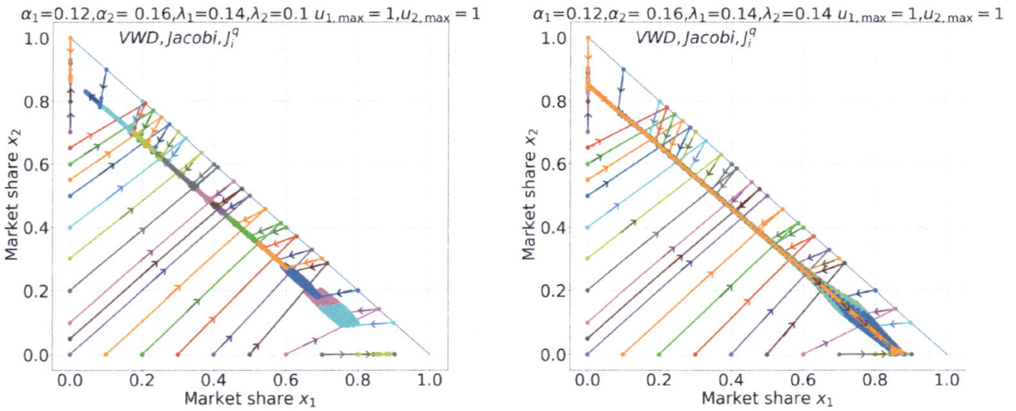

(a) Phase plane plot (b) Phase plane plot

Figure 8.17. *Phase plane plot for the quadratic index J_i^q. The new feature, with respect to the case of the linear index, is the appearance of multiple equilibrium points as well as limit cycles. The initial market shares determine the outcome of the game, which is either an equilibrium or a limit cycle. The equilibrium points lie on a straight line (shown as dashed dark blue line in the figure), which is parallel to the saturated market line $x_1 + x_2 = 1$. The limit cycles are also to be found in a neighborhood of this line.*

8.4.2 ▪ Summary of observations from numerical experiments on the VWD model with no targets stipulated

Using the terminology of λ-gap and α-gap, the behavior of the VWD dynamics under one step ahead optimal control with linear and quadratic performance indices, and using the Gauss–Seidel and Jacobi procedures, can be summarized as follows.

Linear performance index

1. With zero gaps, the Gauss–Seidel procedure leads to a stable limit cycle, with the market shares of each firm oscillating between the same upper and lower bounds, around the same mean value, but out of phase by one period. With the Jacobi procedure, the oscillations are in phase, between the same upper and lower bounds and around the same mean value.

2. If both the α- and λ-gaps are in favor of the same firm and are not too large, both the Gauss–Seidel and Jacobi dynamics lead to stable limit cycles, in which the favored firm's market share oscillates around a larger mean value than its competitor. The gap between the mean values of the market shares is larger for the Gauss–Seidel procedure than that for the Jacobi procedure.

3. If the α- and λ-gaps are not aligned, i.e., one gap favors firm i and the other favors firm j, as long as the gaps are small and roughly of the same size, once again, both procedures lead to stable limit cycles, although there may exist more than one limit cycle for the Jacobi case.

4. Keeping one gap, say the λ-gap, fixed in favor of firm 2 and increasing the α-gap in favor of firm 1, there exists a threshold above which the market share of firm 2 converges to zero, and vice versa. This threshold is larger for the Jacobi procedure than for the Gauss–Seidel procedure.

Quadratic performance index

1. With zero α- and λ-gaps, the use of the quadratic performance index J_i^q by both firms, for both the Gauss–Seidel and Jacobi procedures, there are no longer any global equilibrium points or limit cycles. The new phenomenon is that trajectories starting from different initial conditions may converge to different equilibria. However, all these equilibria lie on a straight line parallel to, and below, the saturated market line ($x_1 + x_2 = 1$).

2. With any mismatch between the α and λ parameters, the trajectories display the winner take all property, where the winner is defined by a relative advantage in either the α-gap or the λ-gap, or even both.

3. The advertising effort (control) is smoother than in the case of a linear performance index. As a result, the evolution of the market shares is also smoother, not presenting large oscillations.

8.4.3 ▪ One step ahead control of the VWD model with target market shares

For brevity, only two phase plane plots are shown in Fig. 8.18, for the Gauss–Seidel procedure, illustrating competition in the situation that the target market shares of the firms sum to an

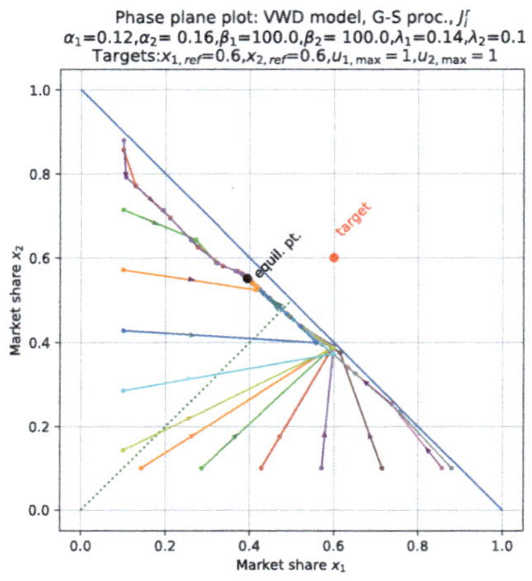

(a) Phase plane plot for parameter set 1, shown in the figure title.

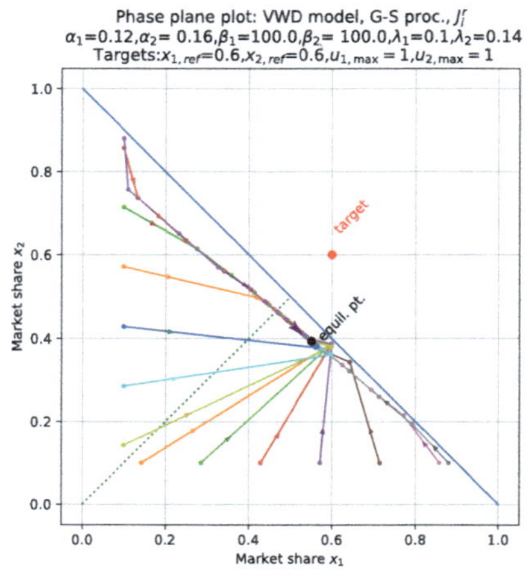

(b) Phase plane plot for parameter set 2, shown in the figure title.

Figure 8.18. (a) *Phase plane plot with α-gap favoring firm* 1 *and λ-gap favoring firm* 2. (b) *Phase plane plot with α- and λ-gaps favoring firm* 1, *for the VWD duopoly game, with specified targets and quadratic index J_i^r, following the Gauss–Seidel procedure.*

unattainable value greater than one. Global convergence occurs to an equilibrium point that is below the saturated market line and "close" to the target.

8.5 ▪ Numerical examples for the ABK and DST models

This section exhibits a few samples of phase plane plots for the other models, without attempting to be exhaustive.

8.5.1 ▪ One step ahead control of the ABK model with target market shares

For brevity, only two phase plane plots are shown in Fig. 8.19, for the Gauss–Seidel procedure, illustrating competition in the situation that the target market shares of the firms sum to an unattainable value greater than one. Global convergence occurs to an equilibrium point that is on the saturated market line and "close" to the target.

8.5.2 ▪ One step ahead control of the DST model with target market shares

For brevity, only two phase plane plots are shown in Fig. 8.20, for the Gauss–Seidel procedure, illustrating competition in the situation that the target market shares of the firms sum to an unattainable value greater than one. Global convergence occurs to an equilibrium point that is on the saturated market line and "close" to the target.

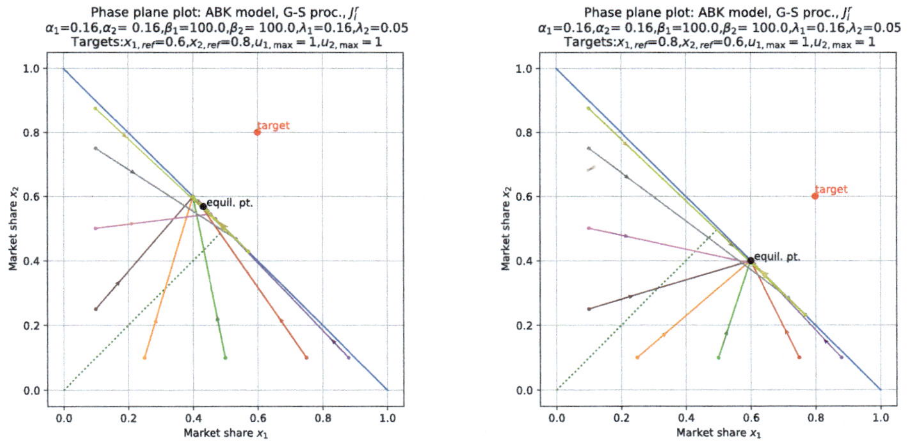

(a) Phase plane plot for parameter set 1, shown in the figure title.

(b) Phase plane plot for parameter set 2, shown in the figure title.

Figure 8.19. *Phase plane plots for the duopoly game based on the ABK model, with specified targets and quadratic index J_i^r, following the Gauss–Seidel procedure. In both cases, the equilibrium point attained lies on the saturated market line, as close as possible to the unattainable target.*

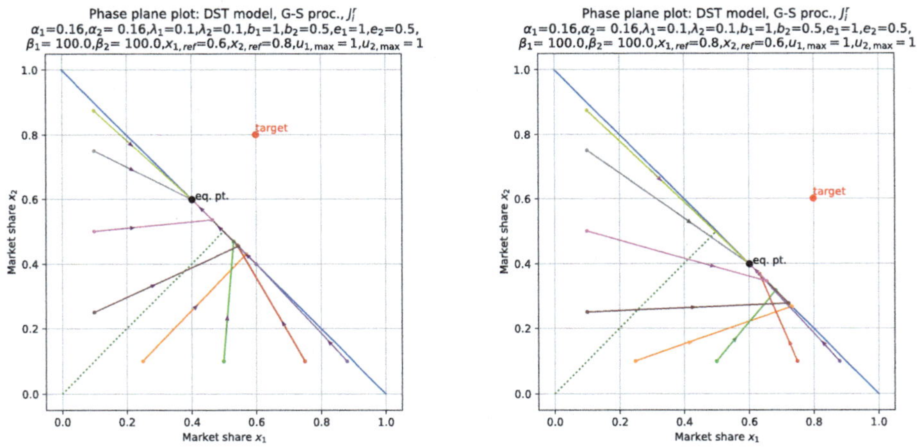

(a) Phase plane plot for parameter set 1, shown in the figure title.

(b) Phase plane plot for parameter set 2, shown in the figure title.

Figure 8.20. *Phase plane plots for the duopoly game based on the DST model, with specified targets and quadratic index J_i^r, following the Gauss–Seidel procedure. In both cases, the equilibrium point attained lies on the saturated market line, as close as possible to the unattainable target.*

8.6 ▪ Chapter summary

This chapter showed that one step ahead optimal control can be applied successfully to duopoly market share models, with or without target market shares for the competing firms. The competition occurs using either the Gauss–Seidel procedure, or the Jacobi procedure. Broadly speaking, without specified targets, for the same configuration of parameters (α-, λ-, and other parameter gaps), and with linear performance indices, both procedures lead to similar results, although, for the VWD dynamic game, the Gauss–Seidel procedure tends to lead to unique stable limit cycles with high period, while the Jacobi procedure leads to different limit cycles, depending on the initial conditions, but generally with smaller periods than those obtained with the Gauss–Seidel procedure. Though not illustrated in the text, it can be shown that the ABK and DST (Jacobi) dynamic games show convergence to a unique equilibrium point, determined by the parameters, and do not display limit cycle behavior. The DST Gauss–Seidel game shows winner-takes-all behavior favoring the leader.

When target market shares are specified in the (quadratic) performance indices of each firm, the result is convergence to an equilibrium, for all the models considered. Furthermore, all models show similar behavior under one step ahead optimal control with target market shares specified, despite their different information requirements about the adversary. These observations provide guidelines to the user, who has qualitative knowledge of the market share behavior, on the best choice of model.

Notes and references

A predominant form of market structure is the oligopoly which represents a market with few enterprises and a large number of buyers from the demand side [Fri83]. The simplest type of oligopoly is the duopoly, where the market consists of two companies offering similar or identical products [Man20]. Markets are dynamic so that the strategies of competition existing in the firms which conform the market such as price, quality, publicity are also influenced by market changes [Eri09]. Advertising results can be assessed by communication impacts and the effects on sales and profits [AK18] and, under different hypotheses, corresponding classes of models have been developed and are surveyed in [WW01]. Studies of duopoly models based on differential games, and mainly focused on the solution of the Hamilton–Jacobi–Bellman equations, are carried out in Fruchter [Fru99], Dockner et al. [Doc+00], Wang and Wu [WW01], Fletcher [FH17], Wang et al. [Wan+16] and Jørgensen and Sigué [JS16]. Differential games related to the leader-follower game were studied in [Jør82; JZ04].

Limit cycles in economic systems and continuous-time dynamic games have been studied in [Fei92; FN94; FNW94].

Differential games are treated in [Bau16; BO99; Hes17].

Switched affine advertising policies in models of duopolies with churn were studied in [BK13].

There is a strong connection between limit cycles of large period and the eventual appearance of the so-called deterministic chaos [Hil85; SJ05]. Many examples in this chapter indeed have large period limit cycles, but the investigation of possible chaos is not the focus of this book. In fact, there are many studies of chaos in general duopoly models, such as the Bertrand and Cournot models, and the interested reader can consult [Bis+10; Puu03] and the references therein.

Nash equilibria in quadratic noncooperative games, in which acquisition of information incurs delays, are studied in [Oli+20].

Finally, it should be pointed out that the approach taken in this chapter is also applicable to cooperative games.

Chapter 9
Conclusions

The idea of writing this book occurred to the authors while teaching a course on control and optimization in business dynamics. This course was offered to senior undergraduate engineering students majoring in control and automation.

In business dynamics, the formulation of mathematical models, managerial objectives, and the presence of uncertainties conceptually leads to the formulation of a stochastic dynamic programming (SDP) problem. The well known numerical difficulties in obtaining solutions to such problems based on SDP led us to the search for simpler alternatives. The concept of greedy or myopic algorithms used in many different disciplines suggested itself and inspired us to use what we refer to in this book as the "one step ahead optimization-based optimal control" approach, with the new terminology being chosen in an effort to avoid the adjectives greedy and myopic, which are sometimes associated with negative connotations. One step ahead optimal control is, of course, the simplest possible version of predictive control. However, we chose to avoid this term as well, for two reasons. The first is that one step ahead is intrinsic to the difference equation description of a discrete dynamical system, of the form $\mathbf{x}(k+1) = f(\mathbf{x}(k), \mathbf{u}(k), \mathbf{e}(k))$. The second is that the term "model predictive" might intimidate many potential users outside the control community.

The one step ahead optimal approach, based on simple optimization techniques, has also been shown to perform quite well in most of the problems treated in this book, when compared to the gold standard of globally optimal solutions, referred to as "omniscient" in the book, since they require information over the whole planning horizon. In other words, the degree of suboptimality of solutions obtained by the one step ahead method is acceptable and in some cases it even matches the optimal solution, as in some instances of the debt amortization and cash balance problems discussed in earlier chapters. As discussed in many of the example problems above, the dynamics of many business processes involves bookkeeping (e.g., outflow = inflow − losses), so there is little or no uncertainty in the process model. This is a scenario that is very favorable to the use of one step ahead optimal control. At the other extreme, when there is a large amount of uncertainty, it is possible to conjecture that, once again, using one step ahead control is likely to be better than m-step ahead control (for $m > 1$), because the uncertainties will accumulate rapidly after the first few steps, seriously reducing the accuracy and hence the usefulness of the computed controls.

Advantages of the proposed approach include the fact that it is made to order for real time online implementation, using only current and past data, and using mathematical programming formulations which are rapidly solvable with commercial optimization software. The low dimension of the mathematical programming problem to be solved at each step also means that the approach is scalable, i.e., can be used with large scale problems. Another important aspect is that the one step ahead solutions are feedback controls, thus inheriting some robustness to uncertainty in the problem data.

The authors are well aware that the models treated in this book are quite simple. An important observation in this respect is that many models in business dynamics are linear or piecewise linear, and performance indices are often either linear or quadratic, which implies that the proposed approach, based on formulating the one step ahead optimal control problem as a simple mathematical program, can be applied in many other, possibly more complex, situations. The chapters on market share dynamics use models which are modifications of predator-prey models used, for instance, in mathematical ecology and epidemiology. This indicates that the proposed one step ahead optimal approach can be usefully employed in these fields as well. We hope that this book will inspire students and other researchers to tackle new problems using this approach.

Bibliography

[ABK20] Walter Aliaga, Amit Bhaya, and Eugenius Kaszkurewicz. "Dynamics of duopoly models with undecided clients under decentralized affine feedback advertising policies". In: *Complexity* 2020 (Jan. 2020), pp. 1–11. DOI: 10.1155/2020/5371492.

[AFFR08] Julián Andrada-Félix and Fernando Fernández-Rodríguez. "Improving moving average trading rules with boosting and statistical learning methods". In: *Journal of Forecasting* 27.5 (Aug. 2008), pp. 433–449. DOI: 10.1002/for.1068.

[AHM51] Kenneth J. Arrow, Theodore Harris, and Jacob Marschak. "Optimal inventory policy". In: *Econometrica* 19 (July 1951), pp. 250–272.

[AK18] Gary Armstrong and Philip Kotler. *Marketing: An Introduction*. 4th ed. Hoboken, New Jersey: Pearson Education, 2018.

[AN11] A. Aravindakshan and P. A. Naik. "How does awareness evolve when advertising stops? The role of memory". In: *Marketing Letters* 22.3 (2011), pp. 315–326.

[Arn92] Vladimir I. Arnol'd. *Ordinary Differential Equations*. Berlin: Springer, 1992.

[Baş87] Tamer Başar. "Relaxation techniques and asynchronous algorithms for on-line computation of non-cooperative equilibria". In: *Journal of Economic Dynamics and Control* 11 (1987), pp. 531–549.

[Bau16] Dario Bauso. *Game Theory with Engineering Applications*. Vol. 30 of Advances in Design and Control. Philadelphia: SIAM, 2016.

[Bau52] W. Baumol. "The transaction demand for cash – an inventory theoretic approach". In: *The Quarterly Journal of Economics* 66 (1952), pp. 545–556.

[BBG14] A. Bemporad, L. Bellucci, and T. Gabbriellini. "Dynamic option hedging via stochastic model predictive control based on scenario simulation". In: *Quantitative Finance* 14.10 (2014), pp. 1739–1751.

[Ber05] Dimitri P. Bertsekas. "Dynamic Programming and Suboptimal Control: A Survey from ADP to MPC". In: *European Journal of Control* 11 (2005), pp. 310–334.

[Ber17] Dimitri P. Bertsekas. *Dynamic Programming and Optimal Control, Vol. I*. 4th ed. Belmont, Massachusetts: Athena Scientific, 2017.

[Bez+17] Jeff Bezanson et al. "Julia: A fresh approach to numerical computing". In: *SIAM Review* 59.1 (2017), pp. 65–98. DOI: 10.1137/141000671.

[BG21] Lakdere Benkherouf and Brian H. Gilding. "Optimal policies for a deterministic continuous-time inventory model with several suppliers". In: *RAIRO-Operations Research* 55. Supplement (2021), pp. S947–S966. DOI: 10.1051/ro/2020037.

[BIP10] Dimitris Bertsimas, Dan A. Iancu, and Pablo A. Parrilo. "Optimality of affine policies in multistage robust optimization". In: *Mathematics of Operations Research* 35.2 (2010), pp. 363–394.

[Bis+10] G. I. Bischi et al. *Nonlinear Oligopolies: Stability and Bifurcations*. Berlin: Springer, 2010.

[BK06] Amit Bhaya and Eugenius Kaszkurewicz. *Control Perspectives on Numerical Algorithms and Matrix Problems*. Vol. 10 of Advances in Design and Control. Philadelphia: SIAM, 2006.

[BK13] Amit Bhaya and Eugenius Kaszkurewicz. "Duopolistic dynamics in markets with competitive advertising and churn". In: *9th Asian Control Conference (ASCC)*. Istanbul, 2013, pp. 1–6.

[BKR20] Amit Bhaya, Eugenius Kaszkurewicz, and Luiz Carlos Roth. "One step ahead optimal control of a single echelon supply chain using mathematical programming". In: *Proceedings of the 9th International Conference on Operations Research and Enterprise Systems - Volume 1: ICORES*. INSTICC. SciTePress, 2020, pp. 233–240. DOI: 10.5220/0009130702330240.

[BLL92] William Brock, Josef Lakonishok, and Blake LeBaron. "Simple technical trading rules and the stochastic properties of stock returns". In: *The Journal of Finance* 47.5 (Dec. 1992), pp. 1731–1764. DOI: 10.1111/j.1540-6261.1992.tb04681.x.

[BO99] Tamer Başar and Geert Jan Olsder. *Dynamic Noncooperative Game Theory*. 2nd ed. Vol. 23 of Classics in Applied Mathematics. Philadelphia: SIAM, 1998.

[BOP16] Dimitris Bertsimas, Allison K. O'Hair, and William R. Pulleyblank. *The Analytics Edge*. Belmont, Massachusetts: Dynamic Ideas LLC, 2016.

[Boy+17] Stephen Boyd et al. "Multi-period trading via convex optimization". In: *Foundations and Trends in Optimization* 3.1 (2017), pp. 1–76. DOI: 10.1561/2400000023.

[BPY05] Tomasz R. Bielecki, Stanley Pliska, and Jiongmin Yong. "Optimal investment decisions for a portfolio with a rolling horizon bond and a discount bond". In: *International Journal of Theoretical and Applied Finance* 8.07 (2005), pp. 871–913.

[CA07] Eduardo F. Camacho and Carlos Bordons Alba. *Model Predictive control*. 2nd ed. London: Springer-Verlag, 2007.

[CCP70] Michael D. Canon, Clifton D. Cullum, and Elijah Polak. *Theory of Optimal Control and Mathematical Programming*. New York: McGraw-Hill, 1970.

[Cha13] Ernest P. Chan. *Algorithmic Trading: Winning Strategies and Their Rationale*. Hoboken, New Jersey: John Wiley, 2013.

[CSL09] Xin Chen and David Simchi-Levi. "A new approach for the stochastic cash balance problem with fixed costs". In: *Probability in the Engineering and Informational Sciences* 23.04 (Oct. 2009), 545–562. DOI: 10.1017/S0269964809000242.

[CV02] J. Y. Campbell and L. M. Viceira. *Strategic Asset Allocation: Portfolio Choice for Long-Term Investors*. Clarendon Lectures in Economics. New York: Oxford University Press, 2002.

[CŻ13] E. K. P. Chong and S. H. Żak. *An Introduction to Optimization*. 4th ed. John Wiley: Hoboken, New Jersey, 2013.

[Dea79] Kenneth R. Deal. "Optimising advertising expenditures in a dynamic duopoly". In: *Operations Research* 27.4 (1979), pp. 682–692.

[Deb01] Kalyanmoy Deb. *Multi-objective Optimization using Evolutionary Algorithms*. Chichester, London: Wiley, 2001.

[Dev92] R. L. Devaney. *A First Course in Chaotic Dynamical Systems: Theory and Experiment*. Boston, Massachusetts: Addison-Wesley, 1992.

[DHL17] Iain Dunning, Joey Huchette, and Miles Lubin. "JuMP: A modeling language for mathematical optimization". In: *SIAM Review* 59.2 (2017), pp. 295–320. DOI: 10.1137/15M1020575.

[Doc+00] E. J. Dockner et al. *Differential Games in Economics and Management Science*. Cambridge: Cambridge University Press, 2000.

[Dok07] Nikolai Dokuchaev. "Discrete time market with serial correlations and optimal myopic strategies". In: *European Journal of Operational Research* 177 (2007), pp. 1090–1104.

[DSS58] Robert Dorfman, Paul A. Samuelson, and Robert M. Solow. *Linear Programming and Economic Analysis*. Republished by Dover Publications, 1987. New York: McGraw Hill, 1958.

[DST79] Kenneth R. Deal, Suresh P. Sethi, and Gerald L. Thompson. "A bilinear-quadratic differential game in advertising". In: *Control Theory in Mathematical Economics*. New York: Marcel Dekker, 1979, pp. 91–109.

[Dug16] Jim Duggan. *Systems Dynamics Modeling with R*. Switzerland: Springer International, 2016.

[Edi97] R. D. Edie. "On the optimal control of the Vidale-Wolfe advertising model". In: *Optimal Control Applications and Methods* 18 (1997), pp. 59–72.

[El +16] Fouad El Ouardighi et al. "Advertising and Quality-Dependent Word-of-Mouth in a Contagion Sales Model". In: *Journal of Optimization Theory and Applications* 170.1 (2016), pp. 323–342.

[EP05] Craig A. Ellis and Simon A. Parbery. "Is smarter better? A comparison of adaptive, and simple moving average trading strategies". In: *Research in International Business and Finance* 19.3 (Sept. 2005), pp. 399–411. DOI: 10.1016/j.ribaf.2004.12.009.

[Eri03] Gary M. Erickson. *Dynamic Models of Advertising Competition*. 2nd ed. Dordrecht: Kluwer Academic Publishers, 2003.

[Eri09] Gary M. Erickson. "An oligopoly model of dynamic advertising competition". In: *European Journal of Operational Research* 197.1 (2009), pp. 374–388.

[Eri95] Gary M. Erickson. "Differential game models of advertising competition". In: *European Journal of Operational Research* 83 (1995), pp. 431–438.

[Fei92] Gustav Feichtinger. "Limit cycles in dynamic economic systems". In: *Annals of Operations Research* 37.1 (Dec. 1992), 313–344. 10.1007/BF02071063.

[FH17] Chloe A. Fletcher and Jason S. Howell. "Dynamic modeling of nontargeted and targeted advertising strategies in an oligopoly". In: *Journal of Dynamics and Games* 4.2 (2017), pp. 97–124. DOI: 10.3934/jdg.2017007.

[FHS94] Gustav Feichtinger, Richard F. Hartl, and Suresh P. Sethi. "Dynamic optimal control models in advertising: Recent developments". In: *Management Science* 40.2 (1994), pp. 195–226.

[FL07] Eugene A. Feinberg and Mark E. Lewis. "Optimality inequalities for average cost Markov decision processes and the stochastic cash balance problem". In: *Mathematics of Operations Research* 32.4 (2007), pp. 769–783. DOI: 10.1287/moor.1070.0269.

[FN94] Gustav Feichtinger and Andreas J. Novak. "Differential game model of the dynastic cycle: 3D-canonical system with a stable limit cycle". In: *Journal of Optimization Theory and Applications* 80.3 (Mar. 1994), pp. 407–423. DOI: 10.1007/BF02207772.

[FNW94] Gustav Feichtinger, Andreas J. Novak, and Franz Wirl. "Limit cycles in intertemporal adjustment models". In: *Journal of Economic Dynamics and Control* 18.2 (Mar. 1994), pp. 353–380. DOI: 10.1016/0165-1889(94)90013-2.

[For61] Jay W. Forrester. *Industrial Dynamics*. Cambridge, Massachusetts: M.I.T. Press, 1961.

[For68] Jay W. Forrester. *Principles of Systems*. Cambridge, Massachusetts: Wright-Allen Press, 1968.

[Fri83] James Friedman. *Oligopoly Theory*. Cambridge: Cambridge University Press, 1983.

[Fru99] Gila E Fruchter. "Oligopoly advertising strategies with market expansion". In: *Optimal Control Applications and Methods* 20.4 (1999), pp. 199–212.

[GM07] F. M. Gormley and N. Meade. "The utility of cash flow forecasts in the management of corporate cash balances". In: *European journal of operational research* 182.2 (2007), pp. 923–935.

[HBT07] K. Hoberg, J. R. Bradley, and U. W. Thonemann. "Analyzing the effect of the inventory policy on order and inventory variability with linear control theory". In: *European Journal of Operational Research* 176 (2007), pp. 1620–1642.

[HCI16] Carlos Antonio Herrera-Cáceres and Asier Ibeas. "Model predictive control of cash balance in a cash concentration and disbursements system". In: *Journal of the Franklin Institute* 353.18 (Dec. 2016), pp. 4885–4923. DOI: 10.1016/j.jfranklin.2016.09.007.

[Hes17] João P. Hespanha. *Noncooperative Game Theory: An Introduction for Engineers and Computer Scientists*. Princeton, New Jersey: Princeton University Press, 2017.

[Hil85] Robert C. Hilborn. *Chaos and Nonlinear Dynamics*. 2nd ed. Oxford: Oxford University Press, 1985.

[HLL12] J. Huang, M.-M. Leng, and L.-P. Liang. "Recent developments in dynamic advertising research". In: *European Journal of Operational Research* 220 (2012), pp. 591–609. URL: http://doi.org/10.1016/j.ejor.2012.02.031.

[HW01] Karl Hinderer and K.-H. Waldmann. "Cash management in a randomly varying environment". In: *European Journal of Operational Research* 130.3 (2001), pp. 468–485.

[Ign12] P. Ignaciuk. "Dead-time compensation in continuous-review perishable inventory systems with multiple supply alternatives". In: *Journal of Process Control* 22.5 (2012), pp. 915–924.

[Iva+18] Dmitry Ivanov et al. "A survey on control theory applications to operational systems, supply chain management, and Industry 4.0". In: *Annual Reviews in Control* 46 (Oct. 2018), pp. 134–147. DOI: 10.1016/j.arcontrol.2018.10.014.

[JKF11] M. M. Jansen, T. G. de Kok, and J. C. Fransoo. "Lead time anticipation in supply chain operations planning". In: *OR Spectrum* 35.1 (2011), pp. 251–290. DOI: 10.1007/s00291-011-0267-y.

[JOP21] Vaidas Jusevičius, Richard Oberdieck, and Remigijus Paulavičius. "Experimental analysis of algebraic modelling languages for mathematical optimization". In: *Informatica* 32.2 (2021), pp. 283–304. DOI: 10.15388/21-INFOR447.

[Jør82] Steffen Jørgensen. "A survey of some differential games in advertising". In: *Journal of Economic Dynamics and Control* 4 (1982), pp. 341–369.

[JS16] Steffen Jørgensen and Simon Pierre Sigué. "A dynamic advertising game with market growth". In: *Dynamic Perspectives on Managerial Decision Making: Essays in Honor of Richard F. Hartl*. Ed. by Herbert Dawid et al. Cham, Switzerland: Springer International Publishing, 2016, pp. 491–520. DOI: 10.1007/978-3-319-39120-5_5.

[JZ04] Steffen Jørgensen and Georges Zaccour. *Differential Games in Marketing*. Dordrecht: Kluwer Academic Publishers, 2004.

[KB00] Eugenius Kaszkurewicz and Amit Bhaya. *Matrix Diagonal Stability in Systems and Computation*. Boston/Switzerland: Birkhäuser Boston/Springer Nature, 2000.

[KB18] Eugenius Kaszkurewicz and Amit Bhaya. "Modeling market share dynamics under advertising effort and word-of-mouth interactions between customers". In: *IEEE Transactions on Computational Social Systems* 5.2 (2018), pp. 382–390. DOI: 10.1109/TCSS.2018.2810242.

[KC16] F. S. N. Karan and S. Chakraborty. "Dynamics of a repulsive voter model". In: *IEEE Transactions on Computational Social Systems* 3.1 (2016), pp. 13–22.

[Kim57] G. E. Kimball. "Some industrial applications of military operations research methods". In: *Operations Research* 5.2 (1957), pp. 201–204.

[KS91] M. I. Kamien and N. L. Schwartz. *Dynamic Optimization: The Calculus of Variations and Optimal Control in Economics and Management*. 2nd ed. Vol. 31 of Advanced Textbooks in Economics. Amsterdam: North-Holland, Elsevier, 1991.

[KW19] Mykel J. Kochenderfer and Tim A. Wheeler. *Algorithms For Optimization*. Code: https://github.com/algorithmsbooks/algforopt-notebooks. Cambridge, Massachusetts: The MIT Press, 2019. URL: https://algorithmsbook.com/optimization/files/optimization.pdf.

[Kwo21] Changhyun Kwon. *Julia Programming for Operations Research*. 2nd ed. 2021. URL: https://juliabook.chkwon.net/book/optimization.

[Lan16] Frederick William Lanchester. *Aircraft in Warfare: The Dawn of the Fourth Arm*. London: Constable & Co. Ltd., 1916. URL: https://archive.org/details/aircraftinwarfa00lancgoog.

[Lav00] E. Lavretsky. "Greedy Optimal Control". In: *American Control Conference (ACC)*. Chicago, IL, 2000, pp. 3888–3892.

[Lin+17] Junyi Lin et al. "The extension and exploitation of the inventory and order based production control system archetype from 1982 to 2015". In: *International Journal of Production Economics* 194 (2017), pp. 135–152. DOI: 10.1016/j.ijpe.2016.12.003.

[Lit79] J. D. C. Little. "Aggregate advertising models: The state of the art". In: *Operations Research* 27 (1979), pp. 629–667.

[LN19] Junyi Lin and Mohamed Naim. "Why do nonlinearities matter? The repercussions of linear assumptions on the dynamic behaviour of assemble-to-order systems". In: *International Journal of Production Research* 57.20 (Jan. 2019), pp. 6424–6451. DOI: 10.1080/00207543.2019.1566669.

[LNS19] Junyi Lin, Mohamed Naim, and Virginia Spiegler. "Delivery time dynamics in an assemble-to-order inventory and order based production control system". In: *International Journal of Production Economics* 223 (Oct. 2019), 107531. DOI: 10.1016/j.ijpe.2019.107531.

[LSZ16] Guowei Liu, Suresh P. Sethi, and Jianxiong Zhang. "Myopic vs. far-sighted behaviours in a revenue-sharing supply chain with reference quality effects". In: *International Journal of Production Research* 54.5 (2016), pp. 1334–1357. DOI: 10.1080/00207543.2015.1068962.

[LT14] Shuren Liu and Pei Tang. "The stochastic cash balance problem with fixed costs: The risk-averse case". In: *Journal of Systems Science and Information* 2.6 (2014), pp. 520–531.

[Lue98] David G. Luenberger. *Investment Science*. New York: Oxford University Press, 1998.

[LX08] B. Liu and C. Xin. "An online model for managing cash: An alternative approach to the Miller-Orr model". In: *2008 Fourth International Conference on Natural Computation*. Vol. 5. New York: IEEE. 2008, pp. 314–317. DOI: 10.1109/ICNC.2008.310.

[Man20] N. Gregory Mankiw. *Principles of Microeconomics*. 9th ed. Boston, Massachusetts: Cengage Learning, 2020.

[Mar52] Harry Markowitz. "Portfolio selection". In: *The Journal of Finance* 7.1 (1952), pp. 77–91.

[MDN16] Xiaoling Mei, Victor DeMiguel, and Francisco J. Nogales. "Multiperiod portfolio optimization with multiple risky assets and general transaction costs". In: *Journal of Banking and Finance* 69 (2016), pp. 108–120.

[Mer69] Robert C. Merton. "Lifetime portfolio selection under uncertainty: The continuous-time case". In: *The Review of Economics and Statistics* 51.3 (1969), pp. 247–257.

[Mer90] Robert C. Merton. *Continuous-Time Finance*. Cambridge, Massachusetts: Basil Blackwell, 1990.

[MH03] S. M. Maurer and B. A. Huberman. "Competitive dynamics of web sites". In: *Journal of Economic Dynamics and Control* 27 (2003), pp. 2195–2206.

[MH04] Bernard McGarvey and Bruce Hannon. *Dynamic Modeling for Business Management: An Introduction*. New York: Springer, 2004.

[Miz10] N. Mizik. "The theory and practice of myopic management". In: *Journal of Marketing Research* XLVII (2010), pp. 594–611.

[MN13] M. B. C. Moraes and M. S. Nagano. "Cash management policies by evolutionary models: A comparison using the Miller-Orr Model". In: *Journal of Information Systems and Technology Management* 10.3 (2013), pp. 561–576. DOI: 10.4301/S1807-17752013000300006.

[MN14] M. B. C. Moraes and M. S. Nagano. "Evolutionary models in cash management policies with multiple assets". In: *Economic Modelling* 39 (April 2014), pp. 1–7. DOI: 10.1016/j.econmod.2014.02.010.

[MNS15] M. B. C. Moraes, M. S. Nagano, and V. A. Sobreiro. "Stochastic cash flow management models: A literature review since the 1980s". In: *Decision Models in Engineering and Management*, Ed. by P. Guarnieri, Springer, Switzerland. 2015. Chap. 2, pp. 11–28. DOI: 10.1007/978-3-319-11949-6_2.

[MO66] M. Miller and D. Orr. "A model of the demand for money by firms". In: *The Quarterly Journal of Economics* 81 (1966), pp. 413–435.

[Mor07] J. Morecroft. *Strategic Modelling and Business Dynamics: A Feedback Systems Approach*. Chichester: John Wiley, 2007.

[Mos68] J. Mossin. "Optimal multiperiod portfolio policies". In: *The Journal of Business* 41.2 (1968), pp. 215–229.

[MS10] John A. Muckstadt and Amar Sapra. *Principles of Inventory Management: When You Are Down to Four, Order More*. New York: Springer, 2010.

[Mur06] Katta G. Murty. *Forecasting for Supply Chain and Portfolio Management*. Preprint. 2006. URL: http://www-personal.umich.edu/~murty/forecastSCM-PFOLIO2.pdf.

[NA62] M. Nerlove and K. J. Arrow. "Optimal advertising policy under dynamic conditions". In: *Economica* 29 (1962), pp. 129–142.

[Nea70] E. H. Neave. "The stochastic cash balance problem with fixed costs for increases and decreases". In: *Management Science* 16 (1970), pp. 472–490.

[NZ96] Anna Nagurney and Ding Zhang. *Projected Dynamical Systems and Variational Inequalities with Applications*. New York: Springer, 1996.

[OL04] M. Ortega and L. Lin. "Control theory applications to the production inventory problem: A review". In: *International Journal of Production Research* 42.11 (2004), pp. 2303–2322.

[Oli+20] Tiago Roux Oliveira et al. "Nash equilibrium seeking in quadratic noncooperative games under two delayed information-sharing schemes". In: *Journal of Optimization Theory and Applications* 191 (2021), pp. 700–735. DOI: 10.1007/s10957-020-01757-z.

[Orl19] E. V. Orlova. "Model for discrete optimal control of the enterprise's financial processes". In: *Journal of Physics: Conference Series* 1368 (2019), 042054. ITNT 2019, pp. 1–11. DOI: 10.1088/1742-6596/1368/4/042054.

[OT12] A. F. Osorio and H. H. Toro. "An MIP model to optimize a Colombian cash supply chain". In: *International Transactions in Operational Research* 19 (2012), pp. 659–673.

[Paa+17] K. Paarporn et al. "Networked SIS epidemics with awareness". In: *IEEE Transactions on Computational Social Systems* 4.3 (2017), pp. 93–103.

[Pek17] Teemu Heikki August Pekkarinen. *The Lower Bounds on Nominal Interest Rates*. Master's thesis, Faculty of Social Sciences, Department of Political and Economic Studies, University of Helsinki. 2017.

[PLYG03] Edgar Perea-López, B. Erik Ydstie, and Ignacio Grossmann. "A model predictive control strategy for supply chain optimization". In: *Computers & Chemical Engineering* 27 (Sept. 2003), pp. 1201–1218. DOI: 10.1016/S0098-1354(03)00047-4.

[Pra10] Puchong Praekhaow. "Determination of trading points using the moving average methods". In: *International Conference for a Sustainable Greater Mekong Subregion (GMSTEC 10)*. Bangkok, Thailand, 2010, pp. 1–6.

[PSS22] Jesse Perla, Thomas J. Sargent, and John Stachurski. *Quantitative Economics with Julia*. Lectures. 2022. URL: https://julia.quantecon.org/intro.html.

[Puu03] Tönu Puu. *Attractors, Bifurcations, & Chaos: Nonlinear Phenomena in Economics*. 2nd ed. Berlin: Springer, 2003.

[Qin+16] J. Qin et al. "Online modified greedy algorithm for storage control under uncertainty". In: *IEEE Transactions on Power Systems* 31.3 (2016), pp. 1729–1743. ISSN: 1558-0679. DOI: 10.1109/TPWRS.2015.2440355.

[Rap] *Rapid API. Alpha Vantage API Documentation*. 2022. URL: https://rapidapi.com/alphavantage/api/alpha-vantage.

[Rev22] J. Revels. `BenchmarkTools`*: Julia Language Package*. 2022. URL: https://github.com/JuliaCI/BenchmarkTools.jl.

[RH12] Matthias Ruth and Bruce Hannon. *Modeling Economic Dynamic Systems*. 2nd ed. New York: Springer, 2012.

[RP05] D. E. Rivera and M. D. Pew. "Evaluating PID control for supply chain management: A freshman design project". In: *Proceedings of the 44th IEEE Conference on Decision and Control*. 2005, pp. 3415–3419. DOI: 10.1109/CDC.2005.1582690.

[RTJ65] A. A. Robichek, D. Teichroew, and J. M. Jones. "Optimal short term financing decision". In: *Management Science* 12.1 (1965), pp. 1–36.

[Sam69] Paul A. Samuelson. "Lifetime portfolio selection by dynamic stochastic programming". In: *The Review of Economics and Statistics* 51.3 (1969), pp. 239–246.

[SE14] L. Servi and S. B. Elson. "A mathematical approach to gauging influence by identifying shifts in the emotions of social media users". In: *IEEE Transactions on Computational Social Systems* 1.4 (2014), pp. 180–190.

[Set19] Suresh P. Sethi. *Optimal Control Theory: Applications to Management Science and Economics*. 3rd ed. Switzerland: Springer Nature, 2019.

[Set73] Suresh P. Sethi. "Optimal control of the Vidale-Wolfe model". In: *Operations Research* 21 (1973), pp. 998–1013.

[Set77] Suresh P. Sethi. "Dynamic optimal control models in advertising: A survey". In: *SIAM Review* 19.4 (1977), pp. 685–725. DOI: 10.1137/1019106.

[SJ05] Heinz Georg Schuster and Wolfram Just. *Deterministic Chaos: An Introduction*. 4th ed. Weinheim: Wiley-VCH, 2005.

[SKM15] Hartmut Stadtler, Christoph Kilger, and Herbert Meyr. *Supply chain management and advanced planning*. 5th ed. Springer Texts in Business and Economics. Berlin: Springer, 2015.

[SM06] Akihiro Suzuki and Shigeo Muto. "Farsighted behavior leads to efficiency in duopoly markets". In: *Advances in Dynamic Games*. Ed. by Alain Haurie et al. Vol. 8 of Annals of the International Society of Dynamic Games. Boston, Massachusetts: Birkhäuser Boston, 2006, pp. 379–395. DOI: 10.1007/0-8176-4501-2_20.

[SM+17] Francisco Salas-Molina et al. "Empowering cash managers to achieve cost savings by improving predictive accuracy". In: *International Journal of Forecasting* 33 (2017), pp. 403–415.

[SM19] Francisco Salas-Molina. "Fitting random cash management models to data". In: *Computers and Operations Research* 106 (2019), pp. 298–306.

[SM20] Francisco Salas-Molina. "Risk-sensitive control of cash management systems". In: *Operational Research: An International Journal* 20 (2020), pp. 1159–1176.

[SM+20] Francisco Salas-Molina et al. "Multiple-criteria cash-management policies with particular liquidity terms". In: *IMA Journal of Management Mathematics* 31.1-2 (2020), pp. 217–231.

[SM87] B. K. Stone and T. W. Miller. "Daily cash forecasting with multiplicative models of cash flow patterns". In: *Financial Management* 16.4 (1987), pp. 45–54.

[SMPSRA18] Francisco Salas-Molina, David Pla-Santamaria, and Juan A. Rodriguez-Aguilar. "A multi-objective approach to the cash management problem". In: *Annals of Operations Research* 267.1-2 (2018), pp. 515–529.

[SMRAPS20] Francisco Salas-Molina, Juan A. Rodriguez-Aguilar, and David Pla-Santamaria. "A stochastic goal programming model to derive stable cash management policies". In: *Journal of Global Optimization* 76 (2020), pp. 333–346.

[SNT94] John Simon, Mohamed Naim, and Denis R. Towill. "Dynamic analysis of a WIP compensated decision support system". In: *International Journal of Manufacturing System Design* 1.4 (1994), pp. 283–297.

[SRM14] K. Subramanian, J. B. Rawlings, and C. T. Maravelias. "Economic model predictive control for inventory management in supply chains". In: *Computers and Chemical Engineering* 64 (2014), pp. 71–80.

[SSR01] Joel M. Stern, John S. Shiely, and Irwin Ross. *The EVA challenge: Implementing value added change in an organization.* New York: John Wiley, 2001.

[ST00] Suresh P. Sethi and Gerald L. Thompson. *Optimal Control Theory: Applications to Management Science and Economics.* 2nd ed. Boston: Kluwer Academic Publishers, 2000.

[ST70] Suresh P. Sethi and Gerald L. Thompson. "Applications of mathematical control theory to finance: Modeling simple dynamic cash balance problems". In: *The Journal of Financial and Quantitative Analysis* 5.4/5 (1970), pp. 381–394.

[Ste00] John D. Sterman. *Business Dynamics: Systems Thinking and Modeling for a Complex World.* Boston, Massachusetts: Irwin/McGraw-Hill, 2000.

[Ste21] William J. Stevenson. *Operations Management.* 14th ed. New York: McGraw-Hill, 2021.

[Tos+08] S. Tosetti et al. "A new inventory level APIOBPCS-based controller". In: *Proceedings of the 2008 American Control Conference.* Seattle, WA, 2008, pp. 2886–2891.

[Tra68] G. S. Tracz. "A selected bibliography on the application of optimal control theory to economic and business systems, management science, and operations research". In: *Operations Research* 16.1 (1968), pp. 174–186. DOI: 10.1287/opre.16.1.174.

[TZ15] Emmanuel Trélat and Enrique Zuazua. "The turnpike property in finite-dimensional nonlinear optimal control". In: *Journal of Differential Equations* 258 (2015), pp. 81–114. DOI: 10.1016/j.jde.2014.09.005.

[VD13] Gyöngyi Vörösmarty and Imre Dobos. "Analysis of purchasing activity with discounted cash flow inventory models". In: *Periodica Polytechnica: Social and Management Sciences* 21.2 (2013), pp. 67–70. DOI: 10.3311/PPso.7085.

[VW57] M. L. Vidale and H. B. Wolfe. "An operations research study of sales response to advertising". In: *Operations Research* 5 (1957), pp. 370–381.

[Wan+16] Fengjun Wang et al. "Optimal investment strategy on advertisement in duopoly". In: *Management* 12.2 (2016), pp. 625–636.

[Wan+19] Jun Wang et al. "Myopic versus farsighted behaviors in a low-carbon supply chain with reference emission effects". In: *Complexity* 2019 (2019), 3123572. DOI: 10.1155/2019/3123572.

[WH18] J. Wu and Q. Huang. "Myopic and far-sighted pricing strategies in a duopoly market with e-WOM effect". In: *International Journal of Electronic Commerce* 22.4 (2018), pp. 609–630. DOI: 10.1080/10864415.2018.1485087.

[Wil06] H. P. Williams. "The formulation and solution of discrete optimisation models". In: *Handbook on Modelling for Discrete Optimization.* Ed. by Gautam Appa, Leonidas Pitsoulis, and H. Paul Williams. Boston, Massachusetts: Springer, 2006. Chap. 1, pp. 3–38.

[WRK07] W.-L. Wang, D. E. Rivera, and K. G. Kempf. "Model predictive control strategies for supply chain management in semiconductor manufacturing". In: *International Journal of Production Economics* 107 (2007), pp. 56–77.

[WW01] Qinan Wang and Zhang Wu. "A duopolistic model of dynamic competitive advertising". In: *European Journal of Operational Research* 128.1 (2001), pp. 213–226.

[Yan14] Xin-She Yang. *Nature-Inspired Optimization Algorithms*. 1st ed. Amsterdam: Elsevier, 2014. ISBN: 978-0-12-416743-8.

[Zas17] Alexander J. Zaslavski. *Discrete-Time Optimal Control and Games on Large Intervals*. Cham, Switzerland: Springer, 2017.

[ZC17] Yafei Zu and Lianghua Chen. "Myopic versus far-sighted behaviors in dynamic supply chain coordination through advertising with reference price effect". In: *Discrete Dynamics in Nature and Society* (2017), 9759561. DOI: 10.1155/2017/9759561.

[ZC21] Fan Zhang and Susu Cheng. "Behavioral choices in a dynamic duopoly with process innovation and sticky price: Myopia versus farsightedness". In: *Managerial and Decision Economics* 42.3 (2021), pp. 662–674. DOI: 10.1002/mde.3263.

[ZZ09] Yingzi Zhu and Guofu Zhou. "Technical analysis: An asset allocation perspective on the use of moving averages". In: *Journal of Financial Economics* 92.3 (June 2009), pp. 519–544. DOI: 10.1016/j.jfineco.2008.07.002.

Index